An Introduction to Data Science

An Introduction to Data Science

Jeffrey S. Saltz

Syracuse University

Jeffrey M. Stanton

Syracuse University

Los Angeles | London | New Delhi
Singapore | Washington DC | Melbourne

FOR INFORMATION:

SAGE Publications, Inc.
2455 Teller Road
Thousand Oaks, California 91320
E-mail: order@sagepub.com

SAGE Publications Ltd.
1 Oliver's Yard
55 City Road
London EC1Y 1SP
United Kingdom

SAGE Publications India Pvt. Ltd.
B 1/I 1 Mohan Cooperative Industrial Area
Mathura Road, New Delhi 110 044
India

SAGE Publications Asia-Pacific Pte. Ltd.
3 Church Street
#10-04 Samsung Hub
Singapore 049483

Acquisitions Editor: Leah Fargotstein
Content Development Editor: Laura Kirkhuff
Production Editor: Kelly DeRosa
Copy Editor: Alison Hope
Typesetter: C&M Digitals (P) Ltd.
Proofreader: Wendy Jo Dymond
Indexer: Sheila Bodell
Cover Designer: Michael Dubowe
Marketing Manager: Susannah Goldes

Printed in the United States of America

Library of Congress Cataloging-in-Publication Data

Names: Saltz, Jeffrey S., author. | Stanton, Jeffrey M., 1961- author.

Title: An introduction to data science / Jeffrey S. Saltz—Syracuse University, Jeffrey M. Stanton—Syracuse University, USA.

Description: First edition. | Los Angeles : SAGE, [2018] | Includes bibliographical references and index.

Identifiers: LCCN 2017011487 | ISBN 9781506377537 (pbk. : alk. paper)

Subjects: LCSH: Databases. | R (Computer program language)

Classification: LCC QA76.9.D32 S38 2018 | DDC 005.74—dc23
LC record available at https://lccn.loc.gov/2017011487

This book is printed on acid-free paper.

SUSTAINABLE FORESTRY INITIATIVE

Certified Chain of Custody
Promoting Sustainable Forestry
www.sfiprogram.org
SFI-01268

SFI label applies to text stock

18 19 20 21 10 9 8 7 6 5 4 3 2

CONTENTS

Preface   viii

About the Authors   x

Introduction: Data Science, Many Skills   xii

    What Is Data Science?   1

    The Steps in Doing Data Science   2

    The Skills Needed to Do Data Science   3

Chapter 1 • About Data   8

    Storing Data—Using Bits and Bytes   10

    Combining Bytes Into Larger Structures   11

    Creating a Data Set in R   13

Chapter 2 • Identifying Data Problems   16

    Talking to Subject Matter Experts   17

    Looking for the Exception   18

    Exploring Risk and Uncertainty   19

Chapter 3 • Getting Started With R   22

    Installing R   24

    Using R   24

    Creating and Using Vectors   25

Chapter 4 • Follow the Data   30

    Understand Existing Data Sources   31

    Exploring Data Models   32

Chapter 5 • Rows and Columns   34

    Creating Dataframes   36

    Exploring Dataframes   39

    Accessing Columns in a Dataframe   43

Chapter 6 • Data Munging   48

    Reading a CSV Text File   49

    Removing Rows and Columns   51

Renaming Rows and Columns 53

Cleaning Up the Elements 54

Sorting Dataframes 57

Chapter 7 • Onward With RStudio® **60**

Using an Integrated Development Environment 61

Installing RStudio 62

Creating R Scripts 62

Chapter 8 • What's My Function? **68**

Why Create and Use Functions? 69

Creating Functions in R 69

Testing Functions 73

Installing a Package to Access a Function 77

Chapter 9 • Beer, Farms, and Peas and the Use of Statistics **80**

Historical Perspective 81

Sampling a Population 82

Understanding Descriptive Statistics 83

Using Descriptive Statistics 85

Using Histograms to Understand a Distribution 88

Normal Distributions 91

Chapter 10 • Sample in a Jar **96**

Sampling in R 98

Repeating Our Sampling 99

Law of Large Numbers and the Central Limit Theorem 101

Comparing Two Samples 105

Chapter 11 • Storage Wars **110**

Importing Data Using RStudio 112

Accessing Excel Data 114

Accessing a Database 120

Comparing SQL and R for Accessing a Data Set 124

Accessing JSON Data 128

Chapter 12 • Pictures Versus Numbers **138**

A Visualization Overview 139

Basic Plots in R 141

Using ggplot2 142

More Advanced ggplot2 Visualizations 150

Chapter 13 • Map Mashup **158**

Creating Map Visualizations With ggplot2 159

Showing Points on a Map 162

A Map Visualization Example 165

Chapter 14 • Word Perfect **174**

Reading in Text Files 176

Using the Text Mining Package 180

Creating Word Clouds 183

Chapter 15 • Happy Words? **188**

Sentiment Analysis 189

Other Uses of Text Mining 193

Chapter 16 • Lining Up Our Models **196**

What Is a Model? 197

Linear Modeling 197

An Example—Car Maintenance 199

Chapter 17 • Hi Ho, Hi Ho—Data Mining We Go **210**

Data Mining Overview 211

Association Rules Data 212

Association Rules Mining 213

Exploring How the Association Rules Algorithm Works 219

Chapter 18 • What's Your Vector, Victor? **230**

Supervised and Unsupervised Learning 231

Supervised Learning via Support Vector Machines 231

Support Vector Machines in R 233

Chapter 19 • Shiny® Web Apps **246**

Creating Web Applications in R 247

Deploying the Application 254

Chapter 20 • Big Data? Big Deal! **260**

What Is Big Data? 261

The Tools for Big Data 264

Index **271**

PREFACE

Welcome to *Introduction to Data Science*! This book began as the key ingredient to one of those massive open online courses, or MOOCs, and was written from the start to welcome people with a wide range of backgrounds into the world of data science. In the years following the MOOC we kept looking for, but never found, a better textbook to help our students learn the fundamentals of data science. Instead, over time, we kept refining and improving the book such that it has now become in integrated part of how we teach data science.

In that welcoming spirit, the book assumes no previous computer programming experience, nor does it require that students have a deep understanding of statistics. We have successfully used the book for both undergraduate and graduate level introductory courses. By using the free and open source R platform (R Core Team, 2016) as the basis for this book, we have also ensured that virtually everyone has access to the software needed to do data science. Even though it takes a while to get used to the R command line, our students have found that it opens up great opportunities to them, both academically and professionally.

In the pages that follow, we explain how to do data science by using R to read data sets, clean them up, visualize what's happening, and perform different modeling techniques on the data. We explore both structured and unstructured data. The book explains, and we provide via an online repository, all the commands that teachers and learners need to do a wide range of data science tasks.

If your goal is to consider the whole book in the span of 14 or 15 weeks, some of the earlier chapters can be grouped together or made optional for those learners with good working knowledge of data concepts. This approach allows an instructor to structure a semester so that each week of a course can cover a different chapter and introduce a new data science concept.

Many thanks to Leah Fargotstein, Yvonne McDuffee, and the great team of folks at SAGE Publications, who helped us turn our manuscript into a beautiful, professional product. We would also like to acknowledge our colleagues at the Syracuse University School of Information Studies, who have been very supportive in helping us get student feedback to improve this book. Go iSchool!

There were a number of reviewers we would like to thank who provided extremely valuable feedback during the development of the manuscript:

- Luis F. Alvarez Leon, University of Southern California

- Youngseek Kim, University of Kentucky

- Nir Kshetri, UNC Greensboro

- Richard N. Landers, Old Dominion University

- John W. Mohr, University of California, Santa Barbara

- Ryan T. Moore, American University and The Lab @ DC

- Fred Oswald, Rice University

- Eliot Rich, University at Albany, State University of New York

- Ansaf Salleb-Aouissi, Columbia University

- Toshiyuki Yuasa, University of Houston

ABOUT THE AUTHORS

Jeffrey S. Saltz, PhD (New Jersey Institute of Technology, 2006), is currently associate professor at Syracuse University, in the School of Information Studies. His research and teaching focus on helping organizations leverage information technology and data for competitive advantage. Specifically, Saltz's current research focuses on the sociotechnical aspects of data science projects, such as how to coordinate and manage data science teams. In order to stay connected to the real world, Saltz consults with clients ranging from professional football teams to Fortune 500 organizations.

Prior to becoming a professor, Saltz's more than 20 years of industry experience focused on leveraging emerging technologies and data analytics to deliver innovative business solutions. In his last corporate role, at JPMorgan Chase, he reported to the firm's chief information officer and drove technology innovation across the organization. Saltz also held several other key technology management positions at the company, including chief technology officer and chief information architect. Saltz has also served as chief technology officer and principal investor at Goldman Sachs, where he invested and helped incubate technology start-ups. He started his career as a programmer, a project leader, and a consulting engineer with Digital Equipment Corp.

Jeffrey M. Stanton, PhD (University of Connecticut, 1997), is associate provost of academic affairs and professor of information studies at Syracuse University. Stanton's research focuses on organizational behavior and technology. He is the author of *Information Nation: Educating the Next Generation of Information Professionals* (2010), with Indira Guzman and Kathryn Stam. Stanton has also published many scholarly articles in peer-reviewed behavioral science journals, such as the *Journal of Applied Psychology, Personnel Psychology,* and *Human Performance.* His articles also appear in *Journal of Computational Science Education, Computers and Security, Communications of the ACM, Computers in Human Behavior,* the *International Journal of Human-Computer Interaction, Information Technology and People,* the *Journal of Information Systems Education,* the *Journal of Digital Information,*

Surveillance and Society, and *Behaviour & Information Technology.* He also has published numerous book chapters on data science, privacy, research methods, and program evaluation. Stanton's methodological expertise is in psychometrics, with published works on the measurement of job satisfaction and job stress. Dr. Stanton's research has been supported through 18 grants and supplements, including the National Science Foundation's CAREER award.

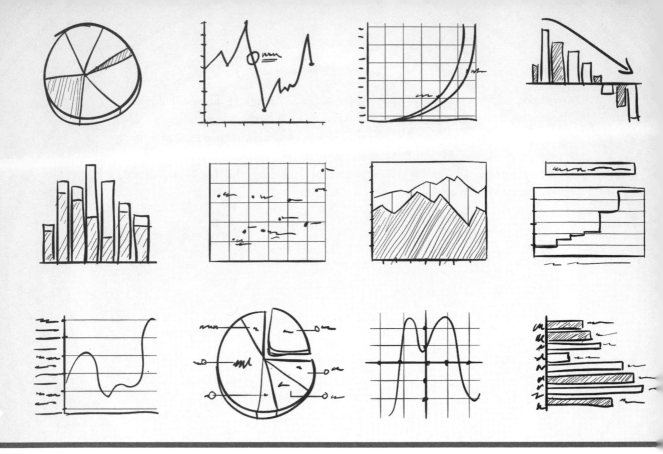

INTRODUCTION: DATA SCIENCE, MANY SKILLS

LEARNING OBJECTIVES

- Articulate what data science is.
- Understand the steps, at a high level, of doing data science.
- Describe the roles and skills of a data scientist.

WHAT IS DATA SCIENCE?

For some, the term *data science* evokes images of statisticians in white lab coats staring fixedly at blinking computer screens filled with scrolling numbers. Nothing could be farther from the truth. First, statisticians do not wear lab coats: this fashion statement is reserved for biologists, physicians, and others who have to keep their clothes clean in environments filled with unusual fluids. Second, much of the data in the world is non-numeric and unstructured. In this context, unstructured means that the data are not arranged in neat rows and columns. Think of a web page full of photographs and short messages among friends: very few numbers to work with there. While it is certainly true that companies, schools, and governments use plenty of numeric information—sales of products, grade point averages, and tax assessments are a few examples—there is lots of other information in the world that mathematicians and statisticians look at and cringe. So, while it is always useful to have great math skills, there is much to be accomplished in the world of data science for those of us who are presently more comfortable working with words, lists, photographs, sounds, and other kinds of information.

In addition, data science is much more than simply analyzing data. There are many people who enjoy analyzing data and who could happily spend all day looking at histograms and averages, but for those who prefer other activities, data science offers a range of roles and requires a range of skills. Let's consider this idea by thinking about some of the data involved in buying a box of cereal.

Whatever your cereal preferences—fruity, chocolaty, fibrous, or nutty—you prepare for the purchase by writing "cereal" on your grocery list. Already your planned purchase is a piece of data, also called a datum, albeit a pencil scribble on the back on an envelope that only you can read. When you get to the grocery store, you use your datum as a reminder to grab that jumbo box of FruityChocoBoms off the shelf and put it in your cart. At the checkout line, the cashier scans the barcode on your box, and the cash register logs the price. Back in the warehouse, a computer tells the stock manager that it is time to request another order from the distributor, because your purchase was one of the last boxes in the store. You also have a coupon for your big box, and the cashier scans that, giving you a predetermined discount. At the end of the week, a report of all the scanned manufacturer coupons gets uploaded to the cereal company so they can issue a reimbursement to the grocery store for all of the coupon discounts they have handed out to customers. Finally, at the end of the month a store manager looks at a colorful collection of pie charts showing all the different kinds of cereal that were sold and, on the basis of strong sales of fruity cereals, decides to offer more varieties of these on the store's limited shelf space next month.

So the small piece of information that began as a scribble on your grocery list ended up in many different places, most notably on the desk of a manager as an aid to decision making. On the trip from your pencil to the manager's desk, the datum went through many transformations. In addition to the computers where the datum might have stopped by or stayed on for the long term, lots of other pieces of hardware—such as the barcode scanner—were involved in collecting, manipulating, transmitting, and storing the datum. In addition, many different pieces of software were used to organize, aggregate, visualize, and present the datum. Finally, many different human systems were involved in working with the datum. People decided which systems to buy and install, who should get access to what kinds of data, and what would happen to the data after its immediate purpose was fulfilled. The personnel of the grocery chain and its partners made a thousand other detailed decisions and negotiations before the scenario described earlier could become reality.

THE STEPS IN DOING DATA SCIENCE

Obviously, data scientists are not involved in all of these steps. Data scientists don't design and build computers or barcode readers, for instance. So where would the data scientists play the most valuable role? Generally speaking, data scientists play the most active roles in the four As of data: data architecture, data acquisition, data analysis, and data archiving. Using our cereal example, let's look at these roles one by one. First, with respect to architecture, it was important in the design of the point-of-sale system (what retailers call their cash registers and related gear) to think through in advance how different people would make use of the data coming through the system. The system architect, for example, had a keen appreciation that both the stock manager and the store manager would need to use the data scanned at the registers, albeit for somewhat different purposes. A data scientist would help the system architect by providing input on how the data would need to be routed and organized to support the analysis, visualization, and presentation of the data to the appropriate people.

Next, acquisition focuses on how the data are collected, and, importantly, how the data are represented prior to analysis and presentation. For example, each barcode represents a number that, by itself, is not very descriptive of the product it represents. At what point after the barcode scanner does its job should the number be associated with a text description of the product or its price or its net weight or its packaging type? Different barcodes are used for the same product (e.g., for different sized boxes of cereal). When should we make note that purchase X and purchase Y are the same product, just in different packages? Representing, transforming, grouping, and linking the data are all tasks that need to occur before the data can be profitably analyzed, and these are all tasks in which the data scientist is actively involved.

The analysis phase is where data scientists are most heavily involved. In this context, we are using analysis to include summarization of the data, using portions of data (samples) to make inferences about the larger context, and visualization of the data by presenting it in tables, graphs, and even animations. Although there are many technical, mathematical, and statistical aspects to these activities, keep in mind that the ultimate audience for data analysis is always a person or people. These people are the data users, and fulfilling their needs is the primary job of a data scientist. This point highlights the need for excellent communication skills in data science. The most sophisticated statistical analysis ever developed will be useless unless the results can be effectively communicated to the data user.

Finally, the data scientist must become involved in the archiving of the data. Preservation of collected data in a form that makes it highly reusable—what you might think of as data curation—is a difficult challenge because it is so hard to anticipate all of the future uses of the data. For example, when the developers of Twitter were working on how to store tweets, they probably never anticipated that tweets would be used to pinpoint earthquakes and tsunamis, but they had enough foresight to realize that geocodes—data that show the geographical location from which a tweet was sent—could be a useful element to store with the data.

THE SKILLS NEEDED TO DO DATA SCIENCE

All in all, our cereal box and grocery store example helps to highlight where data scientists get involved and the skills they need. Here are some of the skills that the example suggested:

Learning the application domain: The data scientist must quickly learn how the data will be used in a particular context.

Communicating with data users: A data scientist must possess strong skills for learning the needs and preferences of users. The ability to translate back and forth between the technical terms of computing and statistics and the vocabulary of the application domain is a critical skill.

Seeing the big picture of a complex system: After developing an understanding of the application domain, the data scientist must imagine how data will move around among all of the relevant systems and people.

Knowing how data can be represented: Data scientists must have a clear understanding about how data can be stored and linked, as well as about metadata (data that describe how other data are arranged).

Data transformation and analysis: When data become available for the use of decision makers, data scientists must know how to transform, summarize, and make inferences from the data. As noted earlier, being able to communicate the results of analyses to users is also a critical skill here.

Visualization and presentation: Although numbers often have the edge in precision and detail, a good data display (e.g., a bar chart) can often be a more effective means of communicating results to data users.

Attention to quality: No matter how good a set of data might be, there is no such thing as perfect data. Data scientists must know the limitations of the data they work with, know how to quantify its accuracy, and be able to make suggestions for improving the quality of the data in the future.

Ethical reasoning: If data are important enough to collect, they are often important enough to affect people's lives. Data scientists must understand important ethical issues such as privacy, and must be able to communicate the limitations of data to try to prevent misuse of data or analytical results.

The skills and capabilities noted earlier are just the tip of the iceberg, of course, but notice what a wide range is represented here. While a keen understanding of numbers and mathematics is important, particularly for data analysis, the data scientist also needs to have excellent communication skills, be a great systems thinker, have a good eye for visual displays, and be highly capable of thinking critically about how data will be used to make decisions and affect people's lives. Of course, there are very few people who are good at all of these things, so some of the people interested in data will specialize in one area, while others will become experts in another area. This highlights the importance of teamwork, as well.

In this *Introduction to Data Science* book, a series of data problems of increasing complexity is used to illustrate the skills and capabilities needed by data scientists. The open source data analysis program known as R and its graphical user interface companion RStudio are used to work with real data examples to illustrate both the challenges of data science and some of the techniques used to address those challenges. To the greatest extent possible, real data sets reflecting important contemporary issues are used as the basis of the discussions.

Note that the field of big data is a very closely related area of focus. In short, big data is data science that is focused on very large data sets. Of course, no one actually defines a "very large data set," but for our purposes we define big data as trying to analyze data sets that are so large that one cannot use RStudio. As an example of a big data problem to be solved, Macy's (an online and brick-and-mortar retailer) adjusts its pricing in near real

time for 73 million items, based on demand and inventory (http://searchcio.techtarget
.com/opinion/Ten-big-data-case-studies-in-a-nutshell). As one might guess, the amount
of data and calculations required for this type of analysis is too large for one computer
running RStudio. However, the techniques covered in this book are conceptually similar
to how one would approach the Macy's challenge and the final chapter in the book provides an overview of some big data concepts.

Of course, no one book can cover the wide range of activities and capabilities
involved in a field as diverse and broad as data science. Throughout the book references to other guides and resources provide the interested reader with access to additional information. In the open source spirit of R and RStudio these are, wherever
possible, web-based and free. In fact, one of guides that appears most frequently in
these pages is Wikipedia, the free, online, user-sourced encyclopedia. Although some
teachers and librarians have legitimate complaints and concerns about Wikipedia,
and it is admittedly not perfect, it is a very useful learning resource. Because it is free,
because it covers about 50 times more topics than a printed encyclopedia, and because
it keeps up with fast-moving topics (such as data science) better than printed sources,
Wikipedia is very useful for getting a quick introduction to a topic. You can't become
an expert on a topic by consulting only Wikipedia, but you can certainly become
smarter by starting there.

Another very useful resource is Khan Academy. Most people think of Khan Academy as a set of videos that explain math concepts to middle and high school students,
but thousands of adults around the world use Khan Academy as a refresher course for a
range of topics or as a quick introduction to a topic that they never studied before. All the
lessons at Khan Academy are free, and if you log in with a Google or Facebook account
you can do exercises and keep track of your progress.

While Wikipedia and Khan Academy are great resources, there are many other
resources available to help one learn data science. So, at the end of each chapter of this
book is a list of sources. These sources provide a great place to start if you want to learn
more about any of the topics the chapter does not explain in detail.

It is valuable to have access to the Internet while you are reading so that you can
follow some of the many links this book provides. Also, as you move into the sections
in the book where open source software such as the R data analysis system is used, you
will sometimes need to have access to a desktop or laptop computer where you can run
these programs.

One last thing: The book presents topics in an order that should work well for people
with little or no experience in computer science or statistics. If you already have knowledge, training, or experience in one or both of these areas, you should feel free to skip
over some of the introductory material and move right into the topics and chapters that
interest you most.

Sources

http://en.wikipedia.org/wiki/E-Science

http://en.wikipedia.org/wiki/E-Science_librarianship

http://en.wikipedia.org/wiki/Wikipedia:Size_comparisons

http://en.wikipedia.org/wiki/Statistician

http://en.wikipedia.org/wiki/Visualization_
(computer_graphics)

http://www.khanacademy.org/

http://www.r-project.org/

http://readwrite.com/2011/09/07/unlocking-big-data-with-r/

http://rstudio.org/

© iStockphoto.com/Vjom

1

ABOUT DATA

The inventor of the World Wide Web, Sir Tim Berners-Lee, is often quoted as having said, "Data is not information, information is not knowledge, knowledge is not understanding, understanding is not wisdom," but this quote is actually from Clifford Stoll, a well-known cyber sleuth.

The quote suggests a kind of pyramid, where data are the raw materials that make up the foundation at the bottom of the pile, and information, knowledge, understanding, and wisdom represent higher and higher levels of the pyramid. In one sense, the major goal of a data scientist is to help people to turn data into information and onward up the pyramid. Before getting started on this goal, though, it is important to have a solid sense of what data actually are. (Notice that this book uses "data" as a plural noun. In common usage, you might hear "data" as both singular and plural.) If you have studied computer science or mathematics, you might find the discussion in this chapter somewhat redundant, so feel free to skip it. Otherwise, read on for an introduction to the most basic ingredient to the data scientist's efforts: data.

A substantial amount of what we know and say about data in the present day comes from work by a U.S. mathematician named Claude Shannon. Shannon worked before, during, and after World War II on a variety of mathematical and engineering problems related to data and information. Not to go crazy with quotes or anything, but Shannon is quoted as having said, "The fundamental problem of communication is that of reproducing at one point either exactly or approximately a message selected at another point" (http://math.harvard.edu/~ctm/home/text/others/shannon/entropy/entropy.pdf, 1). This quote helpfully captures key ideas about data that are important in this book by focusing on the idea of data as a message that moves from a source to a recipient. Think about the simplest possible message that you could send to another person over the phone, via a text message, or even in person. Let's say that a friend had asked you a question, for example, whether you wanted to come to her house for dinner the next day. You can answer yes or no. You can call the person on the phone and say yes or no. You might have a bad connection, though, and your friend might not be able to hear you. Likewise, you could send her a text message with your answer, yes or no, and hope that she has her phone turned on so she can receive the message. Or you could tell your friend face-to-face and hope that she does not have her earbuds turned up so loud that she couldn't hear you. In all three cases, you have a one-bit message that you want to send to your friend, yes or no, with the goal of reducing her uncertainty about whether you will appear at her house for dinner the next day. Assuming that message gets through without being garbled or lost, you will have successfully transmitted one bit of information from you to her. Claude Shannon developed some mathematics, now often referred to as Information Theory, that carefully quantified how bits of data transmitted accurately from a source to a recipient can reduce uncertainty by providing information. A great deal of the computer networking equipment and software in the world today—and especially the huge linked worldwide network we call the Internet—is primarily concerned with this one basic task of getting bits of information from a source to a destination.

STORING DATA—USING BITS AND BYTES

Once we are comfortable with the idea of a bit as the most basic unit of information, either "yes" or "no," we can combine bits to make more-complicated structures. First, let's switch labels just slightly. Instead of "no" we will start using zero, and instead of "yes" we will start using one. So we now have a single digit, albeit one that has only two possible states: zero or one (we're temporarily making a rule against allowing any of the bigger digits like three or seven). This is in fact the origin of the word *bit*, which is a squashed down version of the phrase Binary digIT. A single binary digit can be zero (0) or one (1), but there is nothing stopping us from using more than one binary digit in our messages. Have a look at the example in the table below:

Meaning	2nd Digit	1st digit
No	0	0
Maybe	0	1
Probably	1	0
Definitely	1	1

Here we have started to use two binary digits—two bits—to create a code book for four different messages that we might want to transmit to our friend about her dinner party. If we were certain that we would not attend, we would send her the message 0 0. If we definitely planned to attend, we would send her 1 1. But we have two additional possibilities, "maybe," which is represented by 0 1, and "probably," which is represented by 1 0. It is interesting to compare our original yes/no message of one bit with this new four-option message with two bits. In fact, every time you add a new bit you double the number of possible messages you can send. So three bits would give 8 options and four bits would give 16 options. How many options would there be for five bits?

When we get up to eight bits—which provides 256 different combinations—we finally have something of a reasonably useful size to work with. Eight bits is commonly referred to as a "byte"—this term probably started out as a play on words with the word *bit*. (Try looking up the word *nybble* online!) A byte offers enough different combinations to encode all of the letters of the alphabet, including capital and small letters. There is an old rulebook called ASCII—the American Standard Code for Information Interchange—which matches up patterns of eight bits with the letters of the alphabet, punctuation, and a few other odds and ends. For example, the bit pattern 0100 0001 represents the capital letter A and the next higher pattern, 0100 0010, represents capital B. Try looking up an ASCII table online (e.g., http://www.asciitable.com/) and you can find all of the combinations. Note that the codes might not actually be shown in binary because it is so difficult for people to read long strings of ones and zeroes. Instead, you might see the equivalent codes shown in hexadecimal (base 16), octal (base 8), or the most familiar form that we all use every day, base 10. Although you might remember base conversions from high school math class, it would be a good idea to practice this—particularly the conversions between binary, hexadecimal, and decimal (base 10). You might also enjoy Vi Hart's *Binary Hand Dance* video at Khan Academy (search for this at http://www.khanacademy .org or follow the link at the end of the chapter). Most of the work we do in this book will be in decimal, but more-complex work with data often requires understanding hexadecimal and being able to know how a hexadecimal number, like 0xA3, translates into a bit pattern. Try searching online for "binary conversion tutorial" and you will find lots of useful sites.

COMBINING BYTES INTO LARGER STRUCTURES

Now that we have the idea of a byte as a small collection of bits (usually eight) that can be used to store and transmit things like letters and punctuation marks, we can start to build up to bigger and better things. First, it is very easy to see that we can put bytes together into lists in order to make a string of letters, often referred to as a character string or text string. If we have a piece of text, like "this is a piece of text," we can use a collection of bytes to represent it like this:

```
01110100011010000110100101110011001000000110100101110011001000
00011000010010000000111000001101001011001010110001101100101001
00000011011110110011000100000001110100011001010111100001110100
```

Now nobody wants to look at that, let alone encode or decode it by hand, but fortunately, the computers and software we use these days takes care of the conversion and storage automatically. For example, we can tell the open source data language R to store "this is a piece of text" for us like this:

```
> myText <- "this is a piece of text"
```

We can be certain that inside the computer there is a long list of zeroes and ones that represent the text that we just stored. By the way, in order to be able to get our piece of text back later on, we have made a kind of storage label for it (the word "myText" above). Anytime that we want to remember our piece of text or use it for something else, we can use the label myText to open up the chunk of computer memory where we have put that long list of binary digits that represent our text. The left-pointing arrow made up out of the less-than character (<) and the dash character (–) gives R the command to take what is on the right-hand side (the quoted text) and put it into what is on the left-hand side (the storage area we have labeled myText). Some people call this the assignment arrow, and it is used in some computer languages to make it clear to the human who writes or reads it which direction the information is flowing. Yay! We just explored our first line of R code. But don't worry about actually writing code just yet: We will discuss installing R and writing R code in Chapter 3.

From the computer's standpoint, it is even simpler to store, remember, and manipulate numbers instead of text. Remember that an eight-bit byte can hold 256 combinations, so just using that very small amount we could store the numbers from 0 to 255. (Of course, we could have also done 1 to 256, but much of the counting and numbering that goes on in computers starts with zero instead of one.) Really, though, 255 is not much to work with. We couldn't count the number of houses in most towns or the number of cars in a large parking garage unless we can count higher than 255. If we put together two bytes to make 16 bits we can count from zero up to 65,535, but that is still not enough for some of the really big numbers in the world today (e.g., there are more than 200 million cars in the United States alone). Most of the time, if we want to be flexible in representing an integer (a number with no decimals), we use four bytes stuck together. Four bytes stuck together is a total of 32 bits, and that allows us to store an integer as high as 4,294,967,295.

Things get slightly more complicated when we want to store a negative number or a number that has digits after the decimal point. If you are curious, try looking up "two's complement" for more information about how signed numbers are stored and "floating point" for information about how numbers with digits after the decimal point are stored. For our purposes in this book, the most important thing to remember is that text is stored differently than numbers, and among numbers integers are stored differently than floating point. Later we will find that it is sometimes necessary to convert between these different representations, so it is always important to know how it is represented.

So far, we have mainly looked at how to store one thing at a time, like one number or one letter, but when we are solving problems with data we often need to store a group of related things together. The simplest place to start is with a list of things that are all stored in the same way. For example, we could have a list of integers, where each thing in the list is the age of a person in your family. The list might look like this: 43, 42, 12, 8, 5. The first two numbers are the ages of the parents and the last three numbers are the ages of the kids. Naturally, inside the computer each number is stored in binary, but fortunately we don't have to type them in that way or look at them that way. Because there are no decimal points, these are just plain integers and a 32-bit integer (4 bytes) is more than enough to store each one. This list contains items that are all the same type or mode.

CREATING A DATA SET IN R

The open source data program R refers to a list where all of the items are of the same mode as a vector. We can create a vector with R very easily by listing the numbers, separated by commas and inside parentheses:

```
> c(43, 42, 12, 8, 5)
```

The letter c in front of the opening parenthesis stands for combine, which means to join things together. Slightly obscure, but easy enough to get used to with some practice. We can also put in some of what we learned earlier to store our vector in a named location (remember that a vector is list of items of the same mode/type):

```
> myFamilyAges <- c(43, 42, 12, 8, 5)
```

We have just created our first data set. It is very small, for sure, only five items, but it is also very useful for illustrating several major concepts about data. Here's a recap:

In the heart of the computer, all data are represented in binary. One binary digit, or bit, is the smallest chunk of data that we can send from one place to another.

Although all data are at heart binary, computers and software help to represent data in more convenient forms for people to see. Three important representations are "character" for representing text, "integer" for representing numbers with no digits after the decimal point, and "floating point" for numbers that might have digits after the decimal point. The numbers in our tiny data set just above are integers.

Numbers and text can be collected into lists, which the open source program R calls vectors. A vector has a length, which is the number of items in it, and a mode which is the type of data stored in the vector. The vector we were just working on has a length of five and a mode of integer.

In order to be able to remember where we stored a piece of data, most computer programs, including R, give us a way of labeling a chunk of computer memory. We chose to give the five-item vector up above the name myFamilyAges. Some people might refer to this named list as a variable because the value of it varies, depending on which member of the list you are examining.

If we gather together one or more variables into a sensible group, we can refer to them together as a data set. Usually, it doesn't make sense to refer to something with just one variable as a data set, so usually we need at least two variables. Technically, though, even our very simple myFamilyAges counts as a data set, albeit a very tiny one.

Later in the book we will install and run the open source R data program and learn more about how to create data sets, summarize the information in those data sets, and perform some simple calculations and transformations on those data sets.

Chapter Challenge

Discover the meaning of Boolean Logic and the rules for *and, or, not,* and *exclusive or.* Once you have studied this for a while, write down on a piece of paper, without looking, all the binary operations that demonstrate these rules.

Sources

http://en.wikipedia.org/wiki/Claude_Shannon

http://en.wikipedia.org/wiki/Information_theory

http://cran.r-project.org/doc/manuals/R-intro.pdf

http://www.khanacademy.org/math/vi-hart/v/binary-hand-dance

https://www.khanacademy.org/computing/computer-programming/programming/variables/p/intro-to-variables

http://www.asciitable.com/

2

IDENTIFYING
DATA PROBLEMS

LEARNING OBJECTIVES

- Describe and assess possible strategies for problem identification.
- Explain how to leverage subject matter experts.
- Examine and identify the exceptions.
- Illustrate how data science might be useful.

Apple farmers live in constant fear, first for their blossoms and later for their fruit. A late spring frost can kill the blossoms. Hail or extreme wind in the summer can damage the fruit. More generally, farming is an activity that is first and foremost in the physical world, with complex natural processes and forces, like weather, that are beyond the control of humankind.

In this highly physical world of unpredictable natural forces, is there any role for data science? On the surface, there does not seem to be. But how can we know for sure? Having a nose for identifying data problems requires openness, curiosity, creativity, and a willingness to ask a lot of questions. In fact, if you took away from the first chapter the impression that a data scientist sits in front of a computer all day and works a crazy program like R, that is a mistake. Every data scientist must (eventually) become immersed in the problem domain where she is working. The data scientist might never actually become a farmer, but if you are going to identify a data problem that a farmer has, you have to learn to think like a farmer, to some degree.

TALKING TO SUBJECT MATTER EXPERTS

To get this domain knowledge you can read or watch videos, but the best way is to ask subject matter experts (in this case farmers) about what they do. The whole process of asking questions deserves its own treatment, but for now there are three things to think about when asking questions. First, you want the subject matter experts, or SMEs, as they are sometimes called, to tell stories of what they do. Then you want to ask them about anomalies: the unusual things that happen for better or for worse. Finally, you want to ask about risks and uncertainty: About the situations where it is hard to tell what will happen next, when what happens next could have a profound effect on whether the situation ends badly or well. Each of these three areas of questioning reflects an approach to identifying data problems that might turn up something good that could be accomplished with data, information, and the right decision at the right time.

The purpose of asking about stories is that people mainly think in stories. From farmers to teachers to managers to CEOs, people know and tell stories about success and failure in their particular domain. Stories are powerful ways of communicating wisdom between different members of the same profession and they are ways of collecting a sense of identity that sets one profession apart from another profession. The only problem is that stories can be wrong.

If you can get a professional to tell the main stories that guide how she conducts her work, you can then consider how to verify those stories. Without questioning the veracity of the person that tells the story, you can imagine ways of measuring the different aspects of how things happen in the story with an eye toward eventually verifying (or sometimes debunking) the stories that guide professional work.

For example, the farmer might say that in the deep spring frost that occurred five years ago, the trees in the hollow were spared frost damage while the trees around the ridge of the hill had frost damage. For this reason, on a cold night the farmer places most of the smudge pots (containers that hold a fuel that creates a smoky fire) around the ridge. The farmer strongly believes that this strategy works, but does it? It would be possible to collect time-series temperature data from multiple locations within the orchard, on cold and warm nights, and on nights with and without smudge pots. The data could be used to create a model of temperature changes in the different areas of the orchard, and this model could support, improve, or debunk the story. Of course, just as the story could be wrong, we also have to keep in mind that the data might be wrong. For example, a thermometer might not be calibrated correctly and, hence, would provide incorrect temperature data.

In summary, there is no one correct way of understanding and representing the situation that is inherently more truthful than others. We have to develop a critical lens to be able to assess the possible situations when information might be correct or incorrect.

LOOKING FOR THE EXCEPTION

A second strategy for problem identification is to look for the exception cases, both good and bad. A little later in the book we will learn about how the core of classic methods of statistical inference is to characterize the center—the most typical cases that occur—and then examine the extreme cases that are far from the center for information that could help us understand an intervention or an unusual combination of circumstances. Identifying unusual cases is a powerful way of understanding how things work, but it is necessary first to define the central or most typical occurrences in order to have an accurate idea of what constitutes an unusual case.

Coming back to our farmer friend, in advance of a thunderstorm late last summer a powerful wind came through the orchard, tearing the fruit off the trees. Most of the trees lost a small amount of fruit: The dropped apples could be seen near the base of the trees. One small grouping of trees seemed to lose a much larger amount of fruit, however, and the drops were apparently scattered much farther from the trees. Is it possible that some strange wind conditions made the situation worse in this one spot? Or is it just a matter of chance that a few trees in the same area all lost more fruit than would be typical?

A systematic count of lost fruit underneath a random sample of trees would help to answer this question. The bulk of the trees would probably have each lost about the same amount, but, more important, that typical group would give us a yardstick against which we could determine what would really count as unusual. When we found an unusual set of cases that was truly beyond the limits of typical, we could rightly focus our attention on these to try to understand the anomaly.

EXPLORING RISK AND UNCERTAINTY

A third strategy for identifying data problems is to find out about risk and uncertainty. If you read the previous chapter you might remember that a basic function of information is to reduce uncertainty. It is often valuable to reduce uncertainty because of how risk affects the things we all do. At work, at school, and at home, life is full of risks: Making a decision or failing to do so sets off a chain of events that could lead to something good or something not so good. In general, we would like to narrow things down in a way that maximizes the chances of a good outcome and minimizes the chance of a bad one. To do this, we need to make better decisions, and to make better decisions we need to reduce uncertainty. By asking questions about risks and uncertainty (and decisions) a data scientist can zero in on the problems that matter. You can even look at the previous two strategies—asking about the stories that comprise professional wisdom and asking about anomalies/unusual cases—in terms of the potential for reducing uncertainty and risk.

In the case of the farmer, much of the risk comes from the weather, and the uncertainty revolves around which countermeasures will be cost-effective under prevailing conditions. Consuming lots of expensive oil in smudge pots on a night that turns out to be quite warm is a waste of resources that could make the difference between a profitable or an unprofitable year. So more-precise and more-timely information about local weather conditions might be a key focus area for problem-solving with data. What if a live stream of national weather service Doppler radar could appear on the farmer's smartphone? The app could provide the predicted wind speed and temperature for the farm in general. But, as this example has shown, it is typically helpful to have more data. So, predicting the wind and temperature across the different locations within the farm might be much more useful to the farmer.

Of course, there are many other situations where data science (and big data science) could prove useful. For example, banks have used data science for many years to perform credit analysis for a consumer when they want to take out a loan or obtain a credit card. As mentioned in the Macy's example, retailers have used data science to try to predict inventory and the related concept of pricing their inventory. Online retailers can use data science to cluster people so that the retailer can suggest a related product to someone who liked a certain product (such as a movie). Finally, smart devices can use data science to learn a person's habits, such as a nest thermostat that can predict when a person will be home or away. While it would take an entire book to describe the many different situations where data science has been or could be used, hopefully these examples give you a feel for what is possible when data science is applied to real-world challenges.

To recap, there are many different contexts in which a data scientist might work and doing data science requires much more than sitting in front of a computer and doing R coding. The data scientist needs to understand the domain and data in that domain. Often the data scientist gets this knowledge by talking to or observing SMEs. One strategy for problem identification is to interact with an SME and get that person to tell a story about the situation. A second strategy is to look for good and bad exceptions. Finally, a third strategy is to explore risk and uncertainty.

Chapter Challenge

To help structure discussions with SMEs, an interview guide is useful. Create an interview guide to ask questions of an SME. Try to create one that is general purpose, and then refine it so that you can use it for the farmer in the scenario in this chapter.

Sources

http://blog.elucidat.com/sme-ideas/

http://elearningindustry.com/
working-subject-matter-experts-ultimate-guide

http://info.shiftelearning.com/blog/
communicating-with-smes-elearning

3

© iStockphoto.com/aydinynr

GETTING STARTED WITH R

LEARNING OBJECTIVES

- Know how to install the R software package.
- Gain familiarity with using the R command line.
- Build vectors in R.

If you are new to computers, programming, and/or data science, welcome to an exciting chapter that will open the door to the most powerful free data analytics tool ever created anywhere in the universe, no joke. On the other hand, if you are experienced with spreadsheets, statistical analysis, or accounting software you are probably thinking that this book has now gone off the deep end, never to return to sanity and all that is good and right in user-interface design. Both perspectives are reasonable. The R open source data analysis program is immensely powerful, flexible, and especially extensible (meaning that people can create new capabilities for it quite easily). At the same time, R is command-line oriented, meaning that most of the work that one needs to perform is done through carefully crafted text instructions, many of which have tricky syntax (the punctuation and related rules for making a command that works). In addition, R is not especially good at giving feedback or error messages that help the user to repair mistakes or figure out what is wrong when results look funny.

But there is a method to the madness here. One of the virtues of R as a teaching tool is that it hides very little. The successful user must fully understand what the data situation is, or else the R commands will not work. With a spreadsheet, it is easy to type in a lot of numbers and a formula like =FORECAST() and a result pops into a cell like magic, whether the calculation makes any sense or not. With R you have to know your data, know what you can do with it, know how it has to be transformed, and know how to check for problems. Because R is a programming language, it also forces users to think about problems in terms of data objects, methods that can be applied to those objects, and procedures for applying those methods. These are important metaphors used in modern programming languages, and no data scientist can succeed without having at least a rudimentary understanding of how software is programmed, tested, and integrated into working systems. The extensibility of R means that new modules are being added all the time by volunteers: R was among the first analysis programs to integrate capabilities for drawing data directly from the Twitter(r) social media platform. So you can be sure that, whatever the next big development is in the world of data, someone in the R community will start to develop a new package for R that will make use of it. Finally, the lessons we can learn by working with R are almost universally applicable to other programs and environments. If you have mastered R, it is a relatively small step to get the hang of the SAS(r) statistical programming language and an even smaller step to being able to follow SPSS(r) syntax. (SAS and SPSS are two of the most widely used commercial statistical analysis programs.) So with no need for any licensing fees paid by school, student, or teacher, it is possible to learn the most powerful data analysis system in the universe and take those lessons with you no matter where you go. It will take some patience though, so please hang in there!

INSTALLING R

Let's get started. Obviously, you will need a computer. If you are working on a tablet device or smartphone, you might want to skip forward to the chapter on RStudio, because regular old R has not yet been reconfigured to work on tablet devices (but there is a workaround for this that uses RStudio). There are a few experiments with web-based interfaces to R, like this one—http://www.r-fiddle.org, but they are still in a very early stage. If your computer has the Windows(r), Mac-OS-X(r), or a Linux operating system, there is a version of R waiting for you at http://cran.r-project.org/. Download and install your own copy. If you sometimes have difficulties with installing new software and you need some help, there is a wonderful little book by Thomas P. Hogan called *Bare-Bones R: A Brief Introductory Guide* (2017, Thousand Oaks, CA: SAGE) that you might want to buy or borrow from your library. There are lots of sites online that also give help with installing R, although many of them are not oriented toward the inexperienced user. I searched online using the term "help installing R," and I got a few good hits. YouTube also had four videos that provide brief tutorials for installing R. Try searching for "install R" in the YouTube search box. The rest of this chapter assumes that you have installed R and can run it on your computer as shown in the screenshot in Figure 3.1. (Note that this screenshot is from the Mac version of R: if you are running Windows or Linux your R screen could appear slightly different from this.)

USING R

The screenshot in Figure 3.1 shows a simple command to type that shows the most basic method of interaction with R. Notice near the bottom of the screenshot a greater - than (>) symbol. This is the command prompt: When R is running and it is the active application on your desktop, if you type a command it appears after the > symbol. If you press the enter or return key, the command is sent to R for processing. When the processing is done, a result will appear just under the >. When R is done processing, another command prompt (>) appears and R is ready for your next command. In the screenshot, the user has typed "1+1" and pressed the enter key. The formula 1+1 is used by elementary school students everywhere to insult each other's math skills, but R dutifully reports the result as 2. If you are a careful observer, you will notice that just before the 2 there is a 1 in square brackets, like this: [1]. That [1] is a line number that helps to keep track of the results that R displays. Pretty pointless when only showing one line of results, but R likes to be consistent, so we will see quite a lot of those numbers in square brackets as we dig deeper.

FIGURE 3.1

```
R version 3.2.2 (2015-08-14) -- "Fire Safety"
Copyright (C) 2015 The R Foundation for Statistical Computing
Platform: x86_64-apple-darwin13.4.0 (64-bit)

R is free software and comes with ABSOLUTELY NO WARRANTY.
You are welcome to redistribute it under certain conditions.
Type 'license()' or 'licence()' for distribution details.

  Natural language support but running in an English locale

R is a collaborative project with many contributors.
Type 'contributors()' for more information and
'citation()' on how to cite R or R packages in publications.

Type 'demo()' for some demos, 'help()' for on-line help, or
'help.start()' for an HTML browser interface to help.
Type 'q()' to quit R.

[R.app GUI 1.66 (6996) x86_64-apple-darwin13.4.0]

[Workspace restored from /Users/jsaltz/.RData]
[History restored from /Users/jsaltz/.Rapp.history]

> 1+1
[1] 2
>
```

CREATING AND USING VECTORS

Remember the list of ages of family members from the About Data chapter? No? Well, here it is again: 43, 42, 12, 8, 5, for Dad, Mom, Sis, Bro, and Dog, respectively. We mentioned that this was a list of items, all of the same mode, namely, an integer. Remember that you can tell that they are OK to be integers because there are no decimal points and therefore nothing after the decimal point. We can create a vector of integers in R using the c() command. Take a look at the screenshot in Figure 3.2.

This is the last time that the whole screenshot from the R console will appear in the book. From here on out we will just look at commands and output so we don't waste

FIGURE 3.2

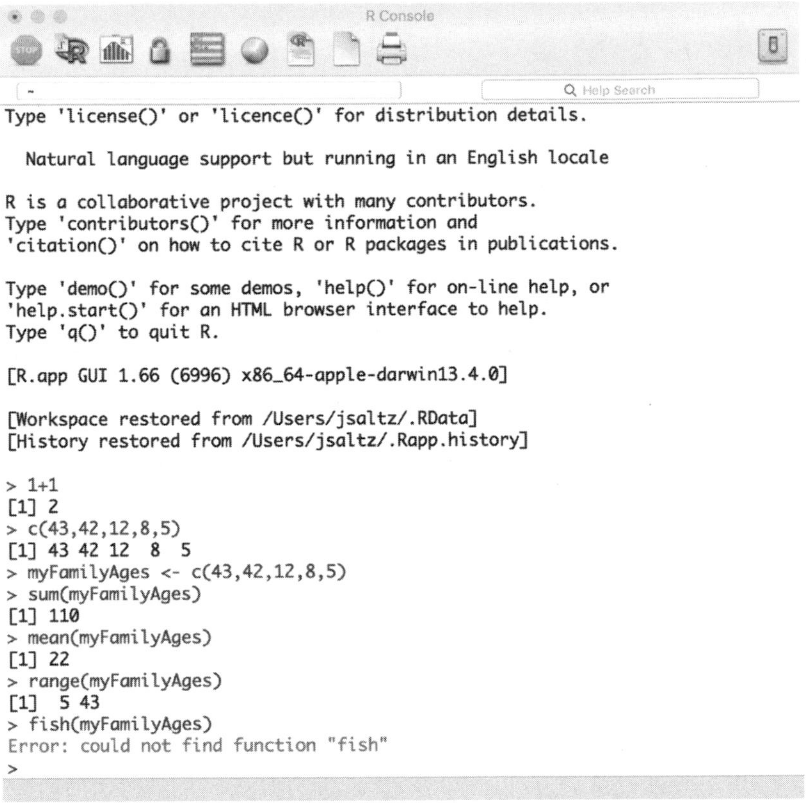

```
Type 'license()' or 'licence()' for distribution details.

  Natural language support but running in an English locale

R is a collaborative project with many contributors.
Type 'contributors()' for more information and
'citation()' on how to cite R or R packages in publications.

Type 'demo()' for some demos, 'help()' for on-line help, or
'help.start()' for an HTML browser interface to help.
Type 'q()' to quit R.

[R.app GUI 1.66 (6996) x86_64-apple-darwin13.4.0]

[Workspace restored from /Users/jsaltz/.RData]
[History restored from /Users/jsaltz/.Rapp.history]

> 1+1
[1] 2
> c(43,42,12,8,5)
[1] 43 42 12  8  5
> myFamilyAges <- c(43,42,12,8,5)
> sum(myFamilyAges)
[1] 110
> mean(myFamilyAges)
[1] 22
> range(myFamilyAges)
[1]  5 43
> fish(myFamilyAges)
Error: could not find function "fish"
>
```

so much space on the page. The first command line in the screenshot is exactly what appeared in an earlier chapter:

```
> c(43, 42, 12, 8, 5)
```

As you can see, when we show a short snippet of code we will make blue and bold what we type, and not blue and bold what R is generating. So, in the preceding example, R generated the >, and then we typed c(43, 42, 12, 8, 5). You don't need to type the > because R provides it whenever it is ready to receive new input. From now on in the book, there will be examples of R commands and output that are mixed together, so always be on the lookout for > because the command after that is what you have to type. Also notice that the output is in black (as opposed to our code that is shown in blue).

You might notice that on the following line in the screenshot R dutifully reports the vector that you just typed. After the line number [1], we see the list 43, 42, 12, 8, and 5. This is because R echoes this list back to us, because we didn't ask it to store the vector anywhere. In the rest of the book, we will show that output from R as follows:

```
[1]  43,  42,  12,  8,  5
```

Combining these two lines, our R console snippet would look as follows:

```
>  c(43,  42,  12,  8,  5)
[1]  43,  42,  12,  8,  5
```

In contrast, the next command line (also the same as in the previous chapter), says:

```
>  myFamilyAges <-  c(43,  42,  12,  8,  5)
```

We have typed in the same list of numbers, but this time we have assigned it, using the left-pointing arrow, into a storage area that we have named myFamilyAges. This time, R responds just with an empty command prompt. That's why the third command line requests a report of what myFamilyAges contains. This is a simple but very important tool. Any time you want to know what is in a data object in R, just type the name of the object and R will report it back to you. In the next command, we begin to see the power of R:

```
>  sum(myFamilyAges)
[1]  110
```

This command asks R to add together all of the numbers in myFamilyAges, which turns out to be 110 (you can check it yourself with a calculator if you want). This is perhaps a weird thing to do with the ages of family members, but it shows how with a very short and simple command you can unleash quite a lot of processing on your data. In the next line (of the screenshot image), we ask for the mean (what non-data people call the average) of all of the ages, and this turns out to be 22 years. The command right afterward, called range, shows the lowest and highest ages in the list. Finally, just for fun, we tried to issue the command fish(myFamilyAges). Pretty much as you might expect, R does not contain a fish() function, and so we received an error message to that effect. This shows another important principle for working with R: You can freely try things out at any time without fear of breaking anything. If R can't understand what you want to accomplish, or you haven't quite figured out how to do something, R will calmly respond with an error message and will not make any other changes until you give it a new command. The error messages from R are not always super helpful, but with some strategies that the book will discuss in future chapters you can break down the problem and figure out how to get R to do what you want.

Finally, it's important to remember that R is case sensitive. This means that myFamilyAges is different from myFamilyages. In R, typing myFamilyages, when we meant myFamilyAges, is treated the same as any other typing error.

```
> myFamilyAges
[1] 43 42 12 8 5
> myFamilyages
Error: object 'myFamilyages' not found
```

Let's take stock for a moment. First, you should definitely try all of the commands noted above on your own computer. You can read about the commands in this book all you want, but you will learn a lot more if you actually try things out. Second, if you try a command that is shown in these pages and it does not work for some reason, you should try to figure out why. Begin by checking your spelling and punctuation, because R is very persnickety about how commands are typed. Remember that capitalization matters in R: myFamilyAges is not the same as myFamilyages. If you verify that you have typed a command just as you see in the book and it still does not work, try going online and looking for some help. There's lots of help at http://stackoverflow.com, at https://stat.ethz.ch, and also at http://www.statmethods.net/. If you can figure out what went wrong on your own you will probably learn something very valuable about working with R. Third, you should take a moment to experiment with each new set of commands that you learn. For example, just using the commands discussed earlier in the chapter you could do this totally new thing:

```
> myRange <- range(myFamilyAges)
```

What would happen if you did that command and then typed "myRange" (without the double quotes) on the next command line to report back what is stored there? What would you see? Then think about how that worked and try to imagine some other experiments that you could try. The more you experiment on your own, the more you will learn. Some of the best stuff ever invented for computers was the result of just experimenting to see what was possible. At this point, with just the few commands that you have already tried, you already know the following things about R (and about data):

How to install R on your computer and run it.

How to type commands on the R console.

The use of the c() function. Remember that c stands for combine, which just means to join things together. You can put a list of items inside the parentheses, separated by commas.

That a vector is pretty much the most basic form of data storage in R, and that it consists of a list of items of the same mode.

That a vector can be stored in a named location using the assignment arrow (a left pointing arrow made of a dash and a less-than symbol, like this: <-).

That you can get a report of the data object that is in any named location just by typing that name at the command line.

That you can run a function, such as mean(), on a vector of numbers to transform them into something else. (The mean() function calculates the average, which is one of the most basic numeric summaries there is.)

That sum(), mean(), and range() are all legal functions in R whereas fish() is not.

That R is case sensitive.

In the next chapter we will move forward a step or two by starting to work with text and by combining our list of family ages with the names of the family members and some other information about them.

Chapter Challenge

Using logic and online resources to get help if you need it, learn how to use the c() function to add another family member's age on the end of the myFamilyAges vector.

Sources

http://a-little-book-of-r-for-biomedical-statistics.readthedocs.org/en/latest/src/installr.html

http://cran.r-project.org/

http://www.r-fiddle.org (an experimental web interface to R)

http://en.wikibooks.org/wiki/R_Programming

https://plus.google.com/u/0/104922476697914343874/posts (Jeremy Taylor's blog: Stats Make Me Cry)

http://stackoverflow.com

https://stat.ethz.ch

http://www.statmethods.net/

© iStockphoto.com/mattjeacock

FOLLOW THE DATA

Hate to nag, but have you had a checkup lately? If you have been to the doctor for any reason you might recall that the doctor's office is awash with data. First, the doctor has loads of digital sensors, everything from blood pressure monitors to ultrasound machines, and all of these produce mountains of data. Perhaps of greater concern in this era of debate about health insurance, the doctor's office is one of the big jumping-off points for financial and insurance data. One of the notable features of the U.S. health-care system is our most common method of health-care delivery: paying by the procedure. When you undergo a procedure at the doctor's office, whether it is a consultation, an examination, a test, or something else, that experience initiates a chain of data events with far-reaching consequences.

If your doctor is typical, the starting point of these events is a paper form. Have you ever looked at one of these in detail? Most of the form will be covered by a large matrix of procedures and codes. Although some of the better-equipped places might use this form digitally on a tablet or other computer, paper forms are still very common. Somewhere, either in the doctor's office or at an outsourced service company, the data on the paper form are entered into a system that begins the insurance reimbursement and/or billing process.

UNDERSTANDING EXISTING DATA SOURCES

Where do these procedure data go? What other kinds of data (such as patient account information) might get attached to them in a subsequent step? What kinds of networks do these linked data travel over, and what kind of security do they have? How many steps are there in processing the data before they arrive at the insurance company? How does the insurance company process and analyze the data before issuing the reimbursement? How is the money transmitted once the insurance company's systems have given approval to the reimbursement? These questions barely scratch the surface: There are dozens or hundreds of processing steps that we haven't yet imagined.

It is easy to see from this example that the likelihood of being able to throw it all out and start designing a better or at least more standardized system from scratch is nil. But what if you had the job of improving the efficiency of the system, or auditing the insurance reimbursements to make sure they were compliant with insurance records, or using the data to detect and predict outbreaks and epidemics, or providing feedback to consumers about how much they can expect to pay out of pocket for various procedures?

The critical starting point for your project would be to follow the data. You would need to be like a detective, finding out in a substantial degree of detail the content, format, senders, receivers, transmission methods, repositories, and users of data at each step in the process and at each organization where the data are processed or housed.

EXPLORING DATA MODELS

Fortunately, there is an extensive area of study and practice called data modeling that provides theories, strategies, and tools to help with the data scientist's goal of following the data. These ideas started in earnest in the 1970s with the introduction by computer scientist Ed Yourdon of a methodology called data flow diagrams. A more contemporary approach, one that is strongly linked with the practice of creating relational databases, is called the entity-relationship model. Professionals using this model develop entity-relationship diagrams, sometimes called an ERD, that describe the structure and movement of data in a system.

Entity-relationship modeling occurs at different levels ranging from an abstract conceptual level to a physical storage level. At the conceptual level, an entity is an object or thing, usually something in the real world. In the doctor's office example, one important entity or object is the patient, and another is the doctor. The patient and the doctor are linked by a relationship: In modern health-care lingo, this is the provider relationship. If the patient is Mr. X and the doctor is Dr. Y, the provider relationship provides a bidirectional link:

Dr. Y is the provider for Mr. X.

Mr. X's provider is Dr. Y.

Naturally there is a range of data that can represent Mr. X: name address, age, and so on. Likewise, there are data that represent Dr. Y: years of experience as a doctor, specialty areas, certifications, licenses. Importantly, there is also a chunk of data that represents the linkage between X and Y, and this is the relationship.

Creating an entity-relationship diagram requires investigating and enumerating all of the entities, such as patients and doctors, as well as all the relationships that might exist among them. As the beginning of the chapter suggested, this might have to occur across multiple organizations (e.g., the doctor's office and the insurance company), depending on the purpose of the information system that is being designed. Eventually, the entity-relationship diagrams must become detailed enough that they can serve as a specification for the physical storage in a database.

In an application area like health care, there are so many choices for different ways of designing the data that it requires some experience and possibly some art to create a workable system. Part of the art lies in understanding the users' current information needs and anticipating how those needs could change in the future. If an organization is redesigning a system, adding to a system, or creating brand-new systems, they are doing so in the expectation of a future benefit. This benefit might arise from greater efficiency, a reduction of errors/inaccuracies, or the hope of providing a new product or service with the enhanced information capabilities.

Whatever the goal, the data scientist has an important and difficult challenge of taking the methods of today—including paper forms and manual data entry—and imagining the methods of tomorrow. Follow the data!

You might be asking yourself, "What does this have to do with data science?" As hinted at in this discussion, data scientists often do not define what data should be collected at the start of the project. Rather, it is likely that a data scientist will need to understand one or more existing systems. Understanding and following the data, perhaps via the SME strategies previously discussed combined with these data modeling concepts, enables the data scientist to get the data. This is important because without the data, there is no data science.

In the next chapter, we look at one of the most common and most useful ways of organizing data, namely, in a rectangular structure that has rows and columns. This rectangular arrangement of data appears in spreadsheets and databases that are used for a variety of applications. Understanding how these rows and columns are organized is critical to most tasks in data science.

Chapter Challenge

Explain the strengths and weaknesses of using an entity relationship diagram versus a data flow diagram. Provide one example when an entity relationship diagram would be better, and one example when a data flow diagram would be more appropriate.

Sources

http://en.wikipedia.org/wiki/Data_modeling   http://en.wikipedia.org/wiki/Entity-relationship_diagram

5

ROWS AND COLUMNS

LEARNING OBJECTIVES

- Explain what a dataframe is and how data are organized in a dataframe.
- Create and use dataframes in R.
- Access columns in a dataframe.
- Gain experience using the following R functions: c, data.frame, str, summary, head, tail.

Although we live in a three-dimensional world, where a box of cereal has height, width, and depth, it is a sad fact of modern life that pieces of paper, chalkboards, whiteboards, and computer screens are still only two dimensional. As a result, most of the statisticians, accountants, computer scientists, and engineers who work with lots of numbers tend to organize them in rows and columns. There's really no good reason for this other than that it makes it easy to fill a rectangular piece of paper with numbers. Rows and columns can be organized any way that you want, but the most common way is to have the rows be cases or instances, and the columns be attributes or variables. Take a look at the nice, two-dimensional representation of rows and columns in Table 5.1:

TABLE 5.1			
Name	Age	Gender	Weight
Dad	43	Male	188
Mom	42	Female	136
Sis	12	Female	83
Bro	8	Male	61
Dog	5	Female	44

Pretty obvious what's going on, right? The top line, in bold, is not really part of the data. Instead, the top line contains the attribute or variable names. Note that computer scientists tend to call them attributes while statisticians call them variables. Either term is OK. For example, age is an attribute that every living thing has, and you could count it in minutes, hours, days, months, years, or other units of time. Here we have the Age attribute calibrated in years. Technically speaking, the variable names in the top line are metadata, or what you could think of as data about data. Imagine how much more difficult it would be to understand what was going on in that table without the metadata. There's lot of different kinds of metadata: Variable names are just one simple type of metadata.

So if you ignore the top row, which contains the variable names, each of the remaining rows is an instance or a case. Again, computer scientists might call them instances, and statisticians might call them cases, but either term is fine. The important thing is that each row refers to an actual thing. In this case, all of our things are living creatures in a family. You could think of the Name column as case labels, in that each of these labels refers to one and only one row in our data. Most of the time when you are working with a large data set, there is a number used for the case label, and that number is unique for each case (i.e., the same number would never appear in more than one row). Computer scientists sometimes refer to this column of unique numbers as a key. A key is very useful, particularly for matching things up from different data sources, and we will run into this idea again later. For now, though, just take note that the Dad row can be distinguished from the Bro row, even though they are both Male. Even if we added an Uncle row that had the same Age, Gender, and Weight as Dad, we would still be able to tell the two rows apart because one would have the name Dad and the other would have the name Uncle.

One other important note: Look at how each column contains the same kind of data all the way down. For example, the Age column is all numbers. There's nothing in the Age column like Old or Young. This is a really valuable way of keeping things organized. After all, we could not run the mean() function on the Age column if it contained a little piece of text, like Old or Young. On a related note, every cell (i.e., an intersection of a row and a column, such as Sis's Age) contains just one piece of information. Although a spreadsheet or a word processing program might allow us to put more than one thing in a cell, a real data handling program will not. Finally, see that every column has the same number of entries so that the whole forms a nice rectangle. When statisticians and other people who work with databases work with a data set, they expect this rectangular arrangement.

CREATING DATAFRAMES

Now let's figure out how to get these rows and columns into R. One thing you will quickly learn about R is that there is almost always more than one way to accomplish a goal. Sometimes the quickest or most efficient way is not the easiest to understand. In this case, we will build each column one by one and then join them together. This is somewhat labor intensive, and not the usual way that we would work with a data set, but it is easy to understand. First, we run this command to make the column of names:

```
> myFamilyNames <- c("Dad","Mom","Sis","Bro","Dog")
```

One thing you might notice is that every name is placed within double quotes. This is how you signal to R that you want it to treat something as a string of characters rather than the name of a storage location. If we had asked R to use Dad instead of "Dad" it would have looked for a storage location (a data object or variable) named Dad. Another thing to notice is that the commas separating the different values are outside of the double quotes. If you were writing a regular sentence this is not how things would look, but for computer programming the comma can only do its job of separating the different values if it is not included inside the quotes. Once you have typed the previous line, remember that you can check the contents of myFamilyNames by typing it on the next command line:

```
> myFamilyNames
```

The output should look like this:

```
[1] "Dad" "Mom" "Sis" "Bro" "Dog"
```

Next, you can create a vector of the ages of the family members, like this:

```
> myFamilyAges <- c(43, 42, 12, 8, 5)
```

Note that this is exactly the same command we used in the last chapter, so if you have kept R running between then and now you would not even have to retype this command because myFamilyAges would still be there. Actually, if you closed R since working the examples from the last chapter, you will have been prompted to save the workspace. If you did so, then R restored all the data objects you were using in the last session. You can always check by typing myFamilyAges on a blank command line. The output should look like this:

```
[1] 43 42 12 8 5
```

Hey, now you have used the c() function and the assignment arrow to make myFamily-Names and myFamilyAges. If you look at the data table earlier in the chapter you should be able to figure out the commands for creating myFamilyGenders and myFamilyWeights. In case you run into trouble, these commands also appear soon, but you should try to figure them out for yourself before you see the commands in this book. In each case, after you type the command to create the new data object, you should also type the name of the data object at the command line to make sure that it looks the way it should. There are four variables, each with five values in it. Two of the variables are character data, and two of the variables are integer data.

Before we show you the R code to create myFamilyGenders and myFamilyWeights, let's explore myFamilyAges some more. We now know that myFamilyAges is a variable, and that is a vector, which means it is a list of numbers. We can access each number individually, using square brackets [ ]. For example, if we want to output just the second element in myFamilyAges, we could do the following:

```
> myFamilyAges[2]
[1] 42
```

Here are those two extra commands, to define myFamilyGenders and myFamily-Weights in case you need them:

```
> myFamilyGenders <-
+         c("Male","Female","Female","Male","Female")
> myFamilyWeights <- c(188,136,83,61,44)
```

Note that the + on the second line was added by R: R knew we were not done after just one line. The + means the line is a continuation of the previous line, as opposed to starting a new R command. So, in the rest of this book, when you see that +, know that R has added it to the command line (just as when R adds the >, you know R is ready for a new command).

Now we are ready to tackle the dataframe. In R, a dataframe is a list (of columns), where each element in the list is a vector. Each vector is the same length, which is how we get our nice rectangular row-and-column setup, and generally each vector also has its own name. The command to make a dataframe is very simple:

```
> myFamily <- data.frame(myFamilyNames, myFamilyAges,
+         myFamilyGenders, myFamilyWeights)
```

Look out! We're starting to get commands that are long enough that they break onto more than one line. If you want, you can type the whole thing as one line in R. Anyway, the data.frame() function makes a dataframe from the four vectors that we previously typed in. Notice that we have also used the assignment arrow to make a new stored location where R puts the dataframe. This new data object, called myFamily, is our dataframe. Once you have gotten that command to work, type myFamily at the command line to get a report back of what the dataframe contains.

```
> myFamily
```

Here's the output you should see:

```
   myFamilyNames myFamilyAges myFamilyGenders
1            Dad           43            Male
2            Mom           42          Female
3            Sis           12          Female
4            Bro            8            Male
5            Dog            5          Female


   myFamilyWeights
1              188
2              136
3               83
4               61
5               44
```

This looks great. Notice that R has put row numbers in front of each row of our data. These are different from the output line numbers we saw in square brackets before, because these are actual indices into the dataframe. In other words, they are the row numbers that R uses to keep track of which row a particular piece of data is in.

EXPLORING DATAFRAMES

With a small data set like this one, only five rows, it is pretty easy just to take a look at all of the data. But when we get to a bigger data set this won't be practical. We need to have other ways of summarizing what we have. The first method reveals the type of structure that R has used to store a data object.

```
> str(myFamily)
'data.frame':    5 obs. of 4 variables:
 $ myFamilyNames : Factor w/ 5 levels
                   "Bro","Dad","Dog",..: 2 4 5 1 3
 $ myFamilyAges :   num 43 42 12 8 5
 $ myFamilyGenders: Factor w/ 2 levels
                   "Female","Male": 2 1 1 2 1
 $ myFamilyWeights: num 188 136 83 61 44
```

OK, so the function str() reveals the structure of the data object that you name between the parentheses. In this case, we pretty well knew that myFamily was a dataframe because we just set that up in a previous command. In the future, however, we will run into many situations where we are not sure how R has created a data object, so it is important to know str() so that you can ask R to report what an object is at any time.

In the first line of output we have the confirmation that myFamily is a dataframe as well as an indication that there are five observations (obs., which is another word that statisticians use instead of cases or instances) and four variables. After that first line of output, we have four sections that each begin with $. For each of the four variables, these sections describe the component columns of the myFamily dataframe object.

Each of the four variables has a mode or type that is reported by R right after the colon on the line that names the variable:

```
$ myFamilyGenders: Factor w/ 2 levels
```

For example, myFamilyGenders is shown as Factor. In the terminology that R uses, Factor refers to a special type of label that can be used to identify and organize groups of cases. R has organized these labels alphabetically and then listed out the first few cases (because our dataframe is so small it actually is showing us all the cases). For myFamilyGenders we see that there are two levels, meaning that there are two different options: female and male. R assigns a number, starting with 1, to each of these levels, so every case that is Female gets assigned a 1 and every case that is Male gets assigned a 2 (Female comes before Male in the alphabet, so Female is the first Factor label and gets a 1). If you have your thinking cap on, you might be wondering why we started out by typing in small strings of text, like Male, but then R has gone ahead and converted these small pieces of text into numbers that it calls Factors. The reason for this lies in the statistical origins of R. For years, researchers have done things like calling an experimental group Exp and a control group Ctl without intending to use these small strings of text for anything other than labels. So R assumes, unless you tell it otherwise, that when you type in a short string like Male that you are referring to the label of a group, and that R should prepare for the use of Male as a Level of a Factor. When you don't want this to happen you can instruct R to stop doing this with an option on the data.frame() function: stringsAsFactors=FALSE. We will look with more detail at options and defaults a little later on.

Phew, that was complicated! By contrast, our two numeric variables, myFamilyAges and myFamilyWeights, are very simple. You can see that after the colon the mode is shown as num (which stands for numeric) and that the first few values are reported:

```
$ myFamilyAges : num 43 42 12 8 5
```

Putting it all together, we have pretty complete information about the myFamily dataframe and we are just about ready to do some more work with it. We have seen first-hand that R has sometimes has cryptic labels for things as well as some obscure strategies for converting this to that. R was designed for experts, rather than novices, so we will just have to take our lumps so that one day we can be experts, too.

Next, we will examine another very useful function called summary(). The summary command provides some overlapping information to the str command but also goes a little farther, particularly with numeric variables. Here's what we get:

```
> summary(myFamily)
myFamilyNames    myFamilyAges
Bro: 1           Min.    : 5
Dad: 1           1st Qu. : 8
Dog: 1           Median  : 12
Mom: 1           Mean    : 22
Sis: 1           3rd Qu. : 42
                 Max.    : 43


myFamilyGenders myFamilyWeights
Female: 3        Min.    : 44
Male : 2         1st Qu. : 61.0
                 Median  : 83.0
                 Mean    : 102.4
                 3rd Qu. : 136.0
                 Max     : 188.0
```

In order to fit on the page properly, these columns have been somewhat reorganized. The name of a column/variable sits up above the information that pertains to it, and each block of information is independent of the others (so it is meaningless, for instance, that Bro: 1 and Min. happen to be on the same line of output). Notice, as with str(), that the output is quite different depending on whether we are talking about a Factor, like myFamilyNames or myFamilyGenders, versus a numeric variable like myFamilyAges and myFamilyWeights. The columns for the Factors list out a few of the names along with the number of occurrences of cases that are coded with that factor. So, for instance, under myFamilyGenders it shows three females and two males. In contrast, for the numeric variables we get five different calculated quantities that help to summarize the variable. There's no time like the present to start to learn about what these are, so here goes:

Min. refers to the minimum or lowest value among all the cases. For this dataframe, five is the age of Dog, and it is the lowest age of all of the family members.

1st Qu. refers to the dividing line at the top of the first quartile. If we took all the cases and lined them up side by side in order of age (or weight) we could then divide up the whole into four groups, where each group had the same number of observations. Just like a number line, the smallest cases would be on the left with the largest on the right. If we're looking at myFamilyAges, the leftmost group, which contains one quarter of all the cases, would start with five on the low end (Dog) and would have eight on the high end (Bro). So the first quartile is the value of age (or another variable) that divides the first quarter of the cases from the other three quarters. Note that if we don't have a number of cases that divides evenly by four, the value is an approximation.

Median refers to the value of the case that splits the whole group in half, with half of the cases having higher values and half having lower values. If you think about it, the median is also the dividing line that separates the second quartile from the third quartile.

Mean, as we have learned before, is the numeric average of all of the values. For instance, the average age in the family is reported as 22.

3rd Qu. is the third quartile. If you remember back to the first quartile and the median, this is the third and final dividing line that splits up all of the cases into four equal sized parts. You might be wondering about these quartiles and what they are useful for. Statisticians like them because they give a quick sense of the shape of the distribution. Everyone has the experience of sorting and dividing things up—pieces of pizza, playing cards into hands, a bunch of players into teams—and it is easy for most people to visualize four equal-sized groups and useful to know how high you need to go in age or weight (or another variable) to get to the next dividing line between the groups.

Finally, Max is the maximum value and, as you might expect, displays the highest value among all of the available cases. For example, in this dataframe Dad has the highest weight: 188. Seems like a pretty trim guy.

Wow, that was a lot of info! Taking a step back, these metrics that we just described are different ways to measure a distribution. Mean and median are measures of central tendency, in that they try to explain the center of the distribution. Another key concept is the measure of dispersion, which lets us understand how stretched out the distribution is. Example of a measure of dispersion that you get from the summary() function include min, max, and quartiles. Other measures, which we discuss in Chapter 9, include variance and standard deviation.

While both the str() and summary() functions are very useful, sometimes we just want to look at a couple of rows in the dataframe. Previously, we typed myFamily at the command line and saw all the rows in the dataframe. However, if the dataframe has many rows, a better way is to use head() or tail().

```
> head(myFamily, 2)
myFamilyNames  myFamilyAges  myFamilyGenders  myFamilyWeights
1         Dad           43            Male              188
2         Mom           42          Female              136
> tail(myFamily, 2)
myFamilyNames  myFamilyAges  myFamilyGenders  myFamilyWeights
4         Bro            8            Male               61
5         Dog            5          Female               44
```

You can see in the code that head() lists the first rows in the dataframe and tail lists the last rows in the dataframe. The actual number of rows to output is the second parameter, in our case, we had R output the first two rows and then the last two rows in the myFamily dataframe.

ACCESSING COLUMNS IN A DATAFRAME

Just one more topic to pack in before ending this chapter: How to access the stored variables in our new dataframe. R stores the dataframe as a list of vectors, and we can use the name of the dataframe together with the name of a vector to refer to each one using the $ to connect the two labels like this:

```
> myFamily$myFamilyAges
[1] 43 42 12 8 5
```

If you're alert, you might wonder why we went to the trouble of typing out that big long thing with the $ in the middle when we could have just referred to myFamilyAges as we did earlier when we were setting up the data. Well, this is a very important point. When we created the myFamily dataframe, we *copied* all of the information from the individual vectors that we had before into a brand-new storage space. So now that we have created the myFamily dataframe, myFamily$myFamilyAges actually refers to a completely separate (but so far identical) vector of values. You can prove this to yourself very easily, and you should, by adding some data to the original vector, myFamilyAges:

```
> myFamilyAges <- c(myFamilyAges, 11)
> myFamilyAges
[1]  43 42 12 8 5 11
> myFamily$myFamilyAges
[1]  43 42 12 8 5
```

Look very closely at the five lines above. In the first line, we use the c() command to add the value 11 to the original list of ages that we had stored in myFamilyAges (perhaps we have adopted an older cat into the family). In the second line, we ask R to report what the vector myFamilyAges now contains. Dutifully, on the third line above, R reports that myFamilyAges now contains the original five values and the new value of 11 on the end of the list. When we ask R to report myFamily$myFamilyAges, however, we still have the original list of five values only. This shows that the dataframe and its component columns/vectors is now a completely independent piece of data. We must be very careful, if we established a dataframe that we want to use for subsequent analysis, that we don't make a mistake and keep using some of the original data from which we assembled the dataframe.

Here's a puzzle that follows on from this question. We have a nice dataframe with five observations and four variables. This is a rectangular data set, as we discussed at the beginning of the chapter. What if we tried to add on a new piece of data on the end of one of the variables? In other words, what if we tried something like the following command?

```
> myFamily$myFamilyAges<-c(myFamily$myFamilyAges, 11)
```

If this worked, we would have a pretty weird situation: The variable in the dataframe that contained the family members' ages would all of a sudden have one more observation than the other variables: no more perfect rectangle! Try it out and see what happens. The result helps to illuminate how R approaches situations like this.

So what new skills and knowledge do we have at this point? Here are a few of the key points from this chapter:

In R, as in other programs, a vector is a list of elements/things that are all of the same kind, or what R refers to as a mode. For example, a vector of mode numeric would contain only numbers.

Statisticians, database experts, and others like to work with rectangular data sets where the rows are cases or instances and the columns are variables or attributes.

In R, one of the typical ways of storing these rectangular structures is in an object known as a dataframe. Technically speaking, a dataframe is a list of vectors where each vector has the exact same number of elements as the others (making a nice rectangle).

In R, the data.frame() function organizes a set of vectors into a dataframe. A dataframe is a conventional, rectangular data object where each column is a vector of uniform mode and having the same number of elements as the other columns in the dataframe. Data are copied from the original source vectors into a new storage area. The variables/columns of the dataframe can be accessed using $ to connect the name of the dataframe to the name of the variable/column.

The str() and summary() functions can be used to reveal the structure and contents of a dataframe (as well as of other data objects stored by R). The str() function shows the structure of a data object, while summary() provides numerical summaries of numeric variables and overviews of non-numeric variables.

The head() and tail() functions can be used to reveal the first or last rows in a dataframe.

A factor is a labeling system often used to organize groups of cases or observations. In R, as well as in many other software programs, a factor is represented internally with a numeric ID number, but factors also typically have labels like Male and Female or Experiment and Control. Factors always have levels, and these are the different groups that the factor signifies. For example, if a factor variable called Gender codes all cases as either Male or Female then that factor has exactly two levels.

Min and max are often used as abbreviations for minimum and maximum; these are the terms used for the highest and lowest values in a vector. Bonus: The range of a set of numbers is the maximum minus the minimum.

The mean is the same thing that most people think of as the average. Bonus: The mean and the median are both measures of what statisticians call central tendency.

Quartiles are a division of a sorted vector into four evenly sized groups. The first quartile contains the lowest-valued elements, for example, the lightest weights, whereas the fourth quartile contains the highest-valued items. Because there are four groups, there are three dividing lines that separate them. The middle dividing line that splits the vector exactly in half is the median. The term *first quartile* often refers to the dividing line to the left of the median that splits up the lower two quarters, and the value of the first quartile is the value of the element of the vector that sits right at that dividing line. Third quartile is the same idea, but to the right of the median and splitting up the two higher quarters. Bonus: quartiles is a measure of dispersion.

Chapter Challenge

Create another variable containing information about family members (e.g., each family member's estimated IQ; you can make up the data). Take that new variable and put it in the existing myFamily dataframe. Rerun the summary() function on myFamily to get descriptive information on your new variable.

Sources

http://en.wikipedia.org/wiki/Central_tendency

http://en.wikipedia.org/wiki/Median

http://en.wikipedia.org/wiki/Relational_model

http://en.wikipedia.org/wiki/Statistical_dispersion

http://stat.ethz.ch/R-manual/R-devel/library/base/html/data.frame.html

http://www.burns-stat.com/pages/Tutor/hints_R_begin.html

http://www.khanacademy.org/math/statistics/v/mean-median-and-mode

R Functions Used in This Chapter

c()	Combines data elements together.
<-	Indicates an assignment arrow.
data.frame()	Makes a dataframe from separate vectors.
head()	Lists the first row in a dataframe.
str()	Reports the structure of a data object.
summary()	Reports data modes/types and a data overview.
tail()	Lists the last row in a dataframe.

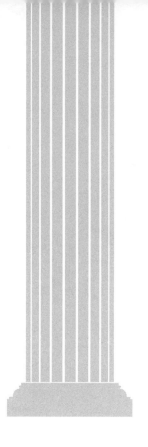
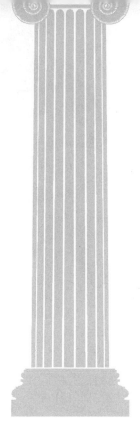

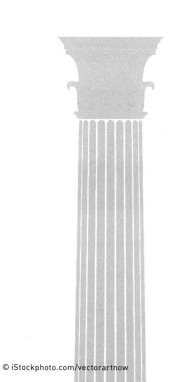

© iStockphoto.com/Tuned_In

6

DATA MUNGING

LEARNING OBJECTIVES

- Describe what data munging is.

- Demonstrate how to read a CSV data file.

- Explain how to select, remove, and rename rows and columns.

- Assess why data scientists need to be able to munge data.

- Demonstrate how to munge data in R while using the following functions: read.csv, url, gsub, rownames, colnames, order.

Data munging is the process of turning a data set with a bunch of junk in it into a nice clean data set. Why is data munging required and why is it important? Well, often R does not guess correctly the structure of the data set, or perhaps R reads a number or a date and thinks it is a simple string. Another issue might be that the data file might have additional information that is useful for humans but not for R. If you think about it, so far we have only explored simple data sets that we created within R. Clearly, the larger the data set, the more difficult it becomes to just type the data into R. Working through these issues so that R can process the data in a dataframe is often a lot of work. It's a big part of data science but perhaps not the most glamorous.

READING A CSV TEXT FILE

So, in this chapter, we explore how to read in a data set that is stored as a comma-delimited text file (known as a CSV file—which stands for comma separated values) that needs to be cleaned up. As we will see in future chapters, there are many formats that we might have to be able to process to get data into R, but for now we will focus on a very common human readable file format. Our first real data set will be U.S. census data. The U.S. Census Bureau has stored population data in many locations on its website, with many interesting data sets to explore. We will use one of the simpler data sets available at www2.census.gov/programs-surveys/popest/tables/2010-2011/state/totals/.

Click on the CSV link for nst-est2011-01.csv; you will either download a CSV (comma separated value file) or your browser will show a bunch of text information, with the first few lines likes like:

```
table with row headers in column A and column headers in rows
3 through 4. (leading dots indicate sub-parts),,,,,,,,,
"Table 1. Annual Estimates of the Population for the
United States, Regions, States, and Puerto Rico: April 1,
2010 to July 1, 2011",,,,,,,,, Geographic Area,"April 1,
2010",,Population Estimates (as of July 1),,,,,,,
Census,Estimates Base,2010,2011,,,,,UnitedStates,"308,
745,538","308,745,538","309,330,219","311,591,
917",,,,,Northeast,"55,317,240","55,317,244","55,366,
108","55,521,598",,,,, Midwest,"66,927,001","66,926,
987","66,976,458","67,158,835",,,,, South,"114,555,
744","114,555,757","114,857,529","116,046,736",,,,,
West,"71,945,553","71,945,550","72,130,124","72,864,
748",,,,,.Alabama,"4,779,736","4,779,735","4,785,401",
"4,802,740",,,,,
```

Now, having the data in the browser isn't useful, so let's write some R code to read in this data set.

```
> urlToRead <-
+ "http://www2.census.gov/programs-surveys/
+     popest/tables/2010-2011/state/totals/
+     nst-est2011-01.csv"
> testFrame <- read.csv(url(urlToRead))
```

The first line of code just defines the location (on the web) of the file to load (note that the URL is so long, it actually takes four lines to define the assignment). As we noted before, since the CSV file is human readable, you can actually cut and paste the URL into a web browser, and the page will show up as a list of rows of data. The next row of code reads the file, using the read.csv command. Note we also use the url() function so R knows that the filename is a URL (as opposed to a local file on the computer).

Next, let's take a look at what we got back. We can use the str() function to create a summary of the structure of testFrame:

```
> str(testFrame)
'data.frame':    66 obs. of 10 variables:
$ table.with.row.headers.in.column.A.and.column.
headers.in.rows.3.through.4...leading.dots.indicate.sub.
parts.: Factor w/ 65 levels "",".Alabama",..: 62 53 1
64 55 54 60 65 2 3 ...
$ X: Factor w/ 60 levels "","1,052,567",..: 1 59 60
27 38 47 10 49 32 50 ...
$ X.1: Factor w/ 59 levels "","1,052,567",..: 1 1 59
27 38 47 10 49 32 50 ...
$ X.2: Factor w/ 60 levels "","1,052,528",..: 1 60 21
28 39 48 10 51 33 50 ...
$ X.3: Factor w/ 59 levels "","1,051,302",..: 1 1 21
28 38 48 10 50 33 51 ...
$ X.4: logi NA NA NA NA NA NA ...
$ X.5: logi NA NA NA NA NA NA ...
$ X.6: logi NA NA NA NA NA NA ...
$ X.7: logi NA NA NA NA NA NA ...
$ X.8: logi NA NA NA NA NA NA ...
```

The last few lines are reminiscent of that late 1960s song entitled, "Na Na Hey Hey Kiss Him Goodbye." Setting aside all the NA NA NA NAs, however, the overall structure is 66 observations of 10 variables, signifying that the spreadsheet contained 66 rows and 10 columns of data. The variable names that follow are pretty bizarre. Now you understand what data scientists mean by junk in their data. The first variable name is

table.with.row.headers.in.column.A.and.column.headers.in.rows.3.through.4... leading.dots.indicate.sub.parts.

REMOVING ROWS AND COLUMNS

What a mess! It is clear that read.csv() treated the upper-leftmost cell as a variable label, but was flummoxed by the fact that this was really just a note to human users of the spreadsheet (the variable labels, such as they are, came on lower rows of the spreadsheet). Subsequent variable names include X, X.1, and X.2: Clearly the read.csv() function did not have an easy time getting the variable names out of this file.

The other worrisome finding from str() is that all of our data are factors. This indicates that R did not see the incoming data as numbers, but rather as character strings that it interpreted as factor data. Again, this is a side effect of the fact that some of the first cells that read.csv() encountered were text rather than numeric. The numbers came much later in the sheet. Clearly, we have some work to do if we are to make use of these data as numeric population values. This is common for data scientists, in that sometimes the data are available but need to be cleaned up before they can be used. In fact, data scientists often use the phrase "data munging" as the verb to describe the act of cleaning up data sets. So, let's get data munging!

First, let's review one way to access a list, a vector or a dataframe. As mentioned briefly in a previous chapter, in R, square brackets allow indexing into a list, vector, or dataframe. For example, myList[3] would give us the third element of myList. Keeping in mind that a dataframe is a rectangular structure, really a two-dimensional structure, we can address any element of a dataframe with both a row and column designator: myFrame[4,1] would give the fourth row and the first column. A shorthand for taking the whole column of a dataframe is to leave the row index empty: myFrame[, 6] would give every row in the sixth column. Likewise, a shorthand for taking a whole row of a dataframe is to leave the column index empty: myFrame[10,] would give every column in the tenth row. We can also supply a list of rows instead of just one row, like this: myFrame[c(1,3,5),] would return rows 1, 3, 5 (including the data for all columns, because we left the column index blank).

Using this knowledge, we will use an easy trick to get rid of stuff we don't need. The Census Bureau put in three header rows that we can eliminate like this:

```
> testFrame <- testFrame[-1:-8,]
```

The minus sign used inside the square brackets refers to the index of rows that should be eliminated from the dataframe. So the notation -1:-8 gets rid of the first eight rows. We also leave the column designator empty so that we can keep all columns for now. So the interpretation of the notation within the square brackets is that rows 1 through 8 should be dropped, all other rows should be included, and all columns should be included. We assign the result back to the same data object, thereby replacing the original with our new, smaller, cleaner version.

Next, we can see that of the 10 variables we got from read.csv(), only the first five are useful to us (the last five seem to be blank). How can we know that the last columns are not useful? Well, we can use the summary command we saw last chapter to explore testFrame but only look at the summary for the last five columns:

```
> summary(testFrame[,6:10])
X.4              X.5              X.6              X.7              X.8
Mode:logical     Mode:logical     Mode:logical     Mode:logical     Mode:logical
NA's:58          NA's:58          NA's:58          NA's:58          NA's:58
```

So, with the summary command, we can see those five columns are all just NA, and so can be removed without removing any data from testFrame. We can use the following command keeps the first five columns of the dataframe:

```
> testFrame <- testFrame[,1:5]
```

In the same vein, the tail() function shows us that the last few rows just contained some Census Bureau notes:

```
> tail(testFrame,5)
```

So we can safely eliminate those like this:

```
> testFrame <- testFrame[-52:-58,]
```

If you're alert you will notice that we could have combined some of these commands, but for the sake of clarity we have done each operation individually. The result is a dataframe with 51 rows and five observations.

RENAMING ROWS AND COLUMNS

Now we are ready to perform a couple of data transformations. But before we start these transformations, let's give our first column a more reasonable name:

```
> testFrame$stateName <- testFrame[,1]
```

We've used a little hack here to avoid typing out the ridiculously long name of that first variable/column. We've used the column notation in the square brackets on the right-hand side of the expression to refer to the first column (the one with the ridiculous name) and simply copied the data into a new column titled stateName.

Rather than create a new column, we could have renamed the column. So, let's also do this renaming, using the colnames() function. If this function is just called with a dataframe as a parameter, then the function returns the column names in the dataframe, as shown below:

```
> colnames(testFrame)
[1]
"table.with.row.headers.in.column.A.and.column.headers
.in.rows.3.through.4...leading.dots.indicate.sub.parts
."
[2] "X"
[3] "X.1"
[4] "X.2"
[5] "X.3"
[6] "stateName"
```

We also can use colnames() to update the column names in the dataframe. We do this by having the colnames() function on the left side of the assignment statement. Putting this together, we first use colnames() to store the current column names, then update the first element to a new name, and finally use colnames() to update the column names in the dataframe:

```
> cnames <- colnames(testFrame)
> cnames[1] <- "newName"
> cnames
[1] "newName" "X"       "X.1"     "X.2"     "X.3"
"stateName"
> colnames(testFrame) <- cnames
> colnames(testFrame)
[1] "newName" "X"       "X.1"     "X.2"     "X.3"
"stateName"
```

This points out one of the good (and bad) aspects of using R—there is often more than one way to get something done. Sometimes there is a better way, but sometimes just an alternative way. In this situation, for very large data sets, renaming columns would typically be slightly better than creating a new column. In any event, since we have created the new column, let's remove the first column (since we already have the column name we want with the last column in the data set).

```
> testFrame <- testFrame[,-1]
```

CLEANING UP THE ELEMENTS

Next, we can change formats and data types as needed. We can remove the dots from in front of the state names very easily with the gsub() command, which replaces all occurrence of a pattern and returns the new string. The g means replace all (it actually stands for global substitute). There is also a sub function, but we want all the dots to be removed, so we will use the gsub() function.

```
> testFrame$stateName <- gsub("\\.","",
+         testFrame$stateName)
```

The two backslashes in the preceding string expression are called escape characters, and they force the dot that follows to be treated as a literal dot rather than as a wildcard character. The dot on its own is a wildcard that matches one instance of any character.

Next, we can use gsub() and as.numeric() to convert the data contained in the population columns to usable numbers. Remember that those columns are now represented as R factors and what we are doing is taking apart the factor labels (which are basically character strings that look like this: 308,745,538) and making them into numbers. First, let's get rid of the commas.

```
> testFrame$april10census <-gsub(",", "", testFrame$X)
> testFrame$april10base <-gsub(",", "", testFrame$X.1)
> testFrame$july10pop <- gsub(",", "", testFrame$X.2)
> testFrame$july11pop <- gsub(",", "", testFrame$X.3)
```

Next, let's get rid of spaces and convert to a number:

```
> testFrame$april10census <- as.numeric(gsub(" ", "",
+     testFrame$april10census))
> testFrame$april10base <- as.numeric(gsub(" ", "",
+     testFrame$april10base))
> testFrame$july10pop <- as.numeric(gsub(" ", "",
+     testFrame$july10pop))
> testFrame$july11pop <- as.numeric(gsub(" ", "",
+     testFrame$july11pop))
```

This code is flexible in that it will deal with both unwanted commas and spaces and will convert strings into numbers whether they are integers or not (i.e., possibly with digits after the decimal point).

Finally, let's remove the columns with the X names:

```
> testFrame <- testFrame[,-1:-4]
```

By the way, the choice of variable names for the new columns in the dataframe was based on an examination of the original data set that was imported by read.csv(). We can confirm that the new columns on the dataframe are numeric by using str() to accomplish this.

```
> str(testFrame)
'data.frame':    51 obs. of  5 variables:
 $ stateName    : chr  "Alabama" "Alaska" "Arizona"
"Arkansas" ...
 $ april10census: num  4779736 710231 6392017 2915918
37253956 ...
 $ april10base  : num  4779735 710231 6392013 2915921
37253956 ...
 $ july10pop    : num  4785401 714146 6413158 2921588
37338198 ...
 $ july11pop    : num  4802740 722718 6482505 2937979
37691912 ...
```

Perfect! Let's take a look at the first five rows:

```
> head(testFrame,5)
   stateName april10census april10base july10pop july11pop
9    Alabama       4779736     4779735   4785401   4802740
10    Alaska        710231      710231    714146    722718
11   Arizona       6392017     6392013   6413158   6482505
12  Arkansas       2915918     2915921   2921588   2937979
13 California      37253956    37253956  37338198  37691912
```

Well, the data look good, but what are the 9, 10, 11, 12, and 13? They are row names—which the read.csv function defined. At the time, those numbers were the same as the row number in the file. But now, these make no sense (if you remember, we deleted the first eight rows in this data set). So, we have to do one more command to remove the confusing row names with the following one line of R code:

```
> rownames(testFrame) <- NULL
```

This line basically tells R that we do not want to have row names and is similar to colnames() but works on the row names, not the column names.

```
> head(testFrame,5)
stateName april10census april10base july10pop july11pop
1    Alabama    4779736    4779735    4785401    4802740
2     Alaska     710231     710231     714146     722718
3    Arizona    6392017    6392013    6413158    6482505
4   Arkansas    2915918    2915921    2921588    2937979
5 California   37253956   37253956   37338198   37691912
```

That's much better. Notice that we've spent a lot of time just conditioning the data we got in order to make it usable for later analysis. Herein lies a very important lesson. An important, and sometimes time-consuming, aspect of what data scientists do is to make sure that data are fit for the purpose to which they are going to be put. We had the convenience of importing a nice data set directly from the web with one simple command, and yet getting those data actually ready to analyze took several additional steps.

SORTING DATAFRAMES

Now that we have a real data set, let's do something with it! How about showing the five states with the highest populations? One way to do this is to sort the data set by the july11pop. But, while we can sort a vector with the sort command, sorting the dataframe is somewhat more challenging. So, let's explore how to sort a column in a dataframe, and basically reorder the dataframe. To accomplish this, we will use the order() function together with R's built-in square bracket notation.

As a reminder, we can supply a list of rows to access the dataframe: myFrame[c(1,3,5),] would return rows 1, 3, 5 (including the data for all columns, because we left the column index blank). We can use this feature to reorder the rows, using the order() function. We tell order() which variable we want to sort on, and it will give back a list of row indices in the order we requested.

Putting it all together yields this command:

```
> sortedStates <-
+     testFrame[order(testFrame$july11pop), ]
```

Working our way from the inside to the outside of the expression above, we want to sort in the order of the population, as defined by the july11pop column. We wrap this inside the order() function. The order() function will provide a list of row indices that reflects the population of the states. We use the square brackets notation to address the rows in the testFrame, taking all of the columns by leaving the index after the comma empty. Finally, we stored the new dataframe in variable sortedStates. Let's take a look at our results:

```
> head(sortedStates,5)
                  stateName april10census april10base
59                  Wyoming        563626      563626
17 District of Columbia           601723      601723
54                  Vermont        625741      625741
43            North Dakota         672591      672591
10                  Alaska         710231      710231

        july10pop    july11pop
51         564554       568158
9          604912       617996
46         625909       626431
35         674629       683932
2          714146       722718
```

Well, that is close, but it's the states with the lowest populations. We wanted the states with the largest (greatest) populations. We can either use the tail command to see the states with the largest population, or do the sort, but tell R to sort largest to smallest. We tell R we want the largest populations first by putting a minus sign (–) next to the vector we want sorted. What this actually does is that it makes the large numbers large negative numbers (so they are smaller), and the small numbers small negative numbers (so they are larger relative to the negative larger numbers). Wow, that's confusing, but it is easy to do in R and is done as follows:

```
> sortedStates <-
+     testFrame[order(-testFrame$july11pop), ]
> head(sortedStates,5)
stateName april10census april10base july10pop july11pop
5  California  37253956    37253956    37338198  37691912
44      Texas  25145561    25145561    25253466  25674681
33   New York  19378102    19378104    19395206  19465197
10    Florida  18801310    18801311    18838613  19057542
14   Illinois  12830632    12830632    12841980  12869257
```

That's it! We can see California has the most people, followed by Texas, and then New York.

In summary, as you have seen, data munging requires lots of knowledge of how to work with dataframes, combined with persistence to get the data into a format that is useful. While we have explored some common challenges related to data munging, there are other challenges we did not get to in this chapter. One classic challenge is working with dates, in that there are many formats such as a year with two or four digits and dates with the month or day is listed first. Another challenge often seen is when we want to combine two data sets. Combining them can be useful, for example when you have a data set with a person's name (or id) and her purchase history. A related data set might have that person's name (or id) and the state where she lives.

Chapter Challenge

Practice reading in a data set; this time the data set is about loans. Go to the lendingClub website (http://www.lendingclub.com/info/download-data.action), download a CSV file and then read in the file (using read.csv). Then, clean up the data set, making sure all the columns have useful information. This means you must explore the data set to understand what needs to be done! One trick to get you started is that you might need to skip one or more lines (before the header line in the CSV file). There is a skip parameter that you can use in your read.csv() command.

Sources

http://www2.census.gov/programs-surveys/popest/

R Commands Used in This Chapter

read.csv()	read in a CSV file
url()	make sure R knows that the file is a URL (not a local file)
gsub()	substitute one string for another
rownames()	get/set the row names for the data
colnames()	get/set the column names for the dataframe
order()	return the indices in the order of the vector supplied

© iStockphoto.com/IvicaNS

7

ONWARD WITH RSTUDIO®

LEARNING OBJECTIVES

- Know how to install the RStudio software package.
- Gain familiarity with using RStudio's interactive development environment.
- Construct and save R scripts.

RStudio is a trademark of RStudio, Inc.

In the previous chapter, we typed a variety of commands into R, using what is known as the R console. Console is an old technology term that dates back to the days when computers were so big that they each occupied its own air-conditioned room. Within that room there was often one master control station where a computer operator could do just about anything to control the giant computer by typing in commands. That station was known as the console. The term *console* is now used in many cases to refer to any interface where you can directly type in commands. We've typed commands into the R console in an effort to learn about the R language as well as to illustrate some basic principles about data structures and statistics.

USING AN INTEGRATED DEVELOPMENT ENVIRONMENT

If we really want to "do" data science, though, we can't sit around typing commands every day. First, it will become boring very fast. Second, whoever is paying us to be a data scientist will get suspicious when he or she notices that we are *retyping* some of the commands we typed yesterday. Third, and perhaps most important, it is way too easy to make a mistake—to create what computer scientists refer to as a bug—if you are doing every little task by hand. For these reasons, one of our big goals within this book is to create something that is reusable: where we can do a few clicks or type a couple of things and unleash the power of many processing steps. Using an integrated development environment (often abbreviated IDE), we can build these kinds of reusable pieces.

Every software engineer knows that if you want to get serious about building something out of code, you must use an IDE. Starting in 2009, Joseph J. Allaire, a serial entrepreneur, a software engineer, and the originator of some remarkable software products, began working with a small team to develop an open source program that enhances the usability and power of R. As mentioned in previous chapters, R is an open source program, meaning that the source code that is used to create a copy of R to run on a Mac, Windows, or Linux computer is available for all to inspect and modify. As with many open source projects, there is an active community of developers who work on R, both on the basic program itself and on the many pieces and parts that can be added on to the basic program.

If you think of R as a piece of canvas rolled up and lying on the floor, RStudio is like an elegant picture frame. R hangs in the middle of RStudio which like any good picture frame, enhances our appreciation of what is inside it. The IDE gives us the capability to open up the process of creation, to peer into the component parts when we need to, and to close the hood and hide them when we don't. Because we are working with data, we also need a way of closely inspecting the data, both its contents and its structure. As you probably noticed, it gets pretty tedious doing this at the R console, where almost every piece of output is a chunk of text and longer chunks scroll off the screen before you can see them. As an IDE for R, RStudio allows us to control and monitor both our code and our text in a way that supports the creation of reusable elements.

INSTALLING RSTUDIO

Before we can get there, though, we have to have RStudio installed on a computer. Perhaps the most challenging aspect of installing RStudio is having to install R first, but if you've already done that in Chapter 2, then RStudio should be a piece of cake. Make sure that you have the latest version of R installed before you begin with the installation of RStudio. There is ample documentation on the RStudio website, http://www.rstudio.org/, so if you follow the instructions there, you should have minimal difficulty. If you reach a page where you are asked to choose between installing RStudio server and installing RStudio as a desktop application on your computer, choose the latter. If you run into any difficulties or you just want some additional guidance about RStudio, you might want to have a look at the book entitled, *Getting Started with R-studio*, by John Verzani (2011, Sebastopol, CA: O'Reilly Media). The first chapter of that book has a general orientation to R and RStudio as well as a guide to installing and updating RStudio. There is also a YouTube video that introduces RStudio here: http://www.youtube.com/watch?v=7sAmqkZ3Be8

If you search for other YouTube videos, be aware that there is a disk recovery program as well a music group that share the RStudio name: You will get a number of these videos if you search on "RStudio" without any other search terms.

Once you have installed RStudio, you can run it immediately in order to get started with the activities in the later parts of this chapter. Unlike other introductory materials, we will not walk through all of the different elements of the RStudio screen. Rather, as we need each feature we will highlight the new aspect of the application. When you run RStudio, you will see three or four sub-windows. Use the File menu to click New and in the sub-menu for New click R Script. This should give you a screen that looks something like Figure 7.1.

CREATING R SCRIPTS

Now let's use RStudio! In the lower-left-hand pane (another name for a sub-window) of RStudio you will notice that we have a regular R console running. You can type commands into this console, just like we did in previous chapters just using R:

FIGURE 7.1

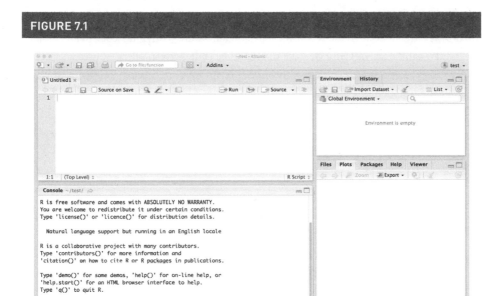

Click in the console pane and type the following:

```
> tinyData <- c(1,2,1,2,3,3,3,4,5,4,5)
> mean(tinyData)
[1] 3
```

As you can see, this behaves the exact same way as just using the R console!

However, it gets much more interesting if we use the upper-left-hand pane, which displays a blank space under the tab title Untitled1. This is the pane that contains your R source code file. If you click on the source code pane (upper-left pane) and then enter the following code:

```
tinyData <- c(1,2,1,2,3,3,3,4,5,4,5)

min(tinyData)
mean(tinyData)
sum(tinyData)
```

You can see, we are now writing R code, but you do not write the >. That is because we are not writing the code in the R console, but instead, we are writing the code in an R source file, which can be saved. Once we have the R source code, we can select "source with echo" to run the commands that you wrote into the R script file (upper-left-hand pane). You will then see the output in the lower-left-hand console pane. Once you have sourced (or run) the commands in the upper-left source pane, the output on the console looks as follows:

```
> tinyData <- c(1,2,1,2,3,3,3,4,5,4,5)
>
> min(tinyData)
[1] 1
> mean(tinyData)
[1] 3
> sum(tinyData)
[1] 33
```

As you can see, it is just as if we had typed the commands into the console window and that the output of min, mean, and sum commands show up in the R console pane. Your RStudio should now look like Figure 7.2.

FIGURE 7.2

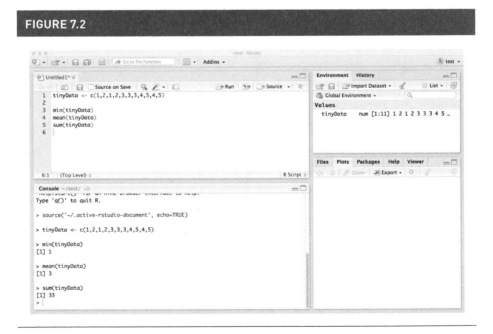

Note that you can also see in the upper right, there is a data element (tinyData). Let's write some more code in our R source file. First, we can create another vector, with each element of the vector being five more than the value in the tinyData vector. We next can create a dataframe using these two vectors. Finally, we can practice changing the column names within the dataframe.

```
biggerData <- tinyData + 5
df <- data.frame(tinyData, biggerData)
colnames(df) <- c("small", "big")
```

Another way to execute the code is to select (highlight) the code in the R source code window, and then press the "run" button. After doing that, you should see something like Figure 7.3.

FIGURE 7.3

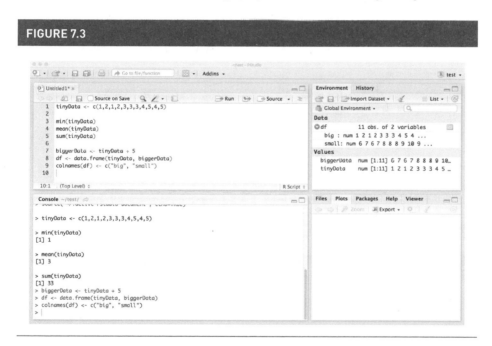

Note that in the upper right the environment window now has the dataframe df as well as the two vectors biggerData and tinyData. We can also explore the contents of df by clicking on the little down arrow (directly to the left of df in the Data part of the Global Environment). The other tab in the upper right is the History tab. This is useful to see the list of previous R commands we have executed. While we have not yet discussed the lower-right window, we will use that window later to see the results of our visualizations.

To recap, this chapter provided a basic introduction to RStudio, an IDE for R. An IDE is useful for helping to build reusable components for handling data and conducting data analysis. From this point forward, we will use RStudio, rather than plain old R, in order to save and be able to reuse our work. Among other things, RStudio makes it easy to manage packages in R, and packages are the key to R's extensibility. In future chapters, we will be routinely using R packages to get access to specialized capabilities. These specialized capabilities come in the form of extra functions that are created by developers in the R community

Chapter Challenge

Explore the global environment window within RStudio. Try to explain the difference between the Data variables and the Values variables.

Sources

http://en.wikipedia.org/wiki/R_(programming_language)

http://en.wikipedia.org/wiki/Joseph_J._Allaire

http://dss.princeton.edu/training/RStudio101.pdf

http://www.youtube.com/watch?v=7sAmqkZ3Be8

https://www.rstudio.com/products/rstudio/features/

R Commands Used in This Chapter

min()	find the minimum number in a vector
mean()	find the average for the entire vector
sum()	find the total for the entire vector
colnames()	define the column names for a dataframe

© iStockphoto.com/NeilStanners

8

WHAT'S MY FUNCTION?

We have previously been using and talking about functions. If you remember, back in Chapter 3 we used functions such as sum() and mean(). We also tried to use fish(), but that function was not defined, so R gave us an error. In this chapter, we will learn to create our own functions. While we will not define the function fish(), by the end of this chapter, if you really wanted, you will be able to create the fish function.

WHY CREATE AND USE FUNCTIONS?

Functions provide two key benefits. First, a key reason to create and use a function is so that we will not have to type the same R code over and over again. That is to say, when we write a function we can easily reuse the code. So, as we start to build more-complicated R programs, due to our desire to reuse R code we will need to create our own functions (as well as using more-advanced functions). The second key benefit of using a function is that, when using the function, we do not need to understand the details of how the function was written. This is known as abstraction. So, if we just want to use a function in our program, we don't have to know how it works inside! In fact, because of abstraction, when we use a function we only need to know the arguments that must be given to the function and what the function returns.

We actually already ran into arguments a little while ago with functions such as mean() and sum(). However, we did not talk about the concept of arguments then—we just used the function. *Argument* is a term used by computer scientists to refer to some extra information that is sent to a function to help it know how to do its job. For the function mean, we passed one argument, the vector on which we should calculate the mean. Other functions take more than one argument. One such function is tail(), which takes two arguments.

CREATING FUNCTIONS IN R

As a start, click in that R source code pane (the upper-left window in RStudio) and type the following:

```
MyMode <- function(myVector)
{
  return(myVector)
}
```

You have just created your first function in R. As was previously mentioned, a function is a bundle of R code that can be used over and over again without having to retype it. Other programming languages also have functions. Other words for function are "procedure" and "subroutine," although these terms can have a slightly different meaning in other languages. We have called our function MyMode. You might remember from a couple of chapters ago that the basic setup of R does not have a statistical mode function in it, even though it does have functions for the two other common central tendency statistics: mean() and median(). We're going to fix that problem by creating our own mode function. Recall that the mode function should count up how many of each value is in a list and then return the value that occurs most frequently. That is the definition of the statistical mode: the most frequently occurring item in a vector of numbers.

A couple of other things to note: The first is the myVector in parentheses on the first line of our function. This is the argument, or input to the function. We have seen and used arguments when we called functions such as mean() and median(). Next, note the curly braces that are used on the second and final lines. These curly braces hold together all of the code that goes in our function. Finally, look at the return() right near the end of our function. This return() is where we send back the result of what our function accomplished. Later on, when we call our new function from the R console, the result that we get back will be whatever is in the parentheses in the return().

Based on that explanation, can you figure out what MyMode() does in this primitive initial form? All it does is return whatever we give it in myVector, completely unchanged. By the way, this is a common way to write code, by incrementally enhancing what we are building. We can test out what we have each step of the way. Let's test out what we have accomplished so far. First, let's make a very small vector of data to work with. In the lower-left-hand pane of RStudio you will remember that we have a regular R console running. You can type commands into this console, just as we did in previous chapters:

```
> tinyData <- c(1,2,1,2,3,3,3,4,5,4,5)
> tinyData
 [1]  1  2  1  2  3  3  3  4  5  4  5
```

Then we can try out our new MyMode() function:

```
> MyMode(tinyData)
Error: could not find function "MyMode"
```

Oops! R doesn't know about our new function yet. We typed our MyMode() function into the code window, but we didn't tell R about it. If you look in the upper-left pane, you will see the code for MyMode() and just above that a few small buttons on a tool bar. One of the buttons looks like a little right pointing arrow with the word "Run" next to it. First, use your mouse to select all of the code for MyMode(), from the first M all the way to the last curly brace. Then click the Run button. You will immediately see the same code appear in the R console window just below. If you have typed everything correctly, there should be no errors or warnings. Now R knows about our MyMode() function and is ready to use it. Now we can type the following:

```
> MyMode(tinyData)
[1]  1 2 1 2 3 3 3 4 5 4 5
```

This did exactly what we expected: It just echoed back the contents of tinyData. You can also see from this example how parameters work. In the command just above, we passed in tinyData as the input to the function. While the function was working, it took what was in tinyData and copied it into myVector for use inside the function. Now we are ready to add the next command to our function:

```
MyMode <- function(myVector)
{
 uniqueValues <- unique(myVector)
 return(uniqueValues)
}
```

Because we made a few changes, the whole function appears again above. Later, when the code gets a little more complicated, we will provide one or two additional lines of code. Let's see what this code does. First, don't forget to select the code and click on the Run button. Then, in the R console, try the MyMode() command again:

```
> MyMode(tinyData)
[1]  1 2 3 4 5
```

Pretty easy to see what the new code does, right? We called the unique() function, and that returned a list of unique values that appeared in tinyData. Basically, unique() took out all of the redundancies in the vector that we passed to it. Now let's build a little more:

```
MyMode <- function(myVector)
{
  uniqueValues <- unique(myVector)
  uniqueCounts <- tabulate(myVector)
  return(uniqueCounts)
}
```

Don't forget to select all of this code and run it before testing it out. This time when we pass tinyData to our function we get back another list of five elements, but this time it is the count of how many times each value occurred:

```
> MyMode(tinyData)
[1]  2  2  3  2  2
```

Now we're basically ready to finish our MyMode() function, but let's make sure we understand the two pieces of data we have in uniqueValues and uniqueCounts. In Table 8.1 we have lined up a row of the elements of uniqueValues just above a row of the counts of how many of each of those values we have. Just for illustration purposes, in the top/label row we have also shown the index number. This index number is the way that we can address the elements in either of the variables that are shown in the rows. For instance, element number 4 (index 4) for uniqueValues contains the number 4, whereas element number 4 for uniqueCounts contains the number 2.

TABLE 8.1					
Index	1	2	3	4	5
uniqueValues	1	2	3	4	5
uniqueCounts	2	2	3	2	2

So if we're looking for the most frequently occurring item, we should look along the bottom row for the largest number. When we get there, we should look at the index of that cell. Whatever that index is, if we look in the same cell in uniqueValues, we will have the value that occurs most frequently in the original list. In R, it is easy to accomplish what was described in the last sentence with a single line of code:

```
uniqueValues <- unique(tinyData)
uniqueCounts <- tabulate(tinyData)
uniqueValues[which.max(uniqueCounts)]
```

The which.max() function finds the index of the element of uniqueCounts that is the largest. Then we use that index to address uniqueValues with square brackets. The square brackets let us get at any of the elements of a vector. For example, if we asked for uniqueValues[5] we would get the number 5. If we add this one list of code to our return statement, our function will be finished:

```
MyMode <- function(myVector)
{
 uniqueValues <- unique(myVector)
 uniqueCounts <- tabulate(myVector)
 return(uniqueValues[which.max(uniqueCounts)])
}
```

TESTING FUNCTIONS

We're now ready to test our function. Don't forget to select the whole thing and run it! Otherwise R will still be remembering our old MyMode() function. Let's ask R what tinyData contains, just to remind ourselves, and then we will send tinyData to our MyMode() function:

```
> tinyData
[1]  1 2 1 2 3 3 3 4 5 4 5
> MyMode(tinyData)
[1]  3
```

Hooray! It works. Three is the most frequently occurring value in tinyData. Let's keep testing and see what happens:

```
> tinyData <- c(tinyData,5,5,5)
> tinyData
[1] 1 2 1 2 3 3 3 4 5 4 5 5 5 5
> MyMode(tinyData)
[1] 5
```

It still works! We added three more fives to the end of the tinyData vector. Now tinyData contains five 5s. MyMode() properly reports the mode as 5. Hmm, now let's try to break it:

```
> tinyData <- c(tinyData, 1, 1, 1)
> tinyData
[1] 1 2 1 2 3 3 3 4 5 4 5 5 5 5 5 1 1 1
> MyMode(tinyData)
[1] 1
```

This is interesting: Now tinyData contains five 1s and five 5s. MyMode() now reports the mode as 1. This turns out to be no surprise. In the documentation for which.max() it says that this function will return the first maximum it finds. So this behavior is to be expected. Actually, this is always a problem with the statistical mode: There can be more than one mode in a data set. Our MyMode() function is not smart enough to realize this, nor does it give us any kind of warning that there are multiple modes in our data. It just reports the first mode that it finds.

Here's another problem:

```
> tinyData<-c(tinyData,9,9,9,9,9,9,9)
> MyMode(tinyData)
[1] NA
> tabulate(tinyData)
[1] 5 2 3 2 5 0 0 0 7
```

In the first line, we stuck a bunch of 9s on the end of tinyData. Remember that we had no 6s, 7s, or 8s. Now when we run MyMode() it says NA, which is R's way of saying that something went wrong and you are getting back an empty value. It is probably not obvious why things went wacky until we look at the last command above, tabulate(tinyData). Here we can see what happened: When it was run inside the

MyMode() function, tabulate() generated a longer list than we were expecting, because it added zeroes (0s) to cover the 6s, 7s, and 8s that were not there. The maximum value, out at the end is 7, and this refers to the number of 9s in tinyData. But look at what the unique() function produces:

```
> unique(tinyData)
[1] 1 2 3 4 5 9
```

There are only six elements in this list, so it doesn't match up as it should. (Take another look at Table 8.1 and imagine if the bottom row stuck out farther than the row just above it.) We can fix this with the addition of the match() function to our code:

```
MyMode <- function(myVector)
{
 uniqueValues <- unique(myVector)
 uniqueCounts <- tabulate(match(myVector,
                   uniqueValues))

 return(uniqueValues[which.max(uniqueCounts)])
}
```

Now instead of tabulating every possible value, including the ones for which we have no data, we tabulate only those items where there is a match between the list of unique values and what is in myVector. Now when we ask MyMode() for the mode of tinyData we get the correct result:

```
> MyMode(tinyData)
[1] 9
```

Aha! Now it works the way it should. After our last addition of seven 9s to the data set, the mode of this vector is correctly reported as 9.

Before we leave this activity, make sure to save your work. Click anywhere in the code window and then click on the File menu and then on Save. You will be prompted to choose a location and provide a filename. You can call the file MyMode, if you like. Note that R adds the R extension to the filename so that it is saved as MyMode.R. You can open this file at any time and rerun the MyMode() function in order to define the function in your current working version of R.

A couple of other points deserve attention. First, notice that when we created our own function we had to do some testing and repairs to make sure it ran the way we wanted it to. This is a common situation when working on anything related to computers, including spreadsheets, macros, and pretty much anything else that requires precision and accuracy. Second, we introduced at least four new functions in this exercise, including unique(), tabulate(), match(), and which.max(). Where did these come from and how did we know that these functions existed? R has so many functions that it is very difficult to memorize them all. There's almost always more than one way to do something, as well. So it can be quite confusing to create a new function if you don't know all of the ingredients and there's no one way to solve a particular problem. This is where the community comes in. Search online and you will find dozens of instances where people have tried to solve similar problems to the one you are solving, and you will also find that they have posted the R code for their solutions. These code fragments are free to borrow and test. In fact, learning from other people's examples is a great way to expand your horizons and learn new techniques.

The last point leads into the next key topic. We had to do quite a lot of work to create our MyMode function, and we are still not sure that it works perfectly on every variation of data it might encounter. Maybe someone else has already solved the same problem. If they did, we might be able to find an existing package to add onto our copy of R to extend its functions. In fact, for the statistical mode there is an existing package that does just about everything you could imagine doing with the mode. As shown in Figure 8.1, this package is called modeest, which is short for 'mode-estimator.'

FIGURE 8.1

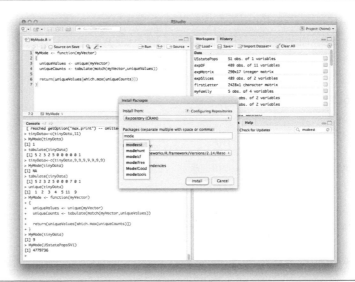

INSTALLING A PACKAGE
TO ACCESS A FUNCTION

To install this package, look in the lower-right-hand pane of RStudio. There are several tabs there, and one of them is Packages. Click on this and you will get a list of every package that you already have available in your copy of R (it might be a short list) with checkmarks for the ones that are ready to use. It is unlikely that modeest is already on this list, so click on the button that says Install Packages. This will give a dialog that looks like what you see in Figure 8.1. Type the beginning of the package name in the appropriate area, and RStudio will start to prompt you with matching choices. Finish typing "modeest" or choose it from the list. There might be a checked box for Install Dependencies, and if so leave this checked. In some cases, an R package will depend on other packages, and R will install all of the necessary packages in the correct order if it can. Once you click the Install button in this dialog, you will see some commands running on the R console (the lower-left pane). Generally, this works without a hitch and you should not see any warning messages. Once the installation is complete you will see modeest added to the list in the lower-right pane (assuming you have clicked the Packages tab). One last step is to click the check box next to it. This runs the library() function on the package, which prepares it for further use.

Let's try out the mfv() function. This function returns the most frequent value in a vector, which is generally what we want in a mode function:

```
> mfv(tinyData)
[1] 9
```

So far, so good! This seems to do exactly what our MyMode() function did, though it probably uses a different method. In fact, it is easy to see what strategy the authors of this package used just by typing the name of the function at the R command line:

```
> mfv
function (x, ...)
{
    f <- factor(x)
    tf <- tabulate(f)
    return(as.numeric(levels(f)[tf == max(tf)]))
}
<environment: namespace:modeest>
```

This is one of the great things about an open source program: You can easily look under the hood to see how things work. Notice that, while trying to understand this function at this time is beyond what we know, we can see that this code is quite different from how we built MyMode(), although it, too, uses the tabulate() function. The final line, that begins with the word "environment" has importance for more-complex feats of programming, since it indicates which variable names mfv() can refer to when it is working. The other aspect of this function, which is probably not so obvious, is that it will correctly return a list of multiple modes when such a list exists in the data you send to it:

```
> multiData <- c(1,5,7,7,9,9,10)
> mfv(multiData)
[1] 7 9
> MyMode(multiData)
[1] 7
```

In the first command line above, we made a small new vector that contains two modes, 7 and 9. Each of these numbers occurs twice, whereas the other numbers occur only once. When we run mfv() on this vector it correctly reports both 7 and 9 as modes. When we use our function, MyMode(), it only reports the first of the two modes.

To recap, by creating our own function we have learned that functions take arguments as their inputs and provide a return value. A return value is a data object, so it could be a single number (technically a vector of length one), or it could be a list of values (a vector) or even a more complex data object. We can write and reuse our own functions, which we will do quite frequently later in the book, or we can use other people's functions by installing their packages and using the library() function to make the contents of the package available. Once we have used library(), we can inspect how a function works by typing its name at the R command line. (Note that this works for many functions, but there are a few that were created in a different computer language, like C, and we will not be able to inspect the code for those as easily.)

Chapter Challenge

Write and test a new function called MyVectorInfo() that takes as input a vector and returns the key characteristics of the vector, such as the min, the max, and the mean of the vector. Make sure to give careful thought about the parameters you will need to pass to your function and what kind of data object your function will return.

Sources

https://www.cs.utah.edu/~zachary/computing/lessons/uces-10/uces-10/node11.html

R Commands Used in This Chapter

function()	Creates a new function
return()	Completes a function by returning a value
tabulate()	Counts occurrences of integer-valued data in a vector
unique()	Creates a list of unique values in a vector
match()	Takes two lists and returns values that are in each
mfv()	Most frequent value (from the modeest package)

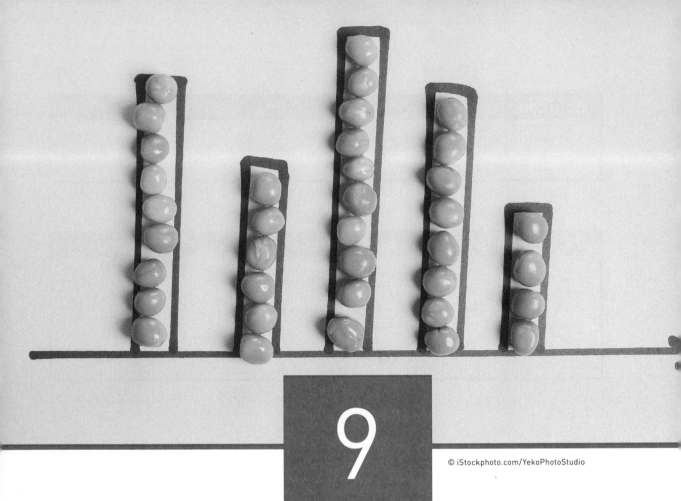

9

BEER, FARMS, AND PEAS AND THE USE OF STATISTICS

LEARNING OBJECTIVES

- Explain why we need to sample from a population.
- Compare the basic concepts of descriptive statistics such as mean, median, range, mode, variance, standard deviation.

- Use histograms to explain the concepts of central tendency and measures of dispersion.

- Understand and be able to generate a normal distribution.

- Demonstrate how to usethe following R functions: mean, median, var, sd, hist, rnorm.

HISTORICAL PERSPECTIVE

The end of the 1800s and the early 1900s were a time of astonishing progress in mathematics and science. Given enough time, paper, and pencils, scientists and mathematicians of that age imagined that just about any problem facing humankind—including the limitations of people themselves—could be measured, broken down, analyzed, and rebuilt to become more efficient. Four Englishmen who epitomized both this scientific progress and these idealistic beliefs were Francis Galton, Karl Pearson, William Sealy Gosset, and Ronald Fisher.

First on the scene was Francis Galton, a half-cousin to the more widely known Charles Darwin, but quite the intellectual force himself. Galton was a gentleman of independent means who studied Latin, Greek, medicine, and mathematics, and who made a name for himself as an explorer in Africa. He created the statistical concept of correlation and regression. He was also the first to apply statistical methods to the study of human differences and the inheritance of intelligence, which led to him coining the phrase "nature versus nurture." Alas, he also introduced the concept of eugenics. Eugenics was the idea that the human race could be improved through selective breeding. Galton studied heredity in peas, rabbits, and people and concluded that certain people should be paid to get married and have children because their offspring would improve the human race. For many people, the concept of eugenics is in itself a bad concept. Unfortunately, these ideas were perverted and used, most notably by the Nazis, as a justification for killing people.

For all his studying and theorizing, Galton was not an outstanding mathematician, but he had a junior partner, Karl Pearson, who is often credited with founding the field of mathematical statistics. Pearson refined the math behind correlation and regression and did a lot else besides to contribute to our modern abilities to manage numbers. Like Galton, Pearson was a proponent of eugenics, but he also is credited with inspiring some of Einstein's thoughts about relativity and was an early advocate of women's rights.

Next to the statistical party was William Sealy Gosset, a wizard at both math and chemistry. It was probably the latter expertise that led the Guinness brewery in Dublin, Ireland, to hire Gosset after college. As a forward-looking business, the Guinness brewery was on the lookout for ways of making batches of beer more consistent in quality. Gosset stepped in and developed what we now refer to as small sample statistical techniques—ways of generalizing from the results of a relatively few observations. Of course, brewing a batch of beer is a time-consuming and expensive process, so in order to draw conclusions from experimental methods applied to just a few batches, Gosset had to figure out the role of chance in determining how each batch beer turned out. Guinness frowned on academic publications, so Gosset had to publish his results under the modest pseudonym, "Student." If you ever hear someone discussing the "Student's t-Test," that is where the name came from.

Last but not least among the born-in-the-1800s bunch was Ronald Fisher, another mathematician who also studied the natural sciences, in his case biology and genetics. Unlike Galton, Fisher was not a gentleman of independent means. In fact, during his early married life he and his wife struggled as subsistence farmers. One of Fisher's professional postings was to an agricultural research farm called Rothhamsted Experimental Station. Here, he had access to data about variations in crop yield that led to his development of an essential statistical technique known as the analysis of variance. Fisher also pioneered the area of experimental design, which includes matters of factors, levels, experimental groups, and control groups that we noted in the previous chapter.

Of course, these four are certainly not the only 19th- and 20th-century mathematicians to have made substantial contributions to practical statistics, but they are notable with respect to the applications of mathematics and statistics to the other sciences (and "Beer, Farms, and Peas" makes a good chapter title as well).

SAMPLING A POPULATION

One of the critical distinctions woven throughout the work of these four is between the sample of data that you have available to analyze and the larger population of possible cases that might or do exist. When Gosset ran batches of beer at the brewery, he knew that it was impractical to run every possible batch of beer with every possible variation in recipe and preparation. Gosset knew that he had to run a few batches, describe what he had found, and then generalize or infer what might happen in future batches. This is a fundamental aspect of working with all types and amounts of data: Whatever data you have, there's always more out there. There are data that you might have collected by changing the way things are done or the way things are measured. There are future data that hasn't been collected yet and might never be collected. There are even data that we might have gotten using the exact same strategies we did use but that would have come out subtly different just due to randomness. Whatever data you have, it is just a snapshot, or sample, of what might be out there. This leads us to the conclusion that we can never, ever 100% trust the data we have. We must always hold back and keep in mind that there is always uncertainty in data. A lot of the power and goodness in statistics comes from the capabilities that people like Fisher developed to help us characterize and quantify that uncertainty and for us to know when to guard against putting too much stock in what a sample of data has to say. So remember that while we can always *describe* the sample of data we have, the real trick is to *infer* what the data could mean when generalized to the larger population of data that we don't have. This is the key distinction between descriptive and inferential statistics.

UNDERSTANDING DESCRIPTIVE STATISTICS

We have already encountered several descriptive statistics in previous chapters, but for the sake of practice here they are again, this time with the more-detailed definitions:

The mean (technically the arithmetic mean), is a measure of central tendency that is calculated by adding together all of the observations and dividing by the number of observations.

The median is another measure of central tendency but one that cannot be directly calculated. Instead, you make a sorted list of all of the observations in the sample and then go halfway up that list. Whatever the value of the observation is at the halfway point, that is the median.

The range is a measure of dispersion—how spread out a bunch of numbers in a sample are—calculated by subtracting the lowest value from the highest value.

The mode is another measure of central tendency. The mode is the value that occurs most often in a sample of data. Like the median, the mode cannot be directly calculated. You just have to count up how many of each number there are and then pick the category that has the most.

To this list we should add two more descriptive statistics that you will run encounter in a variety of situations.

First, the variance is a measure of dispersion. Like the range, the variance describes how spread out a sample of numbers is. Unlike the range, though, which uses just two numbers to calculate dispersion, the variance is obtained from all of the numbers through a simple calculation that compares each number to the mean. If you remember the ages of the family members from the previous chapter and the mean age of 22, you will be able to make sense out of Table 9.1.

TABLE 9.1

Who	Age	Age−Mean	(Age−Mean)^2
Dad	43	43 − 22 = 21	21 * 21 = 441
Mom	42	42 − 22 = 20	20 * 20 = 400
Sis	12	12 − 22 = −10	−10 * −10 = 100
Bro	8	8 − 22 = −14	−14 * −14 = 196
Dog	5	5 − 22 = −17	−17 * −17 = 289
		Total:	1426
		Total/4:	356.5

Table 9.1 shows the calculation of the variance, which begins by obtaining the deviations from the mean and then squares them (multiply each one times itself) to take care of the negative deviations (e.g., −14 from the mean for Bro). We add up all of the squared deviations and then divide by the number of observations to get a kind of average squared deviation. Note that it was not a mistake to divide by 4 instead of 5—the reasons for this is beyond the scope of this book but is related to the concept of degrees of freedom. This result is the variance, a very useful mathematical concept that appears all over the place in statistics. While it is mathematically useful, it is not too nice to look at. For instance, in this example we are looking at the 356.5 squared-years of deviation from the mean. Who measures anything in squared years? Squared feet maybe, but that's a different discussion. So, to address this weirdness, statisticians have also provided us with the next descriptive statistic.

The standard deviation is another measure of dispersion and a cousin to the variance. The standard deviation is simply the square root of the variance, which puts us back in regular units like years. In the previous example, the standard deviation would be about 18.88 years (rounding to two decimal places, which is plenty in this case).

Now let's have R calculate some statistics for us:

```
> var(myFamily$myFamilyAges)
[1]  356.5
> sd(myFamily$myFamilyAges)
[1]  18.88121
```

Note that these commands carry on using the data we used in the previous chapter, including the use of the $ to address variables within a dataframe. If you do not have the data from the previous chapter you can also do this:

```
> var(c(43,42,12,8,5))
[1]  356.5
> sd(c(43,42,12,8,5))
[1]  18.88121
```

USING DESCRIPTIVE STATISTICS

This was a pretty boring example, though, and not very useful for the rest of the chapter, so let's analyze our previously discussed U.S. population data set. Since we will use this data set many times, let's create a readCensus function. In the code that follows, note how comments are used (anything after the #) so that if we go back to this code, we can understand what was done. If some of this code does not make sense, go back to the previous chapter on data munging and review how we worked on this data set to get it into something useful.

```
#read in the census data set
readCensus <- function() {
  urlToRead <-
  "http://www2.census.gov/programs-surveys/
    popest/tables/2010-2011/state/totals/
    nst-est2011-01.csv"
```

```
#read the data from the web
testFrame <- read.csv(url(urlToRead))

#remove the first 8 rows ('header information')
testFrame<-testFrame[-1:-8,]
#only keep the first 5 columns
testFrame<-testFrame[,1:5]

#rename the first column
testFrame$stateName <- testFrame[,1]
testFrame<-testFrame[,-1]

#remove the last rows (tail info)
testFrame<-testFrame[-52:-58,]

#remove the 'dot' from the state name
testFrame$stateName <- gsub("\\.","",
testFrame$stateName)

#convert the columns to actual numbers and rename
#columns
testFrame$april10census <-Numberize(testFrame$X)
testFrame$april10base <-Numberize(testFrame$X.1)
testFrame$july10pop <-Numberize(testFrame$X.2)
testFrame$july11pop <-Numberize(testFrame$X.3)
testFrame <- testFrame[,-1:-4]

#remove the old rownames, which are now confusing
rownames(testFrame) <- NULL


return(testFrame)
}
```

Note that we actually created an additional function, Numberize, listed on page 87. This is because some of the code to remove commas and spaces from a string, and then convert it into a number, was sufficiently repetitive that it seemed to make sense to create a function call to do it—and it also might be useful with other R data munging that we might need to do. A lesson from our chapter on functions is that it is important and valuable to try to automate as many of these steps as possible. So when we saw that numbers had gotten stored as factor labels, we moved to create a general function that would convert these to numbers. Not only does this save a lot of future typing, but it also prevents mistakes from creeping into our processes.

```
# Numberize() - Gets rid of commas and other junk and
# converts to numbers
# Assumes that the inputVector is a list of data that
# can be treated as character strings
Numberize <- function(inputVector)
{
  # Get rid of commas
  inputVector<-gsub(",","", inputVector)
  # Get rid of spaces
  inputVector<-gsub(" ","", inputVector)

  return(as.numeric(inputVector))
}
```

Now that we have the function, let's read in the data:

```
> USstatePops <- readCensus()
>
> USstatePops$april10census[1:3]
[1]  4779736 710231 6392017
```

This would be a great moment to practice your skills from the previous chapter by using the str() and summary() functions on our new data object called USstatePops. Did you notice anything interesting from the results of these functions? One thing you might have noticed is that there are 51 observations instead of 50. Can you guess why? If not, go back and look at your original data from the spreadsheet or the U.S. Census site.

Now we're ready to have some fun with a good-sized list of numbers. Here are the basic descriptive statistics on the population of the states:

```
> mean(USstatePops$april10census)
[1]  6053834
```

```
> median(USstatePops$april10census)
[1]  4339367
> mode(USstatePops$april10census)
[1]  "numeric"
> var(USstatePops$april10census)
[1]  4.656676e+13
> sd(USstatePops$april10census)
[1]  6823984
```

Some great summary information there, but wait—a couple things have gone awry:

The mode() function has returned the data type of our vector of numbers instead of the statistical mode. As we previously discussed, the basic R package does not have a statistical mode function! This is partly due to the fact that the mode is only useful in a very limited set of situations, but as we saw previously, there is an add-on package, modeest, that can be used to get the statistical mode through the function mfv.

The variance is reported as 4.656676e+13. This is the first time that we have seen the use of scientific notation in R. If you haven't seen this notation before, the way you interpret it is to imagine 4.656676 multiplied by 10,000,000,000,000 (also known as 10 raised to the 13th power). You can see that this is 10 trillion, a huge and unwieldy number, and that is why scientific notation is used. If you would prefer not to type all of that into a calculator, another trick to see what number you are dealing with is just to move the decimal point 13 digits to the right.

USING HISTOGRAMS TO UNDERSTAND A DISTRIBUTION

Other than these two issues, we now know that the average population of a U.S. state is 6,053,834 with a standard deviation of 6,823,984. You might be wondering, What does it mean to have a standard deviation of almost 7 million? The mean and the standard deviation are OK, and they certainly are mighty precise, but for most of us, it would make much more sense to have a *picture* that shows the central tendency and the dispersion of a large set of numbers. So here we go. Run this command:

```
> hist(USstatePops$april10census)
```

You should get the output shown in Figure 9.1.

FIGURE 9.1

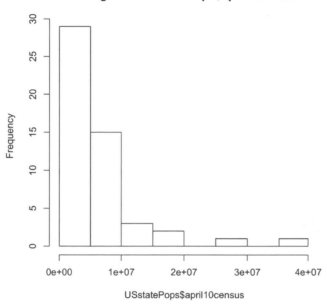

Histogram of USstatePops$april10census

A histogram is a specialized type of bar graph designed to show frequencies. The word *frequencies* here means how often a particular value or range of values occurs in a data set. This histogram shows a very interesting picture. There are nearly 30 states with populations under 5 million, another 10 states with populations under 10 million, and then a very small number of states with populations greater than 10 million. Having said all that, how do we glean this kind of information from the graph? First, look along the Y-axis (the vertical axis on the left) for an indication of how often the data occur. The tallest bar is just to the right of this and it is nearly up to the 30 mark. To know what this tall bar represents, look along the X-axis (the horizontal axis at the bottom) and see that there is a tick mark for every two bars. We see scientific notation under each tick mark. The first tick mark is 1e+07, which translates to 10,000,000. So each new bar (or an empty space where a bar would go) goes up by 5 million in population. With these points in mind it should now be easy to see that there are nearly 30 states with populations under 5 million.

If you think about presidential elections, or the locations of schools and businesses, or how a single U.S. state might compare with other countries in the world, it is interesting to know that there are two really giant states and then lots of much smaller states. Once you have some practice reading histograms, all the knowledge is available at a glance.

On the other hand, there is something unsatisfying about this diagram. With more than 40 of the states clustered into the first couple of bars, there might be some more details hiding in there that we would like to know about. This concern translates into the number of bars shown in the histogram. There are eight shown here, so why did R pick eight?

The answer is that the hist() function has an algorithm, or recipe, for deciding on the number of categories/bars to use by default. The number of observations and the spread of the data and the amount of empty space there would be are all taken into account. Fortunately, it is possible and easy to ask R to use more or fewer categories/bars with the breaks parameter, like this:

```
hist(USstatePops$april10census, breaks=20)
```

FIGURE 9.2

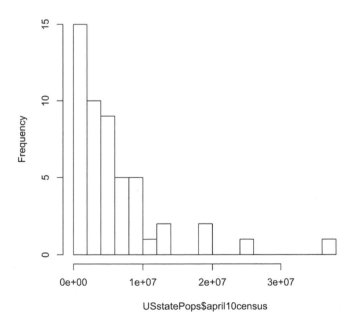

Histogram of USstatePops$april10census

This gives us five bars per tick mark, or about 2 million for each bar. So the new histogram, shown in Table 9.2, shows very much the same pattern as before: 15 states with populations under 2 million. The pattern that you see here is referred to as a distribution. This is a distribution that starts off tall on the left and swoops downward quickly as it moves to the right. You might call this a reverse-J distribution because it looks a little like the shape a *J* makes, although flipped around vertically. More technically, this could be referred to as a Pareto distribution (named after the economist Vilfredo Pareto). We don't have to worry about why it might be a Pareto distribution at this stage, but we can speculate on why the distribution looks the way it does. First, you can't have a state with no people in it or, worse yet, a negative population. It just doesn't make any sense. So a state has to have at least a few people in it, and if you look through U.S. history every state began as a colony or a territory that had at least a few people in it. On the other hand, what does it take to grow really large in population? You need a lot of land, first, and then a good reason for lots of people to move there or lots of people to be born there. So there are lots of limits to growth: Rhode Island is too small to have a bazillion people in it, and Alaska, although it has tons of land, is too cold for lots of people to want to move there. So all states probably started small and grew, but it is very difficult to grow really huge. As a result, we have a distribution where most of the cases are clustered near the bottom of the scale and just a few push up higher and higher. But as you go higher, there are fewer and fewer states that can get that big, and by the time you are out at the end, there's only one state that has managed to grow to be in excess of 30 million people. By the way, do you know or can you guess what that humongous state is?

NORMAL DISTRIBUTIONS

There are lots of other distribution shapes. The most common one that almost everyone has heard of is sometimes called the bell curve because it is shaped like a bell. The technical name for this is the normal distribution. The term *normal* was first introduced by Carl Friedrich Gauss (1777–1855), who supposedly called it that in a belief that it was the most typical distribution of data that one might find in natural phenomena. The histogram in Figure 9.3 depicts the typical bell shape of the normal distribution.

If you are curious, you might be wondering how R generated the histogram in Figure 9.3, and if you are alert, you might notice that the histogram that appears above has the word "rnorm" in a couple of places. Here's another of the cool features in R: It

FIGURE 9.3

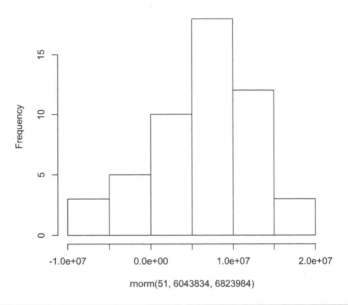

is incredibly easy to generate fake data to work with when solving problems or giving demonstrations. The data in this histogram were generated by R's rnorm() function, which generates a random data set that fits the normal distribution (more closely if you generate a lot of data, less closely if you generate only a little). Some further explanation of the rnorm() command will make sense if you remember that the state population data we were using had a mean of 6,053,834 and a standard deviation of 6,823,984. The command used to generate this histogram was

```
hist(rnorm(51, 6043834, 6823984))
```

The data shown in the histogram in Figure 9.3 are an approximation of what the distribution of state populations might look like if, instead of being a reverse-J distribution (also called Pareto distribution), they were normally distributed. Note that this is our first use of a nested function call: The hist() function that generates the graph surrounds the rnorm() function that generates the new fake data. (Pay close attention to the parentheses!) The inside function, rnorm(), is run by R first, with the results of that sent directly and immediately into the hist() function.

Of course, if we are generating a histogram that others need to look at, the title and x-axis label could be improved. Luckily, that is easy to do in R:

```
hist(rnorm(51, 6043834, 6823984),
  main="Example of Normal Distribution",
  xlab="Distribution with a Mean of 6,043,834 and
  standard deviation of 6,823,984")
```

FIGURE 9.4

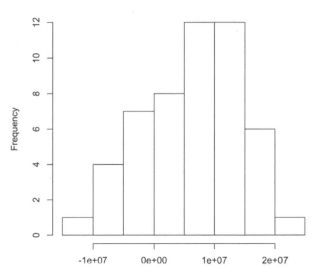

Example of a Normal Distribution

Distribution with a Mean of 6,043,834 and standard deviation of 6,823,984

The normal distribution is used extensively through applied statistics as a tool for making comparisons. For example, look at the right-most bar in Figure 9.4. The label just to the right of that bar is 3e+07, or 30,000,000. We already know from our real state population data that there is only one actual state with a population in excess of 30 million (if you didn't look it up, it is California). So if all of a sudden, someone mentioned to you that he or she lived in a state, *other than California,* that had 30 million people, you would automatically think to yourself, "Wow, that's unusual and I'm not sure I believe it." And the reason that you found it hard to believe was that you had a distribution to compare it to. Not only did that distribution have a characteristic shape (e.g., reverse-J shaped, or bell shaped, or some other shape), it also had a center point, which was the mean, and a spread, which in this case was the standard deviation. Armed with those three pieces of information—the type/shape of distribution, an anchoring point, and a spread (also known as the amount of variability)—you have a powerful tool for making comparisons.

In the next chapter, we will conduct some of these comparisons to see what we can infer about the ways things are, in general, based on just a subset of available data, or what statisticians call a sample.

Chapter Challenge

In this chapter, we used rnorm() to generate random numbers that closely fit a normal distribution. We also learned that the state population data was a Pareto distribution. Do some research to find out which R function generates random numbers using the Pareto distribution. There are two key parameters for the Pareto function—location and dispersion. The location helps define the numbers along the X-axis. In other words, the shape doesn't change, but changing the location changes the scale of the X-axis. The dispersion (sometimes known as shape) defines how fast the distribution goes down (the larger the shape, the more spread out the values will be). It's best to experiment with different values to get a feel for the function, then to run that function with the correct parameters to generate 51 random numbers. (Hint: Experiment with different probability values.) Create a histogram of these random numbers and describe the shape of the distribution.

Sources

http://en.wikipedia.org/wiki/Carl_Friedrich_Gauss

http://en.wikipedia.org/wiki/Francis_Galton

https://en.wikipedia.org/wiki/Pareto_distribution

http://en.wikipedia.org/wiki/Karl_Pearson

http://en.wikipedia.org/wiki/Ronald_Fisher

http://en.wikipedia.org/wiki/William_Sealy_Gosset

http://en.wikipedia.org/wiki/Normal_distribution

http://www2.census.gov/programs-surveys/popest/

http://www.r-tutor.com/elementary-statistics/numerical-measures/standard-deviation

R Functions Used in This Chapter

mean()	Calculates the arithmetic mean.
median()	Locates the median.
mode()	Tells the data type/mode of a data object.
	Note: This is *not* the statistical mode.
var()	Calculates the sample variance.
sd()	Calculates the sample standard deviation.
hist()	Produces a histogram graphic.

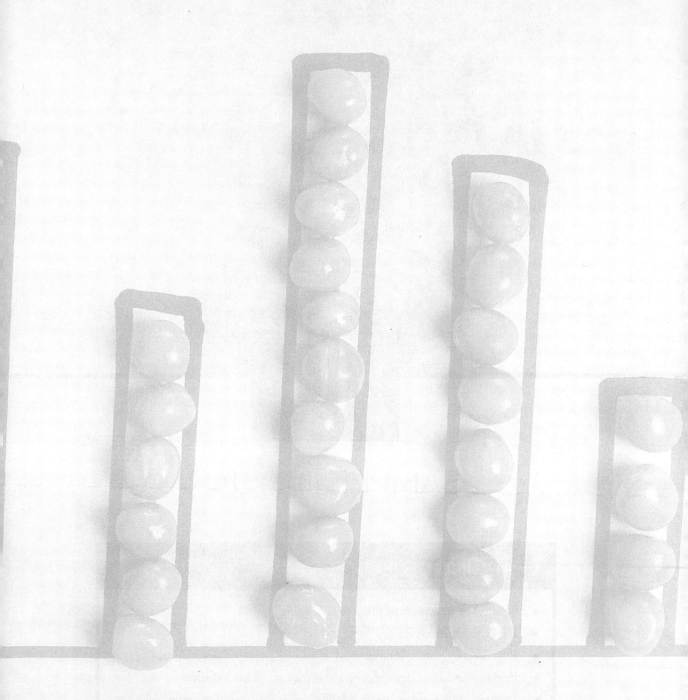

© iStockphoto.com/natalie-claude

10

SAMPLE IN A JAR

LEARNING OBJECTIVES

- Create and interpret sampling distributions.
- Use R to repeat sampling.
- Explain the effects of randomness when one samples a population.
- Explain the law of large numbers and the central limit theorem.
- Demonstrate how to use the following R functions: quantile, replicate, sample, sd, summary.

Imagine a gumball jar full of gumballs of two colors, red and blue. The jar was filled from a source that provided 100 red gumballs and 100 blue gumballs, but when they were all poured into the jar they got mixed together. If you drew eight gumballs from the jar at random, what colors would you get? If things worked out perfectly, which they rarely do, you would get four red and four blue. This is half and half, the same ratio of red and blue that is in the jar as a whole. Of course, it rarely works out this way, does it? Instead of getting four red and four blue, you might get three red and five blue, or any other mix you can think of. In fact, it would be possible, though perhaps not likely, to get eight red gumballs. The basic situation, though, is that we really don't know what mix of red and blue we will get with one draw of eight gumballs. That's uncertainty for you, the forces of randomness affecting our sample of eight gumballs in unpredictable ways.

Here's an interesting idea, though, that is no help at all in predicting what will happen in any one sample but is great at showing what will occur *in the long run*. Pull eight gumballs from the jar, count the number of red ones, and then throw them back. We do not have to count the number of blue gumballs because we can subtract the number of red gumballs from the total (eight gumballs) to know the number of blue gumballs. Mix up the jar again, then draw eight more gumballs, and count the number of red. Keeping doing this many times. Table 10.1 is an example of what you might get.

TABLE 10.1	
Draw	**# red**
1	5
2	3
3	6
4	2

Notice that the left-hand column is just counting the number of sample draws we have done. The right-hand column is the interesting one because it is the count of the number of red gumballs in each particular sample draw. In this example, things are all over the place. In sample draw 4 we only have two red gumballs, but in sample draw 3 we have six red gumballs. But the most interesting part of this example is that if you *average* the number of red gumballs over all of the draws, the average comes out to *exactly four red gumballs* per draw, which is what we would expect in a jar that is half and half. Now this is a contrived example and we won't always get such a perfect result so quickly, but if you did 4,000 draws instead of four, you would get pretty close to the perfect result.

This process of repeatedly drawing a subset from a population is called sampling, and the end result of doing lots of sampling is a sampling distribution. Note that we are using the word *population* in the previous sentence in its statistical sense to refer to the totality of units from which a sample can be drawn. It is just a coincidence that our data set contains the number of people in each state and that this value is also referred to as population. Next, we will get R to help us draw lots of samples from our U.S. state data set.

SAMPLING IN R

Conveniently, R has a function called sample(), that will draw a random sample from a data set with just a single call. We can try it now with our state data:

```
> sample(USstatePops$april10census, size=8,
+    replace=TRUE)
[1]  4533372  19378102  897934  1052567  672591  18801310
[7]  2967297  5029196
```

As a matter of practice, note that we called the sample() function with three arguments. The first argument was the data source. For the second and third arguments, rather than rely on the order in which we specify the arguments, we have used named arguments to make sure that R does what we want it to. The size=8 argument asks R to draw a sample of 8 state data values. The replace=TRUE argument specifies a style of sampling that statisticians use very often to simplify the mathematics of their proofs. For us, sampling with or without replacement does not usually have any practical effects, so we will just go with what the statisticians typically do.

When we're working with numbers such as these state values, instead of counting gumball colors we're more interested in finding out the average, or what you now know as the mean. So we could also ask R to calculate a mean() of the sample for us:

```
> mean(sample(USstatePops$april10census,size=16,
+    replace=TRUE))
[1]  8198359
```

There's the nested function call again. The output no longer shows the 8 values that R sampled from the list of 51. Instead, it used those 8 values to calculate the mean and display that for us. If you have a good memory, or merely took the time to look in the last chapter, you will remember that the actual mean of our 51 observations is 6,053,834. So the mean that we got from this one sample of 8 states is really not even close to the true mean value of our 51 observations. Are we worried? Definitely not! We know that when we draw a sample, whether it is gumballs or states, we will almost never hit the true population mean right on the head.

REPEATING OUR SAMPLING

We're interested not in any one sample but in what happens over the long haul. So now we've got to get R to repeat this process for us, not once, not four times, but 400 or 4,000 times. Like most programming languages, R has a variety of ways of repeating an activity. One of the easiest ones to use is the replicate() function. To start, let's just try four replications:

```
> replicate(4, mean(sample(USstatePops$april10census,
+    size=8,replace=TRUE)),simplify=TRUE)
[1] 10300486 11909337 8536523 5798488
```

Couldn't be any easier. We took the exact same command as before, which was a nested function to calculate the mean() of a random sample of 8 states. This time, we put that command inside the replicate() function so we could run it over and over again. The simplify=TRUE argument asks R to return the results as a simple vector of means, perfect for what we are trying to do. We ran it only four times so that we would not have a big screen full of numbers. From here, though, it is easy to ramp up to repeating the process 400 times. You can try that and see the output, but for here in the book we will encapsulate the whole replicate function inside another mean() so that we can get the average of all 400 of the sample means. Here we go:

```
> mean(replicate(400,mean(
+    sample(USstatePops$april10census, size=8,
+    replace = TRUE)), simplify=TRUE))
[1] 5958336
```

In the command above, the outermost mean() command is what is different from the previous command. So, put into words, this deeply nested command accomplishes the following: (a) Draws 400 samples of size n = 8 from our full data set of 51 states.

(b) Calculates the mean from each sample and keeps it in a list. (c) When finished with the list of 400 of these means, calculates the mean of that list of means. You can see that the mean of 400 sample means is 5,958,336. Now that is still not the exact value of the whole data set, but it is getting close. We're off by about 95,000, which is roughly an error of about 1.6% (more precisely, 95,498/6,053,834 = 1.58%. You might have also noticed that it took a little while to run that command, even if you have a fast computer. There's a lot of work going on there! Let's push it farther and see if we can get closer to the true mean for all of our data:

```
> mean(replicate(4000, mean(
+     sample(USstatePops$april10census, size=8,
+     replace = TRUE)), simplify=TRUE))
[1] 6000972
```

Now we are even closer! We are now less than 1% away from the true population mean value. Note that the results you get might be different, because when you run the commands, each of the 400 or 4,000 samples that is drawn will be slightly different than the

FIGURE 10.1

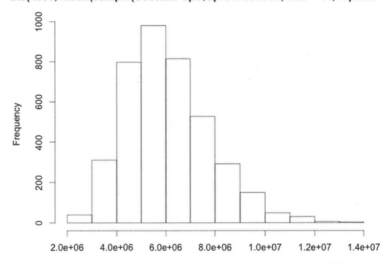

ate(4000, mean(sample(USstatePops$april10census, size = 16, replace = TI

plicate(4000, mean(sample(USstatePops$april10census, size = 16, replace = TRUE)), simplify =

ones that were drawn for the commands above. What will not be much different is the overall level of accuracy.

We're ready to take the next step. Instead of summarizing our whole sampling distribution in a single average, let's look at the distribution of means using a histogram.

The histogram in Figure 10.1 displays the complete list of 4,000 means as frequencies. Take a close look so that you can get more practice reading frequency histograms. This one shows a very typical configuration that is almost bell-shaped but still has some skewness off to the right. The tallest, and therefore most-frequent, range of values is right near the true mean of 6,053,834.

By the way, were you able to figure out the command to generate this histogram on your own? All you had to do was substitute hist() for the outermost mean() in the previous command. In case you struggled, here it is:

```
> hist(replicate(4000,
+     mean(sample(USstatePops$april10census,size=8,
+     replace= TRUE)), simplify=TRUE))
```

LAW OF LARGE NUMBERS AND THE CENTRAL LIMIT THEOREM

This is a great moment to take a breath. We've just covered a couple hundred years of statistical thinking in just a few pages. In fact, there are two big ideas, the law of large numbers and the central limit theorem, that we have just partially demonstrated. These two ideas took mathematicians including Gerolamo Cardano (1501–1576) and Jacob Bernoulli (1654–1705) several centuries to figure out. If you look these ideas up, you might find a lot of bewildering mathematical details, but for our purposes, there are two really important takeaway messages. First, if you run a statistical process a large number of times, it will converge on a stable result. For us, we knew what the average population was of the 50 states plus the District of Columbia. These 51 observations were our population, and we wanted to know how many smaller subsets, or samples, of size n = 8 we would have to draw before we could get a good approximation of that true value. We learned that drawing one sample provided a poor result. Drawing 400 samples gave us a mean that was off by 1.5%. Drawing 4,000 samples gave us a mean that was off by less than 1%. If we had kept going to 40,000 or 400,000 repetitions of our sampling process, we would have come extremely close to the actual average of 6,053,384.

Second, when we are looking at sample means, and we take the law of large numbers into account, we find that the distribution of sampling means starts to create a bell-shaped or normal distribution, and the center of that distribution—the mean of all of those sample means—gets really close to the actual population mean. It gets closer faster for larger samples; in contrast, for smaller samples you have to draw lots and lots of them to get really close. Just for fun, let's illustrate this with a sample size that is larger than 8. Here's a run that repeats only 100 times, but each time draws a sample of n = 51 (equal in size to the population):

```
> mean(replicate(100, mean(
+     sample(USstatePops$april10census,size =
+     51,replace = TRUE)), simplify=TRUE))
[1] 6114231
```

Now, we're off from the true value of the population mean by only about 0.1%. You might be scratching your head now, saying, "Wait a minute. Isn't a sample of 51 the same thing as the whole list of 51 observations?" This is confusing, but it goes back to the question of sampling with replacement that we examined a couple of pages ago (and that appears in the command above as replace=TRUE). Sampling with replacement means that as you draw out one value to include in your random sample, you immediately chuck it back into the list so that, potentially, it could get drawn again either immediately or later. As mentioned before, this practice simplifies the underlying proofs, and it does not cause any practical problems, other than head scratching. In fact, we could go even higher in our sample size with no trouble:

```
> mean(replicate(100, mean(
+     sample(USstatePops$april10census, size=120,
+     replace=TRUE)), simplify=TRUE))
[1] 6054718
```

That command runs 100 replications using samples of size n = 120. Look how close the mean of the sampling distribution is to the population mean now! Remember that this result will change a little every time you run the procedure, because different random samples are being drawn for each run. But the rule of thumb is that the larger your sample size, what statisticians call n, the closer your estimate will be to the true value. Likewise, the more trials you run, the closer your population estimate will be.

So, if you've had a chance to catch your breath, let's move on to making use of the sampling distribution. First, let's save one distribution of sample means so that we have a fixed set of numbers to work with:

```
> SampleMeans <- replicate(10000,
+     mean(sample(USstatePops$april10census,size =
+     5,  replace = TRUE)), simplify=TRUE)
```

We're saving a distribution of sample means to a new vector called SampleMeans. We should have 10,000 of them:

```
> length(SampleMeans)
[1] 10000
```

And the mean of all of these means should be pretty close to our population mean of 6,053,384:

```
> mean(SampleMeans)
[1] 6065380
```

You might also want to run a histogram on SampleMeans and see what the frequency distribution looks like. Right now, all we need to look at is a summary of the list of sample means:

```
> summary(SampleMeans)
Min. 1st Qu. Median Mean 3rd Qu. Max.
799100 3853000 5370000 6065000 7622000 25030000
```

As a reminder, the 1st Qu. (first quartile) is the value that divides the first quarter of the cases from the other three quarters. Median refers to the value of the case that splits the whole group in half, with half of the cases having higher values and half having lower values. The median is also the dividing line that separates the second quartile from the third quartile. If you need a refresher on the median and quartiles, take a look back at Chapter 5, "Rows and Columns."

This summary is full of useful information. First, take a look at the max and the min. The minimum sample mean in the list was 799,100. Think about that for a moment. How could a sample have a mean that small when we know that the true mean is much higher? Wyoming must have been drawn several times in that sample! The answer comes from the randomness involved in sampling. If you run a process 10,000 times you are definitely going to end up with a few weird examples. It's almost like buying a lottery ticket. The vast majority of tickets are the usual—not a winner. Once in a great while, though, there is a very unusual ticket—a winner. Sampling is the same: The extreme events are unusual, but they do happen if you run the process enough times. The same goes for the maximum: At 25,030,000 the maximum sample mean is much higher than the true mean.

At 5,370,000 the median is quite close to the mean but not exactly the same because we still have a little rightward skew. (The tail on the high side is slightly longer than it should be because of the shape of the original distribution.) The median is very useful because it divides the sample exactly in half: 50%, or exactly 5,000 of the sample means are larger than 5,370,000, and the other 50% are lower. So if we were to draw one more sample from the population it would have a 50–50 chance of being above the median. The quartiles help us to cut things up even more finely. The third quartile divides up the bottom 75% from the top 25%. So only 25% of the sample means are higher than 7,622,000. That means if we drew a new sample from the population that there is only a 25% chance that it will be larger than that. Likewise, in the other direction, the first quartile tells us that there is only a 25% chance that a new sample would be less than 3,853,000.

There is a slightly different way of getting the same information from R that will prove more flexible for us in the long run. The quantile() function can show us the same information as the median and the quartiles, like this:

```
> quantile(SampleMeans, probs=c(0.25,0.50,0.75))
     25%       50%       75%
3853167   5370314   7621871
```

You will notice that the values are just slightly different, by less than 0.1%, than those produced by the summary() function. These are actually more precise, although the less-precise ones from summary() are fine for most purposes. One reason to use quantile() is that it lets us control exactly where we make the cuts. To get quartiles, we cut at 25% (0.25 in the command just above), at 50%, and at 75%. But what if we wanted instead to cut at 2.5% and 97.5%? Easy to do with quantile():

```
> quantile(SampleMeans, probs=c(0.025,0.975))
    2.5%       97.5%
 2014580    13537085
```

So, this result shows that, if we drew a new sample, there is only a 2.5% chance that the mean would be lower than 2,014,580. Likewise, there is only a 2.5% chance that the new sample mean would be higher than 13,537,085 (because 97.5% of the means in the sampling distribution are lower than that value).

COMPARING TWO SAMPLES

Now let's put this knowledge to work. Here is a sample of the number of people in a certain area, where each of these areas is some kind of a unit associated with the United States:

3,706,690 159,358 106,405 55,519 53,883

We can easily get these into R and calculate the sample mean:

```
> MysterySample <- c(3706690, 159358, 106405,
+      55519, 53883)
> mean(MysterySample)
[1] 816371
```

The mean of our mystery sample is 816,371. The question is, Is this a sample of U.S. states or is it something else? Just on its own it would be hard to tell. The first observation in our sample has more people in it than Kansas, Utah, Nebraska, and several other states. We also know from looking at the distribution of raw population data from our previous example that there are many, many states that have very few people. Thanks to the work we've done earlier in this chapter, however, we have an excellent basis for comparison. We have the sampling distribution of means, and it is fair to say that if we get a new mean to look at, and the new mean is way out in the extreme areas of the sample distribution, say, below the 2.5% mark or above the 97.5% mark, then it seems much less likely that our MysterySample is a sample of states.

In this case, we can see quite clearly that 816,371 is on the extreme low end of the sampling distribution. Recall that when we ran the quantile() command we found that only 2.5% of the sample means in the distribution were smaller than 2,014,580.

In fact, we could even play around with a more stringent criterion:

```
> quantile(SampleMeans, probs=c(0.005,0.995))
    0.5%      99.5%
 1410883  16792211
```

This quantile() command shows that only 0.5% of all the sample means are lower than 1,410,883. So our MysterySample mean of 816,371 would definitely be a very rare event, if it were truly a sample of states. From this we can infer, tentatively but based on good statistical evidence, that our MysterySample is *not* a sample of states. The mean of MysterySample is just too small to be very likely to be a sample of states.

And this is in fact correct: MysterySample contains the number of people in five different U.S. territories, including Puerto Rico in the Caribbean and Guam in the Pacific. These territories are land masses and groups of people associated with the United States, but they are not states, and they are different from states in many ways. For one thing, they are all islands, so they are limited in land mass. Among the U.S. states, only Hawaii is an island, and it is actually bigger than 10 of the states in the continental United States. The important thing to take away is that the characteristics of this group of data points, notably the mean of this sample, was sufficiently different from a known distribution of means that we could make an inference that the sample *was not drawn from the original population of data.*

This reasoning is the basis for virtually all statistical inference. You construct a comparison distribution, you mark off a zone of extreme values, and you compare any new sample of data you get to the distribution to see if it falls in the extreme zone. If it does, you tentatively conclude that the new sample was obtained from some source other than what you used to create the comparison distribution.

If you feel confused, take heart. There's 400 to 500 years of mathematical developments represented in that one preceding paragraph. Also, before we had cool programs like R that could be used to create and analyze actual sample distributions, most of the material above was taught as a set of formulas and proofs. Yuck! Now let's take note of three additional pieces of information.

First, we looked at the mean of the sampling distribution with mean(), and we looked at its shaped with hist(), but we never quantified the spread of the distribution:

```
> sd(SampleMeans)
[1] 3037318
```

This shows us the standard deviation of the distribution of sampling means. Statisticians call this the standard error of the mean. This chewy phrase would have been clearer, although longer, if it had been something like this: "The standard deviation of the distribution of sample means for samples drawn from a population." Unfortunately, statisticians are not known for giving things clear labels. Suffice to say that when we are looking at a distribution and each data point in that distribution is itself a representation of a sample (e.g., a mean), then the standard deviation is referred to as the standard error.

Second, there is a shortcut to finding out the standard error that does not require actually constructing an empirical distribution of 10,000 (or any other number) of sampling means. It turns out that the standard deviation of the original raw data and the standard error are closely related by some simple algebra:

```
> sd(USstatePops$april10census)/sqrt(5)
[1] 3051779
```

The formula in this command takes the standard deviation of the original state data and divides it by the square root of the sample size. Remember three or four pages ago, when we created the SampleMeans vector by using the replicate() and sample() commands, we used a sample size of n = 5. That's what you see in the formula above, inside of the sqrt() function. In R and other software, sqrt() is the abbreviation for square root and not for squirt as you might expect. So if you have a set of observations and you calculate their standard deviation, you can also calculate the standard error for a distribution of means (each of which has the same sample size), just by dividing by the square root of the sample size. You might notice that the number we got with the shortcut was slightly larger than the number that came from the distribution itself, but the difference is not meaningful (and only arises because of randomness in the distribution). Another thing you might have noticed is that the larger the sample size, the smaller the standard error. This leads to an important rule for working with samples: the bigger, the better.

The last thing is another shortcut. We found out the 97.5% cut point by constructing the sampling distribution and then using quantile to tell us the actual cuts. You can also cut points just using the mean and the standard error. Two standard errors down from the mean is the 2.5% cut point, and two standard errors up from the mean is the 97.5% cut point.

```
> StdError <- sd(USstatePops$april10census)/sqrt(5)
> CutPoint975 <- mean(USstatePops$april10census)+(2 *
```

```
+              StdError)
> CutPoint975
[1] 12157391
```

You will notice again that this value is different from what we calculated with the quantile() function using the empirical distribution. The differences arise because of the randomness in the distribution that we constructed. The preceding value is an estimate that is based on statistical proofs, whereas the empirical SampleMeans list that we constructed is just one of a nearly infinite range of such lists that we could create. We could easily reduce the discrepancy between the two methods by using a larger sample size and by having more replications included in the sampling distribution.

To summarize, with a data set that includes 51 data points with the numbers of people in states, and some work using R to construct a distribution of sampling means, we have learned the following:

Run a statistical process a large number of times and you get a consistent pattern of results.

Taking the means of a large number of samples and plotting them on a histogram shows that the sample means are fairly well normally distributed and that the center of the distribution is very, very close to the mean of the original raw data.

This resulting distribution of sample means can be used as a basis for comparisons. By making cut points at the extreme low and high ends of the distribution, for example, 2.5% and 97.5%, we have a way of comparing any new information we get.

If we get a new sample mean, and we find that it is in the extreme zone defined by our cut points, we can tentatively conclude that the sample that made that mean is a different kind of thing from the samples that made the sampling distribution.

A shortcut and more-accurate way of figuring the cut points involves calculating the standard error based on the standard deviation of the original raw data.

We're not statisticians at this point, but the process of reasoning based on sampling distributions is at the heart of inferential statistics, so if you have followed the logic presented in this chapter, you have made excellent progress toward being a competent user of applied statistics.

Chapter Challenge

Collect a sample consisting of at least 20 data points and construct a sampling distribution. Calculate the standard error and use this to calculate the 2.5% and 97.5% distribution cut points. The data points you collect should represent instances of the same phenomenon. For instance, you could collect the prices of 20 textbooks or count the number of words in each of 20 paragraphs.

Sources

http://en.wikipedia.org/wiki/Central_limit_theorem

http://en.wikipedia.org/wiki/Gerolamo_Cardano

http://en.wikipedia.org/wiki/Jacob_Bernoulli

http://en.wikipedia.org/wiki/Law_of_large_numbers

http://en.wikipedia.org/wiki/List_of_U.S._states_and_territories_by_population

http://www.khanacademy.org/math/statistics/v/central-limit-theorem

R Commands Used in This Chapter

length()	The number of elements in a vector.
mean()	The arithmetic mean or average of a set of values.
quantile()	Calculates cut points based on percents/proportions.
replicate()	Runs an expression/calculation many times.
sample()	Chooses the elements at random from a vector.
sd()	Calculates the standard deviation.
sqrt()	Calculates the square root.
summary()	Summarizes the contents of a vector.

11

STORAGE WARS

LEARNING OBJECTIVES

- Recognize the different data sources that are available for R analysis.
- Use RStudio to import data.
- Build R code to access data that are available in Excel, JSON, and an SQL database.
- Use the sqldf package to access a dataframe as if it was a database.

- Use the R sapply and tapply functions to do summary analysis on a dataframe.

- Understand how to use loops in R.

- Demonstrate the following R functions: getURL, fromJSON, read.xls, str_replace, dbConnect, dbGetQuery, dbListTables, dbWriteTable, unlist, matrix, sqldf, tapply.

Most people who have watched the evolution of technology over recent decades remember a time when storage was expensive and had to be hoarded like gold. Over the past few years, however, the accelerating trend of Moore's Law has made data storage almost "too cheap to meter" (as they used to predict about nuclear power). Although this opens many opportunities, it also means that people keep data around for a long time, since it doesn't make sense to delete anything, and they might keep data around in many different formats. As a result, the world is full of different data formats, some of which are proprietary—designed and owned by a single company such as SAS—and some of which are open, such as the lowly but infinitely useful comma-separated variable, or CSV format.

In fact, one of the basic dividing lines in data formats is whether data are human readable or not. Formats that are not human readable, often called binary formats, are very efficient in terms of how much data they can pack in per kilobyte but are also squirrelly in the sense that it is hard to see what is going on inside the format. As you might expect, human readable formats are inefficient from a storage standpoint but are easy to diagnose when something goes wrong. For high-volume applications, such as credit card processing, the data that are exchanged between systems are almost universally in binary formats. When data sets are archived for later reuse, for example, in the case of government data sets available to the public, they are usually available in multiple formats, at least one of which is a human readable format.

Another dividing line, as mentioned earlier, is between proprietary and open formats. One of the most common ways of storing and sharing small data sets is as Microsoft Excel spreadsheets. Although this is a proprietary format, owned by Microsoft, it has also become a kind of informal and very common standard. Dozens of different software applications can read Excel formats (and there are several different formats that match different versions of Excel). In contrast, the OpenDocument format is an open format, managed by a standards consortium, that anyone can use without worrying what the owner might do. OpenDocument format is based on XML, which stands for extensible markup language. XML is a whole topic in and of itself, but briefly it is a data exchange format designed specifically to work on the Internet and is both human and machine readable. XML is managed by the W3C consortium, which is responsible for developing and maintaining the many standards and protocols that support the web.

As an open source program with many contributors, R offers a wide variety of methods of connecting with external data sources. This is both a blessing and a curse. There is a solution to almost any data access problem you can imagine with R, but there is also a dizzying array of options available such that it is not always obvious what to choose. We'll tackle this problem in two different ways.

In the first part of this chapter we will build on our readCensus function and look at methods for importing existing data sets. These might exist on a local computer or on the Internet, but the characteristic they have in common is that they are contained (usually) within one single file. The main trick here is to choose the right command to import those data into R. In the second half of the chapter, we will consider a different strategy, namely, linking to a source of data that is not a file. Many data sources, particularly databases, exist not as a single discrete file, but rather as a system. The system provides methods or calls to query data from the system, but from the perspective of the user (and of R) the data never really take the form of a file.

IMPORTING DATA USING RSTUDIO

The first and easiest strategy for getting data into R is to use the data import dialog in RStudio. In the upper-right-hand pane of RStudio, the Workspace tab gives views of currently available data objects, but also has a set of buttons at the top for managing the work space. One of the choices there is the Import Dataset button: This enables a drop-down menu where one choice is to import From CSV . . . . If you click this option and choose an appropriate file, you will get a screen that looks like Figure 11.1.

The most important stuff is on the bottom-left side. Heading controls whether or not the first line of the text file is treated as containing variable names. The deliminator drop-down gives a choice of different characters that separate the fields/columns in the data. RStudio tries to guess the appropriate choice here based on a scan of the data. In this case, it guessed right by choosing comma. As mentioned earlier, tab-delimited and comma-delimited are the two most common formats used for interchange between data programs. There are other controls such as if the first row has names for each of column columns and a Quote drop-down, which controls which character is used to contain quoted string/text data. The most common method is double quotes. On the lower-right part of the screen we can also see the code that will be generated when we import the data set.

Of course, we skipped ahead here because we assumed that an appropriate file of data was available. It might be useful to see some examples of human readable data:

FIGURE 11.1

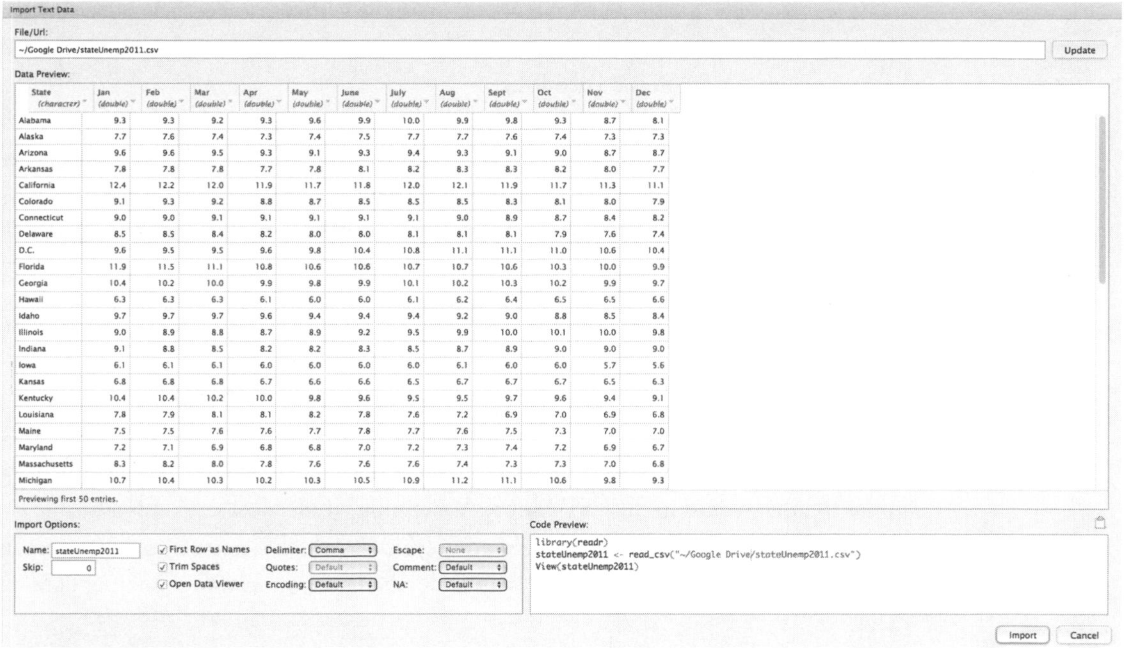

State (character)	Jan (double)	Feb (double)	Mar (double)	Apr (double)	May (double)	June (double)	July (double)	Aug (double)	Sept (double)	Oct (double)	Nov (double)	Dec (double)
Alabama	9.3	9.3	9.2	9.3	9.6	9.9	10.0	9.9	9.8	9.3	8.7	8.1
Alaska	7.7	7.6	7.4	7.3	7.4	7.5	7.7	7.7	7.6	7.4	7.3	7.3
Arizona	9.6	9.6	9.5	9.3	9.1	9.3	9.4	9.3	9.1	9.0	8.7	8.7
Arkansas	7.8	7.8	7.8	7.7	7.8	8.1	8.2	8.3	8.3	8.2	8.0	7.7
California	12.4	12.2	12.0	11.9	11.7	11.8	12.0	12.1	11.9	11.7	11.3	11.1
Colorado	9.1	9.3	9.2	8.8	8.7	8.5	8.5	8.5	8.3	8.1	8.0	7.9
Connecticut	9.0	9.0	9.1	9.1	9.1	9.1	9.1	9.0	8.9	8.7	8.4	8.2
Delaware	8.5	8.5	8.4	8.2	8.0	8.0	8.1	8.1	8.1	7.9	7.6	7.4
D.C.	9.6	9.5	9.5	9.6	9.8	10.4	10.8	11.1	11.1	11.0	10.6	10.4
Florida	11.9	11.5	11.1	10.8	10.6	10.6	10.7	10.7	10.6	10.3	10.0	9.9
Georgia	10.4	10.2	10.0	9.9	9.8	9.9	10.1	10.2	10.3	10.2	9.9	9.7
Hawaii	6.3	6.3	6.3	6.1	6.0	6.0	6.1	6.2	6.4	6.5	6.5	6.6
Idaho	9.7	9.7	9.7	9.6	9.4	9.4	9.4	9.2	9.0	8.8	8.5	8.4
Illinois	9.0	8.9	8.8	8.7	8.9	9.2	9.5	9.9	10.0	10.1	10.0	9.8
Indiana	9.1	8.8	8.5	8.2	8.2	8.3	8.5	8.7	8.9	9.0	9.0	9.0
Iowa	6.1	6.1	6.1	6.0	6.0	6.0	6.0	6.1	6.0	6.0	5.7	5.6
Kansas	6.8	6.8	6.8	6.7	6.6	6.6	6.5	6.7	6.7	6.7	6.5	6.3
Kentucky	10.4	10.4	10.2	10.0	9.8	9.6	9.5	9.5	9.7	9.6	9.4	9.1
Louisiana	7.8	7.9	8.1	8.1	8.2	7.8	7.6	7.2	6.9	7.0	6.9	6.8
Maine	7.5	7.5	7.6	7.6	7.7	7.8	7.7	7.6	7.5	7.3	7.0	7.0
Maryland	7.2	7.1	6.9	6.8	6.8	7.0	7.2	7.3	7.4	7.2	6.9	6.7
Massachusetts	8.3	8.2	8.0	7.8	7.6	7.6	7.6	7.4	7.3	7.3	7.0	6.8
Michigan	10.7	10.4	10.3	10.2	10.3	10.5	10.9	11.2	11.1	10.6	9.8	9.3

Name, Age, Gender

"Fred",22,"M"

"Ginger",21,"F"

The above is a very simple example of a comma-delimited file where the first row contains a header, meaning the information about the names of variables for each of the columns. The second and subsequent rows contain actual data. Each field is separated by a comma, and the text strings are enclosed in double quotes. The same file tab-delimited might look like this:

Name	Age	Gender
"Fred"	22	"M"
"Ginger"	21	"F"

Of course you can't see the tab characters on the screen, but there is one tab character in between each pair of values. In each case, for both comma- and tab-delimited, one line equals one row. The end of a line is marked, invisibly, with a so-called newline character. On occasion, you might run into differences between different operating systems on how this end-of-line designation is encoded.

Files containing comma- or tab-delimited data are very common across the Internet, but sometimes we would like to gain direct access to binary files in other formats. There are a variety of packages that one might use to access binary data. A comprehensive access list appears here:

http://cran.r-project.org/doc/manuals/R-data.html

This page shows a range of methods for obtaining data from a wide variety of programs and formats. In this chapter, we will explore how to read in a data set using three very common methods. First, we will read in an Excel file. As you will see, this will be very similar to how we read in the CSV format. We will also read a data set that is available via a database and via Java Script Object Notation (JSON), which is a structured, but human readable, way of sharing data; JSON is an increasingly common way of sharing data on the web.

ACCESSING EXCEL DATA

Because Excel is such a widely used program for small, informal data sets, we will start with an example here to illustrate both the power and the pitfalls of accessing binary data with R. While we could read an Excel file in a similar way to how we just read in the CSV file (via the import dataset menu), we can also read the file directly in R. There are certainly many packages available to help us read in an Excel file. Interestingly, this is one area where Mac and Linux users are at a disadvantage relative to Windows users. This is perhaps because Excel is a Microsoft product, originally written to be native to Windows, and as a result it is easier to create tools that work with Windows. One example noted here is the package called RODBC. The abbreviation ODBC stands for open database connection, and this is a Windows facility for exchanging data among Windows programs. Although there is a proprietary ODBC driver available for the Mac, most Mac users will want to try a different method for getting access to Excel data. Another Windows-only package for R is called xlsReadWrite. This package provides convenient one-command calls for importing data directly from Excel spreadsheets or exporting it directly to spreadsheets.

Fortunately, a general-purpose data manipulation package called gdata provides essential facilities for importing spreadsheet files. In the example that follows, we will use a function from gdata to read Excel data directly from a website. The gdata package is a kind of Swiss Army knife package containing many different functions for accessing and manipulating data. For example, you might recall that R uses the value NA to represent missing data. Frequently, however, it is the case that data sets contain other values, such as 999, to represent missing data. The gdata package has several functions that find and transform these values to be consistent with R's strategy for handling missing data.

Begin by using install.package() and library() functions to prepare the gdata package for use:

```
> install.packages("gdata")
# ... lots of output here
> library("gdata")
gdata: read.xls support for 'XLS' (Excel 97-2004)
files
gdata: ENABLED.
gdata: read.xls support for 'XLSX' (Excel 2007+) files
ENABLED.
```

It was important here to see the output from the library() function. Note that the gdata package reported some diagnostics about the different versions of Excel data that it supports. Note that this is one of the major drawbacks of binary data formats, particularly proprietary ones: you have to make sure that you have the right software to access the different versions of data that you might encounter. In this case, it looks like we are covered for the early versions of Excel (1997–2004) as well as later versions of Excel (2007+). We must always be on the lookout, however, for data that are stored in even newer versions of Excel that might not be supported by gdata or other packages.

Now that gdata is installed, we can use the read.xls() function that it provides. The documentation for the gdata package and the read.xls() function is located here:

http://cran.r-project.org/web/packages/gdata/gdata.pdf

A review of the documentation reveals that the only required argument to this function is the location of the XLS file, and that this location can be a pathname, a web location with http, or an Internet location with ftp (file transfer protocol, a way of sending and receiving files without using a web browser).

If you think back to an early chapter in this book, you hopefully remember that we accessed some census data that had population counts for all the different U.S. states. Previously, we read the data in a CSV format. For this example, we are going to read the Excel file containing that data directly into a dataframe using the read.xls() function:

```
> testFrame<-read.xls(
+    "http://www2.census.gov/programs-surveys/popest/
+      tables/2010-2011/state/totals/
+      nst-est2011-01.xls")
trying URL
'http://www2.census.gov/programs-surveys/
popest/tables/2010-2011/state/totals/
nst-est2011-01.xls'
Content type 'application/vnd.ms-excel' length 31232
bytes (30 Kb)
opened URL
==================================================
downloaded 30 Kb
```

The command in the first three lines above provides the URL of the Excel file to the read.xls() function. The subsequent lines of output show the function attempting to open the URL, succeeding, and downloading 30 kilobytes of data.

Next, let's take a look at what we got back by using the str() function to create a summary of the structure of testFrame:

```
> str(testFrame)
'data.frame':    65 obs. of 10 variables:
$ table.with.row.headers.in.column.A.and.column.
headers.in.rows.3.through.4...leading.dots.indicate.
sub.parts.: Factor w/ 65 levels "",".Alabama",..: 62
53 1 64 55 54 60 65 2 3 ...
$ X: Factor w/ 60 levels "","1,052,567",..: 1 59 60
     27 38 47 10 49 32 50 ...
$ X.1: Factor w/ 59 levels "","1,052,567",..: 1 1 59
     27 38 47 10 49 32 50 ...
$ X.2: Factor w/ 60 levels "","1,052,528",..: 1 60 21
```

```
        28  39  48  10  51  33  50 ...
 $ X.3: Factor w/ 59 levels "","1,051,302",..: 1 1 21
        28  38  48  10  50  33  51 ...
 $ X.4: logi NA NA NA NA NA NA ...
 $ X.5: logi NA NA NA NA NA NA ...
 $ X.6: logi NA NA NA NA NA NA ...
 $ X.7: logi NA NA NA NA NA NA ...
 $ X.8: logi NA NA NA NA NA NA ...
```

This looks very, very similar to the results of the read.csv function we had previously used to read the comma separated file in an earlier chapter. Not surprisingly, the cleanup is also very similar. As a review, we will briefly go through the steps required to clean up the dataframe. If you need more of a review, please go back and reread the readCensus discussion in Chapter 9.

First, the Census Bureau put in header rows that we can eliminate:

```
> testFrame<-testFrame[-1:-8,]
```

As a reminder, the minus sign used inside the square brackets refers to the index of rows that should be eliminated from the dataframe. So the notation -1:-3 gets rid of the first three rows. We also leave the column designator empty so that, for now, we can keep all columns. So the interpretation of the notation within the square brackets is that rows 1 through 3 should be dropped, all other rows should be included, and all columns should be included. We assign the result back to the same data object, thereby replacing the original with our new, smaller, cleaner version.

Next, we know that of the 10 variables we got from read.xls(), only the first five are useful to us (the last five seem to be blank). So this command keeps the first five columns of the dataframe:

```
> testFrame <- testFrame[,1:5]
```

In the same vein, the tail() function shows us that the last few rows just contained some Census Bureau notes. So we can safely eliminate those like this:

```
> testFrame <- testFrame[-52:-62,]
```

Now we are ready to perform a couple of data transformations. Before we start these, let's give our first column a more reasonable name:

```
> testFrame$stateName <- testFrame[,1]
```

We've used the little hack here to avoid typing out the ridiculously long name of that first variable/column. We've used the column notation in the square brackets on the right-hand side of the expression to refer to the first column (the one with the ridiculous name) and simply copied the data into a new column titled stateName. Let's also remove the offending column with the stupid name so that it does not cause us problems later on:

```
> testFrame <- testFrame[,-1]
```

Next, we can change formats and data types as needed. We can remove the dots from in front of the state names very easily with str_replace():

```
> testFrame$stateName <-
+     str _ replace(testFrame$stateName,"\\.","")
```

The function str_replace() is part of the stringr package, and you will have to use install.packages() and library() to load it if it is not already in place. We previously used gsub, which is a similar function, but gsub replaces each occurrence, whereas str_replace replaces just the first occurrence (of the dot character [.] in our example). The two back-slashes in the string expression above are called escape characters, and they force the dot that follows to be treated as a literal dot rather than as a wildcard character. The dot on its own is a wildcard that matches one instance of any character.

Next, let's use the Numberize function. If you remember from Chapter 9, this function handles both unwanted commas and spaces and will convert strings into numbers whether or not they are integers (i.e., possibly with digits after the decimal point).

```
# Numberize() - Gets rid of commas and other junk and
# converts to numbers
# Assumes that the inputVector is a list of data that
# can be treated as character strings
Numberize <- function(inputVector)
```

```
{
# Get rid of commas
inputVector<-gsub(",","", inputVector)
# Get rid of spaces
inputVector<-gsub(" ","", inputVector)


return(as.numeric(inputVector))
}
```

So we can now run this a few times to create new vectors on the dataframe that contain the numeric values we wanted and to remove the old columns that have column names that are not useful.

```
testFrame$april10census <- Numberize(testFrame$X)
testFrame$april10base <- Numberize(testFrame$X.1)
testFrame$july10pop <- Numberize(testFrame$X.2)
testFrame$july11pop <- Numberize(testFrame$X.3)
testFrame <- testFrame[,-1:-4]
```

As you can see, once we read in the data file, the process of cleaning the data file was very similar to the process used to clean the same data set in CSV format.

Now we are ready to consider the other strategy for getting access to data: querying it from external databases. Depending on your familiarity with computer programming and databases, you might notice that the abstraction is quite different here. Previously, we had a file (sometimes rather messy) that contained a complete copy of the data that we wanted, and we read that file into R and stored it in our local computer's memory (and possibly later on the hard disk for safekeeping). This is a good and reasonable strategy for small- to medium-sized data sets, which we'll define just for the sake of argument as anything up to 100 megabytes.

But what if the data you want to work with is really large—too large to represent in your computer's memory all at once and too large to store on your own hard drive? This situation could occur even with smaller data sets if the data owner did not want people making complete copies of their data but rather wanted everyone who was using it to work from one official version of the data. Similarly, if multiple users need to share data, it is much better to have the data in a database that was designed for this purpose. For the most part R is a poor choice for maintaining data that must be used simultaneously by more than one user. For these reasons, it becomes necessary to do one or both of the following things:

Allow R to send messages to the large, remote database, perhaps via the web, asking for summaries, subsets, or samples of the data.

Allow R to send computation requests to a distributed data processing system asking for the results of calculations performed on the large remote database, perhaps via a web service.

Like most contemporary programming languages, R provides several methods for performing these two tasks. We will explore two basic ways to access these remote data services.

ACCESSING A DATABASE

The first strategy we will explore to access remote systems or data involves using a package that provides a client that can connect up to the database server. The R client supports sending commands—mostly in SQL, structured query language—to the database server. The database server returns a result to the R client, which places it in an R data object (typically a dataframe) for use in further processing or visualization.

The R community has developed a range of client software to enable R to connect up with other databases. Here are the major databases for which R has client software:

RMySQL: Connects to MySQL, perhaps the most popular open source database in the world. MySQL is the M in LAMP, which is the acronym for Linux, Apache, MySQL, and PHP. Together, these four elements provide a complete solution for data driven web applications.

ROracle: Connects with the widely used Oracle commercial database package. Oracle is probably the most widely used commercial database package. Ironically, Oracle acquired Sun Microsystems a few years ago and Sun developers predominate in development and control of the open source MySQL system.

RPostgreSQL: Connects with the well-developed, full-featured PostgreSQL (sometimes just called Postgres) database system. PostgreSQL is a much more venerable system than MySQL and has a much larger developer community. Unlike MySQL, which is effectively now controlled by Oracle, PostgreSQL has a developer community that is independent of any company and a licensing scheme that allows anybody to modify and reuse the code.

RSQlite: Connects with SQlite, another open source, independently developed database system. As the name suggests, SQlite has a very light code footprint, meaning that it is fast and compact.

RMongo: Connects with the MongoDB system, which is the only system here that does not use SQL. Instead, MongoDB uses JavaScript to access data. As such it is well suited for web development applications.

RODBC: Connects with ODBC compliant databases, which include Microsoft's SQLserver, Microsoft Access, and Microsoft Excel, among others. Note that these applications are native to Windows and Windows server, and as such the support for Linux and Mac OS is limited.

For demonstration purposes, we will use RMySQL. This requires installing a copy of MySQL on your computer. Use your web browser to go to this page:

http://dev.mysql.com/downloads/

Then look for the MySQL Community Server. The term *community* in this context refers to the free, open source developer community version of MySQL. Note that there are also commercial versions of SQL developed and marketed by various companies, including Oracle. Download the version of MySQL Community Server that is most appropriate for your computer's operating system and install it. Note that unlike user applications, such as a word processor, there is no real user interface to server software like the MySQL Community Server. Instead, this software runs in the background, providing services that other programs can use. This is the essence of the client-server idea. In many cases the server is on some remote computer to which we do not have physical access. In this case, we will run the server on our local computer so that we can complete the demonstration.

On the Mac installation used in preparation of this chapter, after installing the MySQL server software, it was also important to install the MySQL Preference Pane, in order to provide a simple graphical interface for turning the server on and off. Because we are just doing a demonstration here, and we want to avoid future security problems, it is probably sensible to turn MySQL server off when we are done with the demonstration. In Windows, you can use MySQL Workbench to control the server settings on your local computer.

Returning to R, use install.packages() and library() to prepare the RMySQL package for use. If everything is working the way it should, you should be able to run the following command from the command line:

```
> con <- dbConnect(dbDriver("MySQL"), dbname = "test")
```

The dbConnect() function establishes a linkage or connection between R and the database we want to use. This underscores the point that we are connecting to an external resource and we must therefore manage the connection.

If there were security controls involved (such as username and passwords), this is where we would provide the necessary information to establish that we were authorized users of the database. However, in this case, because we are on a local server of MySQL, we don't need to provide this security information.

The dbDriver() function provided as an argument to dbConnect specifies that we want to use a MySQL client. The database name—specified as dbname = "test"—is just a placeholder at this point. We can use the dbListTables() function to see what tables are accessible to us (for our purposes, a table is just like a dataframe, but it is stored inside the database system):

```
> dbListTables(con)
character(0)
```

The response character(0) means that there is an empty list, so no tables are available to us. This is not surprising because we just installed MySQL and have not used it for anything yet. Unless you have another database available to import into MySQL, we can just use the census data we obtained earlier in the chapter to create a table in MySQL:

```
> dbWriteTable(con, "census", testFrame, overwrite =
+       TRUE)
[1] TRUE
```

Take note of the arguments supplied to the dbWriteTable() function. The first argument provides the database connection that we established with the dbConnect() function. The census argument gives our new table in MySQL a name. We use testFrame as the source of data—as noted earlier a dataframe and a relational database table are very similar in structure. Finally, we provide the argument overwrite=TRUE, which was not really needed in this case—because we know that there were no existing tables—but could be important in other operations where we need to make sure to replace any old table that might have been left around from previous work. The function returns the logical value TRUE to signal that it was able to finish the request that we made. This is important in programming new functions because we can use the signal of success or failure to guide subsequent steps and provide error or success messages.

Now if we run dbListTables() we should see our new table:

```
> dbListTables(con)
[1] "census"
```

Now we can run an SQL query on our table:

```
> dbGetQuery(con, "SELECT stateName, july11pop FROM
+     census WHERE july11pop<1000000")
               stateName    july11pop
1                 Alaska    722718
2               Delaware    907135
3   District of Columbia    617996
4                Montana    998199
5           North Dakota    683932
6           South Dakota    824082
7                Vermont    626431
8                Wyoming    568158
```

Note that the dbGetQuery() call shown above breaks onto two lines, but the string starting with SELECT has to be typed all on one line. The capitalized words in that string are the SQL commands. It is beyond the scope of this chapter to give an SQL tutorial, but, briefly, SELECT chooses a subset of the table and the fields named after select are the ones that will appear in the result. The FROM command chooses the table(s) where the data should come from. The WHERE command specified a condition, in this case that we only wanted rows where the July 2011 population was less than 1 million. SQL is a powerful and flexible language and this just scratches the surface.

In this case we did not assign the results of dbGetQuery() to another data object, so the results were just echoed to the R console. But it would be easy to assign the results to a dataframe and then use that dataframe for subsequent calculations or visualizations.

To emphasize a point made above, the normal motivation for accessing data through MySQL or another database system is that a large database exists on a remote server. Rather than having our own complete copy of those data, we can use dbConnect(), dbGetQuery(), and other database functions to access the remote data through SQL. We can also use SQL to specify subsets of the data, to preprocess the data with sorts and other operations, and to create summaries of the data. SQL is also particularly well suited to joining data from multiple tables to make new combinations. In the present example, we used only one table, it was a very small table, and we had created it ourselves in R from an Excel source, so none of these were very good motivations for storing our data in MySQL, but this was only a demonstration.

COMPARING SQL AND R FOR ACCESSING A DATA SET

In R, there is a library sqldf, that enables us to use a dataframe as a database. So, for example, we can do the same SQL query using sqldf on a dataframe that we previously did using SQL on a database. (Note that the code below assumes that we have already installed and libraried the sqldf package.):

```
> sqldf("select avg(april10base) From testFrame")
  avg(april10base)
1          6162876

> mean(testFrame$april10base)
[1]   6162876

> sqldf("select stateName From testFrame
+     Where july11pop<1000000")
    stateName
1      Alaska
2    Delaware
3     Montana
4 North Dakota
5 South Dakota
6     Vermont
7     Wyoming
```

As you can see, we can do SQL commands using the dataframe as the database. The actual SQL is the same as normal SQL. Since we can perform SQL commands on a dataframe, it is very easy to compare typical SQL tasks with how those tasks can be done in R. That is to say, we can easily compare using SQL commands to doing more-traditional

R commands. For example, in our code we computed the mean of a column in SQL, and we also computed the mean (i.e., the same task) directly in R.

We can also use the tapply command to perform a command similar operation to the Group by SQL command. To show how tapply can be used, we first need to add the region for each state in the country. This way, we can states by region. We are lucky, since there is a state.region vector provided with R this task is very easy. Our only issue is that the census data set includes Washington, D.C. (the District of Columbia). So we first have to remove that row before adding the region column.

```
> testFrame <- testFrame[testFrame$stateName !=
+     "District of Columbia", ]
> testFrame$region <- state.region
```

Now we have the region for each state. With this information, we can determine the average population for each region, based on the states in a specific region.

```
> sqldf("select AVG(july11pop) From testFrame
+        Group by region")
  AVG(july11pop)
1      5596570
2      6169066
3      7214296
4      5604981
```

In R, as just mentioned, we can do something very similar using the tapply command, which takes three parameters. This command applies a function (specified as the third parameter), on a subset of the vector (specified by the first parameter), broken down by a given factor variable (specified by the second parameter). Seeing the tapply in action might make this easier to understand:

```
> tapply(testFrame$april10base, testFrame$region,
+        mean)
    Northeast        South    North Central         West
      6146360      7122127          5577249      5534273
```

In this example, we grouped the april10base column by the region column. Then, for all the states in a specific region (e.g., the South), tapply took the mean of those states. This functionality is the same as the Group by SQL command.

Let's use these region means to do more with R. Specifically, let's store the region mean for each state. This is more complicated than many other tasks we have done: We have four regions but many states. We need to figure out which region mean should be associated with each state.

To do this, just like other R commands, we can store the result of the tapply command and use the results. So we first store the region means in the regionMean variable and the region names in the regionNames variable.

```
> regionMean <- tapply(testFrame$april10base,
+     testFrame$region, mean)
> regionMean
Northeast          South North Central            West
   6146360        7122127         5577249         5534273

> regionNames <- names(regionMean)
> regionNames
[1] "Northeast"    "South"    "North Central"    "West"
```

But how do we create the column with the appropriate region mean for each state? One strategy is to get the indexes of the states within a specific region and to assign those states the appropriate region mean. This is similar in concept to how the order function works to sort a dataframe. As you might remember, order sorts a column and returns the sorted indexes, which is then used to sort the dataframe. In our case, we do not need to sort but, rather, identify which rows have the region. We can use the "which" function to get this info:

```
> which(regionNames[1] == testFrame$region)
[1]   7 19 21 29 30 32 38 39 45
```

We can see the regionNames[1] is the Northeast and use that to let R determine the appropriate index into regionNames, as shown below:

```
> which(regionNames[regionNames=="Northeast"] ==
+     testFrame$region)
[1]   7 19 21 29 30 32 38 39 45
```

Either way, we can get the appropriate rows and can use that information to define those rows to have the region mean of the Northeast. We can do similar commands for the other regions.

```
> testFrame$regionMean <- 0
> testFrame$regionMean[which(regionNames[1] ==
+     testFrame$region)] <- regionMean[1]
> testFrame$regionMean[which(regionNames[2] ==
+     testFrame$region)] <- regionMean[2]
> testFrame$regionMean[which(regionNames[3] ==
+     testFrame$region)] <- regionMean[3]
> testFrame$regionMean[which(regionNames[4] ==
+     testFrame$region)] <- regionMean[4]
```

As you can see in the code above, we had to repeat the code four times (one for each region). If you are thinking there must be a way to not have to cut and paste the code four times, you are correct. In R, there is a concept of loops. We will use a simple "for" loop to do the same line of code on each of the regions.

```
> for (x in 1:4) {
+     indexes <- which(regionNames[x] ==
+           testFrame$region)
+     testFrame$regionMean[indexes] <- regionMean[x]
+     }
```

In this code, we defined a variable x, and x changes in value each time through the loop. The first time, x is equal to 1, and the code works for the Northeast. The second time through the loop, x is equal to 2, and the code works for the South. When we say the "second time through the loop," what happens is that the code between the { and the } is executed four times. The first time, x is equal to 1; the second time, x is equal to 2. This continues for x equals 3, and then, finally, x equals 4. As you can probably guess, the 1:4 defines the start and end values for x within the loop.

In many programming languages, loops are fundamental, and are used extensively. However, in R we can do many, many operations without doing loops. For people with experience with other programming languages, it is often tempting to use loops more than needed. For example, in other programming languages, one might need to use a loop to add two vectors together, but in R, that is one line of code. This is an example of the power of R. We can see that using "for" loops adds more code and is not as easy to read:

```
> a <- c(10:19)
> b <- c(20:29)
> c <- a + b
> c
 [1]  30 32 34 36 38 40 42 44 46 48
> for(x in 1:10) {
+     d[x] <- a[x] + b[x]
+  }
> d
 [1]  30 32 34 36 38 40 42 44 46 48
```

So, while sometimes we need to use loops, always try to think if there is a way to do the same thing in R without a loop.

ACCESSING JSON DATA

The second strategy we will explore involves the use of an application programming interface (API) to communicate with another application or database system. We will explore JSON (Java Script Object Notation), an increasingly common way to share data on the web. JSON is a structured, but human readable, way of sending back some data from an application or a website. Sometimes those data are static, but other times a website will use JSON to supply up-to-the-minute information. JSON was created by Douglas Crockford in the early 2000s, while he was working at a start-up funded by Tesla Ventures. Although originally derived from the JavaScript scripting language, JSON is a language-independent data format and code for sharing data. JSON is available for many programming languages, including R!

We will start by exploring how Google shares geocode information. We will use the Google geocoding API, which is pretty easy to use, does not require an account or application ID, and allows about 2,500 address conversions per day. The Google geocode API allows a user (program or person) to supply an address, and Google will return the latitude and longitude of that address. The API can be accessed over the web, using what is called an HTTP GET request. Note that the terms of service for the Google geocoding API are very specific about how the interface can be used—most notably on the point that the geocodes must be used on Google maps. Make sure you read the terms of service before you create any software applications that use the geocoding service. See the link in the list of sources at the end of the chapter. The list has a link to an article with dozens of other geocoding APIs if you disagree with Google's terms of service.

These abbreviations probably look familiar. HTTP is the hyper text transfer protocol, and it is the standard method for requesting and receiving web page data. A GET request consists of information that is included in the URL string to specify some details about the information we are hoping to get back from the request. Here is an example GET request to the Google geocoding API:

http://maps.googleapis.com/maps/api/geocode/json?address=1600+Pennsylvania+ Avenue,+Washington,+DC&sensor=false

This request can be typed into a web browser as a web address. The first part of the web address should look familiar: The http://maps.googleapis.com part of the URL specifies the domain name just like a regular web page. The next part of the URL, /maps/api/ geocode, tells Google which API we want to use. Then the json indicates that we would like to receive our result in Java Script Object Notation.

The address appears next, and we are apparently looking for the White House at 1600 Pennsylvania Avenue in Washington, D.C. Finally, sensor=false is a required parameter indicating that we are not sending our request from a mobile phone. As previously mentioned, you can type that whole URL into the address field of any web browser, and you should get a sensible result back. The JSON notation is not beautiful, but you will see that it makes sense and provides the names of individual data items along with their values. Here's a small excerpt that shows the key parts of the data object that we are trying to get our hands on:

```
{
    "results" : [
        {
            "address _ components" : [
            "geometry" : {
                "location" : {
                    "lat" : 38.8791981,
                    "lng" : -76.9818437
                },
    "status" : "OK"
}
```

Perhaps a bit surprisingly, the actual coordinates you get might be different from what was shown earlier. That is because Google might be improving the accuracy of its geocodes. There are tons more data in the JSON object that Google returned, and we can use RJSONIO to extract the data we need from the structure without having to parse it ourselves.

In order to get R to send the HTTP GET requests to Google, we will also need to use the RCurl package. This will give us a single command to send the request and receive the result back—essentially doing all of the quirky steps that a web browser takes care of automatically for us. To get started, use install.packages() and library() on the two packages that we will need—RCurl and RJSONIO. If you are working on a Windows machine, you might need to jump through a hoop or two to get RCurl, but it is available for Windows even if it is not in the standard CRAN repository. Search for RCurl Windows if you run into trouble.

Next, we will create a new helper function to take the address field and turn it into the URL that we need:

```
# Format an URL for the Google Geocode API
MakeGeoURL <- function(address)
{
  root <- "http://maps.google.com/maps/api/geocode/"
  url <- paste(root, "json?address=", address,
        "&sensor=false", sep = "")
  return(URLencode(url))
}
```

There are three simple steps here. The first line initializes the beginning part of the URL into a string called root. Then we use paste() to glue together the separate parts of the string (note the sep="" so we don't get spaces between the parts). This creates a string that looks almost like the one in the earlier White House example. The final step converts the string to a legal URL using a utility function called URLencode() that RCurl provides. Let's try it:

```
> MakeGeoURL("1600 Pennsylvania Avenue, Washington,
+       DC")
[1]
```

```
"http://maps.google.com/maps/api/geocode/json?address=
1600%20Pennsylvania%20Avenue,%20Washington,%20DC&senso
r=false"
```

Looks good! Just slightly different from the original example (%20 instead of the plus [+] character), but hopefully that won't make a difference. Remember that you can type this function at the command line or you can create it in the script editing window in the upper-left-hand pane of RStudio. The latter is the better way to go; if you click the Source on Save checkmark, RStudio will make sure to update R's stored version of your function every time you save the script file. Now we are ready to use our new function, MakeGeoURL(), in another function that will actually request the data from the Google API:

```
Addr2latlng <- function(address)
{
  url <- MakeGeoURL(address)
  apiResult <- getURL(url)
  geoStruct <- fromJSON(apiResult, simplify = FALSE)
  lat <- NA
  lng <- NA
  try(lat <-
      geoStruct$results[[1]]$geometry$location$lat)
  try(lng <-
      geoStruct$results[[1]]$geometry$location$lng)
  return(c(lat, lng))
}
```

We have defined this function to receive an address string as its only argument. The first thing it does is to pass the URL string to MakeGeoURL() to develop the formatted URL. Then the function passes the URL to getURL(), which actually does the work of sending the request out onto the Internet. The getURL() function is part of the RCurl package. This step is just like typing a URL into the address box of your browser.

We capture the result in an object called apiResult. If we were to stop and look inside this, we would find the JSON structure that appeared earlier. We can pass this structure to the function fromJSON()—we put the result in an object called geoStruct. This is a regular

R dataframe such that we can access any individual element using regular $ notation and the array index [[1]]. Note that our results are two lists (not vectors). One thing to remember when working with lists is that we need to use double square brackets: [[ ]]. If you compare the variable names geometry, location, lat, and lng to the preceding JSON example, you will find that they match perfectly. The fromJSON() function in the RJSONIO package has done all the heavy lifting of breaking the JSON structure into its component pieces.

Note that this is the first time we have encountered the try() function. When programmers expect the possibility of an error, they frequently use methods that are tolerant of errors or that catch errors before they disrupt the code. If our call to getURL() returns something unusual that we aren't expecting, then the JSON structure might not contain the fields that we want. By surrounding our command to assign the lat and lng variables with a try() function, we can avoid stopping the flow of the code if there is an error. Because we initialized lat and lng to NA, this function will return a two-item list with both items being NA if an error occurs in accessing the JSON structure. There are more-elegant ways to accomplish this same goal. For example, the Google API puts an error code in the JSON structure and we could choose to interpret that instead. We will leave that to the Chapter Challenge!

In the last step, our new Addr2latlng() function returns a two item list containing the latitude and longitude. We can test it out right now:

```
> testData <- Addr2latlng("1600 Pennsylvania Avenue,
+     Washington, DC")
> str(testData)
 num [1:2] 38.9 -77
```

Perfect! we called our new function Addr2latlng() with the address of the White House and got back a list with two numeric items containing the latitude and longitude associated with that address. With just a few lines of R code we have harnessed the power of Google's extensive geocoding capability to convert a brief text street address into mapping coordinates.

Now let's try to read a large JSON data set. Our example that we will parse is a data set about the Citi Bike program in New York City. There are similar programs in many cities. The basic idea is that a person can rent a bike from one bike location and ride it to another location in the city. The person can leave it there. So, for example, maybe you take a bike to work, lock it at a location near work, but in the evening, if it's raining, you can take the train home. The next day, you can ride a different bike to work. Of course, if it rained every afternoon for a week, and everyone acted the same way, eventually, there would be no bikes in some locations (and no empty spaces in other Citi Bike locations).

Hence, Citi Bike makes data available about how many bikes and spaces are available at each of its locations. One of the ways Citi Bike makes this information available is via JSON. To access the data, we will again use the package RJSONIO (there are other JSON packages available in R, such as jsonlite, but we have found RJSONIO to be somewhat more stable in parsing JSON data sets). We will also use the RCurl package, since we will use the getURL function to retrieve the source of the JSON web page.

To start, after loading the RJSONIO and RCurl libraries, we load the JSON data set with the following code:

```
> bikeURL <-
+     "https://feeds.citibikenyc.com/stations/
+     stations.json"
> apiResult <- getURL(bikeURL)
> results <- fromJSON(apiResult)
> length(results)
[1] 2
```

First, we captured the result in an object called apiResult. Note that, as was previously mentioned, just as for a CSV file, JSON is human readable. So if we type the URL into a browser, we can see the results on a web page, just as we did for the Google geocode API. If we were to stop and look inside the apiResult, we would find the JSON structure. We then pass this structure to the function fromJSON()—and put the result in an object called results. This is a regular R dataframe such that we can access any individual element using regular $ notation and the list index using double brackets since our results are two lists (not vectors). The first item in the list describes when the web page (data set) was generated, as we can see from the following code:

```
> when <- results[[1]]
> when
[1]   "2016-01-03 11:56:40 AM"
```

The next results are actually a list of stations:

```
> stations <- results[[2]]
> length(stations)
[1] 508
```

While lists are more of a hassle than dataframes, we are starting to see some real data—specifically, that there are 508 places where someone can get or return a bike. Now let's look at one station to see the type of information available for each station:

```
> str(stations[[1]])
List of 18
$ id                     : num 72
$ stationName            : chr "W 52 St & 11 Ave"
$ availableDocks         : num 5
$ totalDocks             : num 39
$ latitude               : num 40.8
$ longitude              : num -74
$ statusValue            : chr "In Service"
$ statusKey              : num 1
$ availableBikes         : num 34
$ stAddress1             : chr "W 52 St & 11 Ave"
$ stAddress2             : chr ""
$ city                   : chr ""
$ postalCode             : chr ""
$ location               : chr ""
$ altitude               : chr ""
$ testStation            : logi FALSE
    $ lastCommunicationTime : chr"2016-01-03 11:53:24 AM"
$ landMark               : chr ""
```

Now we finally have interesting data! We can see that there are 39 docks (the places to park a bike) at this station and that there are 5 docks available, meaning that there are 34 bikes available, which you can see is another data element later in the list. There are other interesting pieces of information, such as the street addresses. But working with lists is a pain, so let's convert this station list into a dataframe using the following R code. We first get the total number of rows in the list of stations (which is the number of stations to get/park a bike) and the names of all the attributes at each station (which will be our column variables in our dataframe).

```
> numRows <- length(stations)
> nameList <- names(stations[[1]])
```

Next we create the dataframe, by using unlist on the list, which creates one long list of elements, and putting them back into a dataframe, using the structure of the matrix.

```
> dfStations <- data.frame(matrix(unlist(stations),
+ nrow=numRows, byrow=T), stringsAsFactors=FALSE)
```

Finally, we need to name the columns appropriately:

```
> names(dfStations) <- nameList
```

Now we can look at our newly created dataframe:

```
> str(dfStations)
'data.frame':    508 obs. of  18 variables:
 $ id                : chr  "72" "79" "82" "83" ...
 $ stationName       : chr  "W 52 St & 11 Ave"
"Franklin St & W Broadway" ...
 $ availableDocks    : chr  "5" "5" "19" "36" ...
 $ totalDocks        : chr  "39" "33" "27" "62" ...
 $ latitude          : chr  "40.76727216"
"40.71911552" ...
 $ longitude         : chr  "-73.99392888"
"-74.00666661" ...
 $ statusValue       : chr  "In Service"
"In Service" "In Service" "In Service" ...
 $ statusKey         : chr  "1" "1" "1" "1" ...
 $ availableBikes    : chr  "34" "27" "8" "26" ...
 $ stAddress1        : chr  "W 52 St & 11 Ave"
"Franklin St & W Broadway" ...
 $ stAddress2        : chr  "" "" "" "" ...
 $ city              : chr  "" "" "" "" ...
 $ postalCode        : chr  "" "" "" "" ...
 $ location          : chr  "" "" "" "" ...
 $ altitude          : chr  "" "" "" "" ...
```

```
 $ testStation             : chr   "FALSE" "FALSE"
"FALSE" "FALSE" ...
 $ lastCommunicationTime : chr   "2016-01-03 11:53:24
AM" ...
 $ landMark                : chr   "" "" "" "" ...
```

The only thing left to clean up is the fact that R thinks all the columns (variables) are characters, but some are numbers, so we can fix this by doing the following:

```
> dfStations$availableDocks <-
+     as.numeric(dfStations$availableDocks)
> dfStations$availableBikes <-
+     as.numeric(dfStations$availableBikes)
> dfStations$totalDocks <-
+     as.numeric(dfStations$totalDocks)
```

We are done reading in a JSON data set! However, just for fun, before we move on let's take a look at some of the data. Of course, if we rerun the code, we might get different results since these data update throughout the day, every day.

```
> mean(dfStations$availableDocks)
[1]   21.41142
> mean(dfStations$availableBikes)
[1]   10.88386
> bikesAvailDF <-
+     dfStations[dfStations$availableBikes>0,]
> nrow(bikesAvailDF)
[1]   469
```

We can see that there is an average of more than 21 docks available at each station, and there is an average of 10 bikes available at each station. However, there are only 469 stations with at least one bike available (and remember, there is a total of 508 stations).

While we covered a lot in the chapter, the key point is that there are many ways to store and access data. Our job, as data scientists, is to be able to read the data and put it into a usable format within R.

Chapter Challenge

Explore the web for other JSON data sets. Find one that is interesting and read the JSON data set into R. Work with the JSON data set to make sure it can be easily used by creating a dataframe with the key information that was read using JSON.

Sources

http://cran.r-project.org/doc/manuals/R-data.html

http://cran.r-project.org/web/packages/gdata/gdata.pdf

http://www.json.org

http://dev.mysql.com/downloads/

http://en.wikipedia.org/wiki/Comparison_of_relational_database_management_systems

http://gis.stackexchange.com/questions/110942/how-often-does-google-change-the-geo-coordinates-for-a-given-address

R Functions Used in This Chapter

getURL()	Gets the results of a web page.
fromJSON()	Converts a JSON data source to R.
library()	Makes an R package available for use.
Numberize()	This is a custom function created in this chapter.
read.xls()	Imports data from a binary R file; part of the gdata package.
str_replace()	Replaces one character string with another.
str_replace_all()	Replaces multiple instances of a character string with another.
dbConnect()	Connects to an SQL database.
dbGetQuery()	Runs an SQL query and return the results.
dbListTables()	Shows the tables available in a connection.
dbWriteTable()	Sends a data table to an SQL systems.
install.packages()	Gets the code for an R package.
unlist()	Takes a list and returns a simple vector.
matrix()	Takes a vector and converts it into a matrix.
sqldf()	Treats a dataframe as a database for SQL commands.
tapply()	Creates subsets of a vector and performs a specified function on each subset.

© iStockphoto.com/larryrains

12

PICTURES VERSUS NUMBERS

> - Demonstrate how to use the following R functions: ggplot (and building layers in ggplot via ggtitle, geom_histogram, geom_boxlot, geom_line, geom_col, geom_point, geom_text, coord_flip, theme, format, scale_color_continuous).

Sometimes it is really helpful to "see" the data. Seeing the data is typically known as visualization. We can think of visualization as turning data into pictures. More formally, in the book *Interactive Data Visualization* (2015, Boca Raton, FL: CRC Press), Matthew Ward, Georges Grinstein, and Daniel Keim define visualization as the "the communication of information using graphical representations." Information visualization is the use of visual representations of abstract data. In other words, information visualization is used when there is no well-defined two-dimensional or three-dimensional representation of the data. In this chapter we will explore information visualization. In the following chapter, we will explore data that have a geometric component, just as our Citi Bike data had a geometric component of stations (that had a physical address).

Visualization is often useful since human vision has the highest bandwidth of all our senses. It is fast and processes information in parallel. In addition, the eye is trained for pattern recognition—we can scan an image, quickly recognize outliers, and remember that image. For example, quickly reviewing a grid of numbers (perhaps an Excel spreadsheet) and finding the large and small numbers can be difficult. However, if the grid cells are color coded, it is much easier to identify the largest and smallest numbers.

A VISUALIZATION OVERVIEW

There are six key components one can use to create a visualization. We can think of a simple scatter plot when exploring each of these components.

Color:	The color of each symbol in the scatter plot. Color is the most common and was mentioned in our grid of numbers example. Note that some people are color-blind, so the use of color needs to take this into account.
Size:	The size of each symbol in the scatter plot.
Texture:	The shape of the symbol and whether the symbol is a solid color or a pattern.
Proximity:	The location of the symbol on the X-axis and the Y-axis.
Annotation:	Whether we label our scatter plots.

Interactivity: Selecting one or more symbols, or perhaps zooming into a subset of the graph.

Before we start exploring how to create visualizations, one last point to remember is that often, in a visualization, we must focus on making sure that the picture is easy to understand. It is often very easy to create a visualization that has a lot of information, but is difficult to understand. To address this concern, the following are 10 principles that should be useful to think about as you create a visualization:

1. Simplicity. Edward Tufte is famous for suggesting that you should create the simplest graph that conveys the information you want to convey. This is a good rule to remember!

2. Encoding. Consider the type of encoding used, and try to make the encoding intuitive. For example, something that is bigger should be encoded as something longer/thicker/bigger as compared to something that is smaller.

3. Patterns versus details. Focus on visualizing patterns or the details. It is very hard to do both in the same picture.

4. Ranges. Select meaningful ranges for the axes.

5. Transformations. Transforming data can be useful. An example is a log transformation.

6. Density. Rendering semitransparent points can show the density in different parts of the visualization.

7. Connections. Use lines to connect sequential data.

8. Aggregates. Combine data and visualizations in meaningful ways.

9. Comparison. Keep axis ranges as similar as possible when comparing multiple graphs.

10. Color. Select an appropriate color scheme, based on the type and meaning of the data.

Now we are set to begin creating visualizations! In fact, we have used some of the R base graphics during our initial exploration of data sets. For example, when we wanted to understand the distribution of a vector (such as population of states within the United States), we can compute the mean, range, quantiles, and other attributes such as skewness, but often it is much easier to understand information presented in a picture. In this case, to understand the distribution of a vector (or a column in a data set), we used a histogram. This visualization provided a view of the data that complemented our descriptive statistics that we generated in previous chapters.

BASIC PLOTS IN R

So, let's continue to explore the states population data set.

```
> dfStates <- readCensus()
```

We can start by reviewing the R base graphics that we have previously used. For example, if we want to understand the distribution of the state populations, we can show the histogram in Figure 12.1.

```
> hist(dfStates$july11pop)
```

FIGURE 12.1

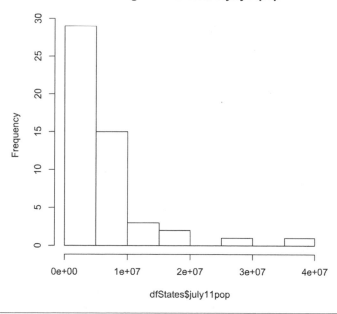

Histogram of dfStates$july11pop

Using R base graphics, we can also show a bar plot (a bar chart), as in Figure 12.2.

```
> barplot(dfStates$july11pop, names.arg =
+      dfStates$stateName, las=2)
```

FIGURE 12.2

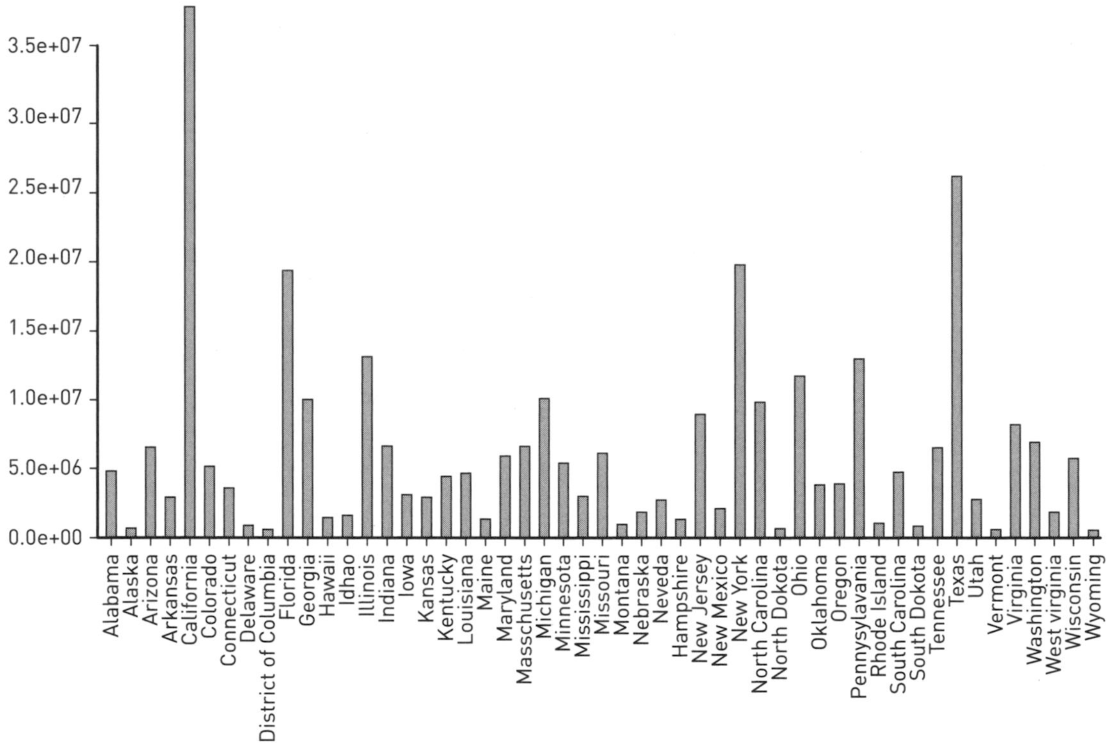

USING GGPLOT2

While doing these simple charts in R's base graphics is very easy, if we want to create more-advanced visualizations, we need to explore a more-advanced visualization package, known as ggplot2. As we will see, doing simple things in ggplot2 is more complicated, but that extra work makes it much easier to build advanced and more useful visualizations.

According to ggplot2's own website (http://ggplot2.org/), "ggplot2 is a plotting system for R, based on the grammar of graphics, which tries to take the good parts of base and lattice graphics and none of the bad parts. It takes care of many of the fiddly details that make plotting a hassle (like drawing legends) as well as providing a powerful model of graphics that makes it easy to produce complex multi-layered graphics." Yup! The gg stands for grammar of graphics. ggplot2 was initially created by Hadley Wickham in 2005 and was refined until 2015. The latest version, ggplot2, is now the most commonly used visualization tool within the R ecosystem. An important concept when using ggplot2 is that we can build up layers of information to be displayed. So, for example, we can have one layer for lines and another layer for points.

To create a ggplot, we need to define three key items. First, we need to define the data, in the form of a dataframe, to be used in the visualization. Next, we need to describe the aesthetics for the visualization. The aesthetics defines how to map attributes, such as color, to columns in the dataframe. The aesthetics also defines which columns get mapped to the X- and Y-axis of the visualization The final component of a ggplot visualization is the geometry, which defines the type of graphics to be used in the visualization (such as a histogram, a scatter plot, or a bar chart). Don't worry if this sounds confusing, as we go through the examples in the chapter, it will become easier to understand!

Before we get started using ggplot, we need to ensure that ggplot2 has been installed and libraried. Rather than do this manually, let's create a function that will assist us and make the activity more repeatable. So here is a function that takes as input the name of a package. It tests whether the package has been downloaded—installed—from the R code repository. If it has not yet been downloaded/installed, the function takes care of this. Then we use a new function, called require() to prepare the package for further use. Let's call our function EnsurePackage, because it ensures that a package is ready for us to use. It might make sense to create this function in a new R source file. If so, you should click the File menu and then click New to create a new file of R script. Then, type or copy/paste the following code:

```
EnsurePackage<-function(x) {
  x <- as.character(x)

  if (!require(x,character.only=TRUE)) {
    install.packages(pkgs=x, repos="http://cran.r-
    project.org")
    require(x,character.only=TRUE)
  }
}
```

On Windows machines, the folder where new R packages are stored has to be configured to allow R to put new files there ("write" permissions). In Windows Explorer, you can right click on the folder and choose Properties->Security, then choose your username and user group, click Edit, enable all permissions, and click OK. If you run into trouble, check out the Windows FAQ at CRAN by searching or using this web address: http://cran.r-project.org/bin/windows/base/rw-FAQ.html.

The require() function does the same thing as library(), which we have used in the previous chapter, but it also returns the value FALSE if the package you requested in the argument x has not yet been downloaded. That same line of code also contains another new feature, the "if" statement. This is what computer scientists call a conditional. It tests the stuff inside the parentheses to see if it evaluates to TRUE or FALSE. If TRUE, the program continues to run the script in between the curly braces (lines 4 and 8). If FALSE, all the stuff in the curly braces is skipped. Also, in the third line, in case you are curious, the arguments to the require() function include x, which is the name of the package that was passed into the function, and character.only=TRUE, which tells the require() function to expect x to be a character string. The last thing to notice about this third line: there is an exclamation mark (!) character that reverses the results of the logical test. Technically, it is the Boolean function NOT. It requires some mental gyration that when require() returns FALSE, the ! inverts it to TRUE, and that is when the code in the curly braces runs.

Once you have this code in a script window, make sure to select the whole function and click Run in the toolbar to make R aware of the function. There is also a checkbox on that same toolbar called Source on Save that will keep us from having to click on the Run button all the time. If you click the checkmark, then every time you save the source code file, RStudio will rerun the code. If you get in the habit of saving after every code change you will always be running the latest version of your function.

Now we are ready to put EnsurePackage() to work

```
> EnsurePackage("ggplot2")
```

Now that we can use ggplot2, let's explore one key aspect of ggplot—the fact that we can build up the plot with layers. The code below shows a histogram being built.

```
> g <- ggplot(dfStates, aes(x=july11pop))
> g <- g + geom _ histogram(binwidth=5000000,
+     color="black", fill="white")
> g <- g + ggtitle("states population histogram")
> g
```

FIGURE 12.3

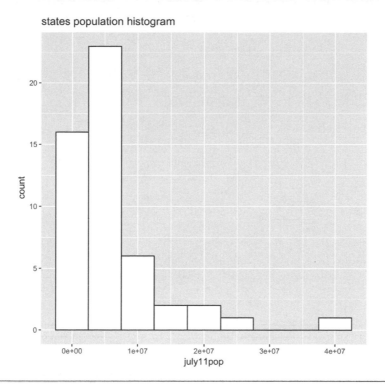

states population histogram

To review the code, the first line creates a ggplot, where the dataframe to be used is dfStates, and the X-axis will be the july11pop population. Note that once we specify the dataframe (dfStates), ggplot looks at the columns within the data set (such as july11pop). The next line states that we want to use a histogram with the bars being white with a black outline (see Figure 12.3); finally, we add a title. Another way to see the distribution within a list of numbers is to create a boxplot as shown in Figures 12.4 and 12.5.

```
> ggplot(dfStates,aes(x=factor(0),july11pop)) +
+    geom _ boxplot()
```

If we want to explore the distribution of the population but put the states into two groups—one group for those states with an increase in population and one group for states with a decrease in population—we can use the following code:

FIGURE 12.4

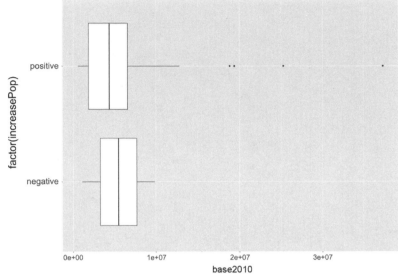

FIGURE 12.5

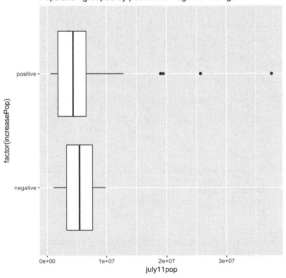

```
> dfStates$popChange <- dfStates$july11pop-
+    dfStates$july10pop
> dfStates$increasePop <- ifelse(dfStates$popChange >
+    0, "positive", "negative")
> g <- ggplot(dfStates,aes(x=factor(increasePop),
+    july11pop))
> g <- g + geom _ boxplot() + coord _ flip()
> g <- g + ggtitle('Population grouped by positive or
+    negative change')
> g
```

FIGURE 12.6

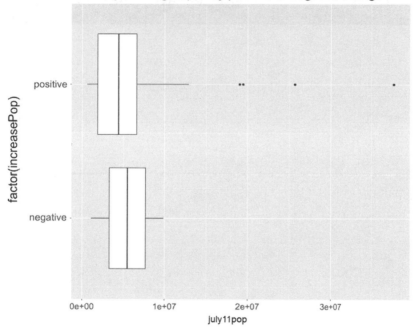

The first line creates a new column in the dfStates dataframe, based on the change in population. The second line of the code creates a new column in the dataframe, noting if the population change was positive or negative. Then we create the boxplot. Note the coord_flip() function, which rotates the chart by 90 degrees.

In addition to histograms and boxplots, we can also use ggplot2 to create line and bar charts. To create a line chart, like that shown in Figure 12.7, we use the geom_line() function; to create a bar chart, like that shown in Figure 12.8, we use the geom_col() function. You can see in the code below that we rotate the x labels (the state names) so that we can easily read the state name. Finally, note that the height of the bar (or line) represents the value in a column of our dataframe (the July 2011 population).

```
> g <- ggplot(dfStates,aes(x=reorder(stateName,
+    july11pop), y=july11pop, group=1))
> g <- g + geom _ line()
> g <- g + theme(axis.text.x = element _ text(angle =
+    90, hjust = 1))
> g
```

FIGURE 12.7

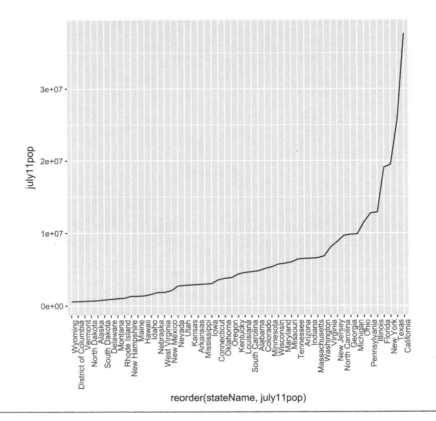

```
> g <- ggplot(dfStates,aes(x=reorder(stateName,
+    jul11ypop), y=july11pop, group=1))
> g <- g + geom _ col()
> g <- g + theme(axis.text.x =
+    element _ text(angle = 90, hjust = 1))
> g
```

FIGURE 12.8

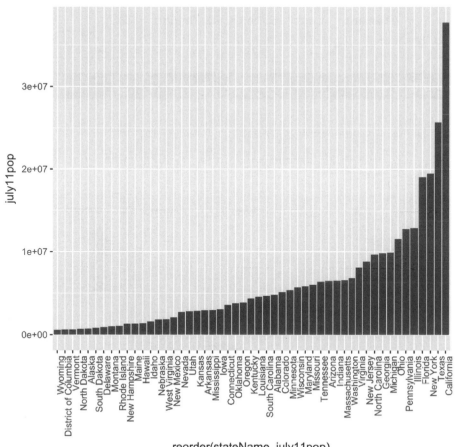

reorder(stateName, july11pop)

MORE ADVANCED
GGPLOT2 VISUALIZATIONS

We can refine the bar chart by having the color of the bars represent another variable. So let's create a visualization where the bar color represents the percent change in population, as in Figure 12.9.

```
> dfStates$percentChange <-
+     dfStates$popChange/dfStates$july10pop * 100
> g <- ggplot(dfStates,aes(x=reorder(stateName,
+     july11pop), y=july11pop,fill=percentChange))
> g <- g + geom _ col()
> g <- g + theme(axis.text.x =
+     element _ text(angle = 90, hjust = 1))
> g
```

FIGURE 12.9

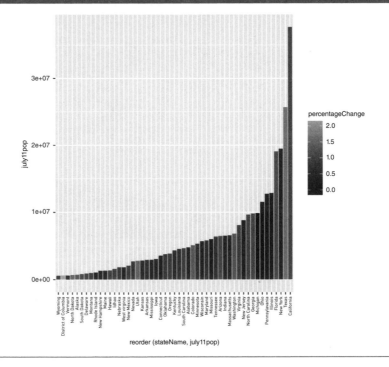

Our last type of visualization we will explore is a scatter plot, which provides a way to look at the data across two dimensions. So let's create a scatter plot where each point represents a state. We can place the point on the two-dimensional grid based on the population change (the X-axis) and the percent change (the Y-axis). In addition, we color the points based on the July 2011 population. We use that population for the size of the point as well, as shown in Figure 12.10.

```
> g <- ggplot(dfStates, aes(x=popChange,
+     y=percentChange))
> g <- g + geom _ point(aes(size=july11pop,
+     color=july11pop))
> g
```

FIGURE 12.10

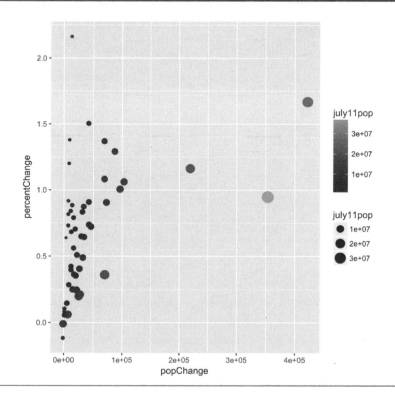

Finally, we add some text to show the name of each state (see Figure 12.11):

```
> g + geom _ text(aes(label=stateName), size=4)
```

FIGURE 12.11

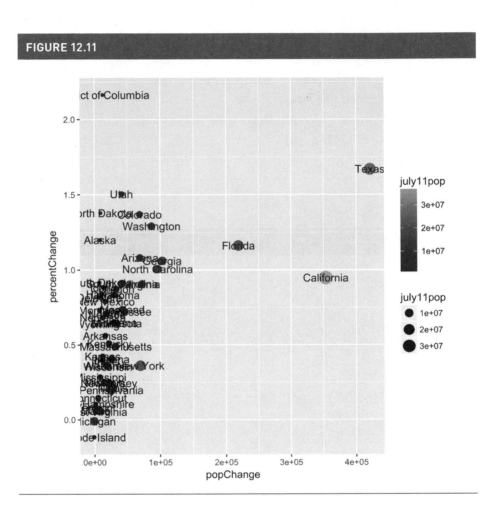

By using this scatter plot, we see some states are outliers (some have large populations, and some have much smaller populations). For example, the District of Columbia has a very small population (and population change) but has the largest percent increase in population. Texas is a large state and has a high percentage change in population.

We can improve the picture (see Figure 12.12) by moving the text (the state name) to be away from the actual symbol by using the hjust and vjust parameters (adjusting the horizontal and vertical position of the text)

```
> g + geom _ text(aes(label=stateName),size=4, hjust=1,
+    vjust=-1)
```

FIGURE 12.12

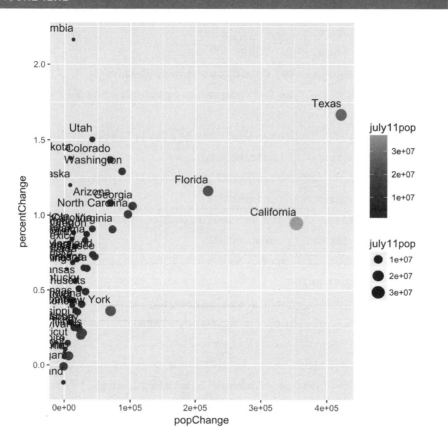

But this is still a cluttered scatter chart. Let's clean it up by doing several actions. First, let's define a set of key (or important) states. These are the states that have a percentage change of at least 1% and a population change of at least 100,000 people.

With these criteria, we can define a new column in the dfStates dataframe, keystate, to be true if that state fits our defined criteria of percentage and population change. In the scatter chart, we show the key states by defining the shape of the symbol within the scatter plot to dependent on the keystate column. We also show the text of the state name only for the key states. Next, we clean up the format of the color key, defining the three values to be shown in the key as well as formatting the numbers to include commas, so the numbers are easier to see. Finally, we change the color scale to range from white to black.

```
> minPerChange <- 1
> minPopChange <- 100000
> dfStates$keystate <- dfStates$popChange >
+       minPopChange & dfStates$percentChange>
minPerChange
> minLabel <- format(min(dfStates$july11pop),
+       big.mark=",", trim=TRUE)
> maxLabel <- format(max(dfStates$july11pop),
+       big.mark=",", trim=TRUE)
> medianLabel <- format(median(dfStates$july11pop),
+       big.mark=",", trim=TRUE)
> g <- ggplot(dfStates, aes(x=popChange,
y=percentChange))
> g <- g + geom _ point(aes(size=july11pop,
+       color=july11pop, shape=keystate))
> g <- g + geom _ text(data=
+       dfStates[dfStates$popChange > minPopChange &
+     dfStates$percentChange > minPerChange,],
+     aes(label=stateName, hjust=1, vjust=-1))
> g + scale _ color _ continuous(name="Pop",
+        breaks = with(dfStates,
+        c(min(july11pop), median(july11pop),
+          max(july11pop))),
+        labels = c(minLabel, medianLabel, maxLabel),
+        low = "white",high = "black")
```

FIGURE 12.13

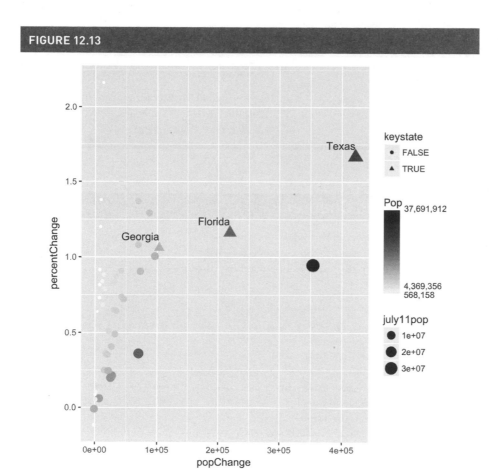

In the visualization in Figure 12.13 it is easy to see the three states of most interest—Georgia, Florida, and Texas.

Wow, we just covered many different ways to create visualizations using ggplot2. In the next chapter we will continue with visualizations but will focus on visualizing data that can be shown on a map.

Chapter Challenge

Create a bar chart, showing the average population in each region of the United States. To do this, you will need to add the region to each state (as was done in the previous chapter, where we added the region to our dataframe and then used tapply). You will need to do something similar here, adding the region to the dfStates dataframe and then figuring out how to calculate and display the mean for each region.

Sources

https://www.rstudio.com/wp-content/uploads/2015/04/
ggplot2-cheatsheet.pdf

http://ggplot2.org

http://www.sthda.com/english/wiki/print.php?id=121

http://www.crcpress.com/Interactive-Data-Visualization-
Foundations-Techniques-and-Applications/Ward-
Grinstein-Keim/p/book/9781482257373

R Functions Used in This Chapter

hist()	Generates a histogram using R's base graphics.
barplot()	Generates a bar chart using R's base graphics.
ggplot()	Starts the creation of a ggplot, defining the dataframe to be used.
Functions to Add Layers to a ggplot	
ggtitle()	Adds a title to the plot.
geom_histogram()	Creates a histogram.
geom_boxplot()	Creates a boxplot.
geom_line()	Creates a line chart.
geom_col()	Creates a bar chart.
geom_point()	Adds points to your plot.
geom_text()	Adds text to your plot.
coord_flip()	Rotates the chart by 90 degrees.
theme()	Refines the visual look of the chart (e.g., text).
format()	Enables a number to be printed in a pretty, easy-to-read format.
scale_color_continuous()	Defines a color range for mapping data to a color.

© iStockphoto.com/JoeGough

13

MAP MASHUP

In this chapter we continue our exploration of visually displaying information, and tackle a mashup challenge. *Mashup* is a term that originated in the music business decades ago related to the practice of overlaying one music recording on top of another one. The term has entered general usage to mean anything that brings together disparate influences or elements. In the application development area, mashup often refers to bringing together various sources of data to create a new product with unique value. There's even a nonprofit consortium called the Open Mashup Alliance that develops standards and methods for creating new mashups.

One of the first examples of a maps mashup was HousingMaps (http://www.housingmaps .com), a web application that grabbed apartment rental listings from the classified advertising service Craigslist and plotted them on an interactive map that shows the location of each listing. This app helped to popularize the idea that it might be useful to show real estate availability on a map. Although it's hard to imagine now, previously, real estate showed properties via lists and images, and then people would have to manually look up the location on a different map!

This housing example shows the power of using maps to display information, and, as data scientists, we need to not only be able to calculate and analyze data, but we also need to be able to display the information in an intuitive manner. Showing a dot where each house is located is far more intuitive than just showing a list of houses available within a city. One could also encode more meaning in the map in that, rather than just a dot for each rental available, we could color-code the symbol and have different types of symbols. So, for example, we could have apartments be one shape and single-family houses be another shape. We could color-code based on price. As you can see, map visualizations are similar in concept to the visualizations we previously discussed, but with the added physical component of the actual map. Since we just mentioned color coding, this might be a good time to explain how we can use color coding and still take into account that many people are color-blind. One approach is to use a gray scale, which we did at the end of the previous chapter, such as ranging from white to black. Another approach is to pick a color range that varies intensity from light to dark (such as ranging from white to blue).

CREATING MAP VISUALIZATIONS WITH GGPLOT2

Let's start with generating a simple map, using, of course, ggplot2. We do this in a similar fashion to other ggplot charts. However, first we need to get a map. Luckily, there is a package that works with ggplot2, known as ggmap. Once that is installed, we can get the map of the United States with the following line of code:

```
> us <- map _ data("state")
```

ggmap also has the list of state names available as a variable (state.names), so we can use this to create a default (dummy) dataframe (since all we want to do now is to show a basic map, without any data). Note that ggplot wants all the state names to be lower case, which is why we used the tolower() command.

```
> dummyDF <- data.frame(state.name,
+       stringsAsFactors=FALSE)
> dummyDF$state <- tolower(dummyDF$state.name)
```

Now that we have a map and a dataframe, we can create a ggplot, specifying a dataframe and the map we want to use. Then we use the geom_map function (similar in spirit to the geom_col or geom_line functions we previously used).

Within the geom_map, we tell ggplot the map to use and tell it to simply fill each state white and have its outline be black. We then expand the limits, based on the longitude and latitude for the United States. Finally, the coord_map function makes sure to keep the map from being distorted or stretched.

```
> map.simple <- ggplot(dummyDF, aes(map _ id = state))
> map.simple <- map.simple + geom _ map(map = us,
+       fill="white", color="black")
> map.simple <- map.simple + expand _ limits(x =
+       us$long, y = us$lat)
> map.simple <- map.simple + coord _ map() +
+       ggtitle("Basic map of continental USA")
> map.simple
```

After doing these commands, we get a real map: see Figure 13.1.

While that's a good start, it becomes much more interesting if we can shade each state, based on some attribute, such as the population of the state. In order to do this mashup, we can to use our function to read the state population data set, and then make sure the state names are all lowercase. As previously mentioned, we need to do this because ggplot expects the state names to be lowercase.

```
> dfStates <- readCensus()
>
> #make sure everything is lowercase
> dfStates$state <- tolower(dfStates$stateName)
```

FIGURE 13.1

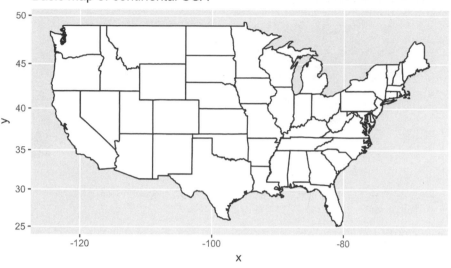

Basic map of continental USA

Now we can easily create a map, and have the fill color represent the population of each state by telling ggplot to fill each state based on the july11pop column of data (see Figure 13.2). Everything else is the same as the simple map we previously created.

```
> map.popColor <- ggplot(dfStates,
+       aes(map _ id = state))
> map.popColor <- map.popColor + geom _ map(map = us,
+       aes(fill=july11pop))
> map.popColor <- map.popColor + expand _ limits(x =
+       us$long, y = us$lat)
> map.popColor <- map.popColor+ coord _ map() +
+       ggtitle("state population")
> map.popColor
```

In looking at Figure 13.2, we can see the states with the highest population are California, Texas, and New York. So now we have created two maps—one that is a simple map without any info (map.simple) and one that has the population shown as the color within each state (map.color). These two R objects are stored and ready to use.

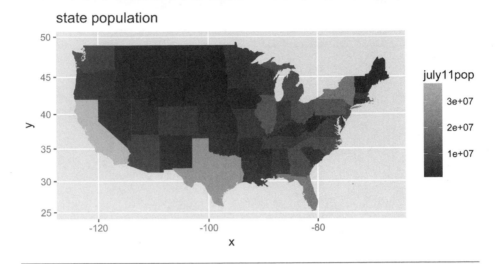

SHOWING POINTS ON A MAP

Let's now add points to the map. Let's start by just hard coding the latitude and longitude of a specific location. For example, let's demonstrate this with a made-up point somewhere in Texas:

```
> map.simple + geom _ point(aes(x = -100, y = 30))
```

Look carefully in Figure 13.3 for the dot in southern Texas. We used geom_point to create that single point, specified by x (longitude) and y (latitude) within the geom_point function.

Next, let's show a point on the map, using a logical location. A logical location is the address of a location, as opposed to specific latitude and longitude coordinates. Let's find where Syracuse, New York, is located on the map. To do this, we need to use the function geocode from the ggmap package, as you can see with the following code:

```
> latlon <- geocode("syracuse, ny")
Source :
```

FIGURE 13.3

Basic map of continental USA

```
https://maps.googleapis.com/maps/api/geocode/json?addr
ess=syracuse%2C%20ny

> latlon
       lon       lat
1  -76.14742  43.04812
```

We can see the geocode function returns an x (longitude) and y (latitude) for the address provided. You can also see that the geocode function uses the Google web service to obtain the latitude and longitude, and that the Google service encodes the results using JSON (the web data format we previously explored). In fact, we could have used the function we created, Addr2latlng, as opposed the ggmap's geocode function. Since they both use the Google API, they both would have returned the same information.

Note that if we use the geocode function or our Addr2latlng function, the Google geocoding application programming interface (API) is pretty easy to use, does not require an account or application ID, and allows about 2,500 address conversions per day. As a reminder, the terms of service for the Google geocoding API are very specific about how the interface can be used—most notably on the point that the geocodes must be used on Google maps. Make sure you read the terms of service before you create any software applications that use the geocoding service. See the link in the bibliography at the end of the chapter. The bibliography has a link to an article with dozens of other geocoding APIs if you disagree with Google's terms of service.

We can use that x and y location to draw a point on the map at the logical location of the address.

```
> map.popColor + geom _ point(aes(x = latlon$lon, y =
+      latlon$lat), color="darkred", size = 3)
```

If you look at the map in Figure 13.4, you can see a darker, slightly larger dot in the state of New York.

FIGURE 13.4

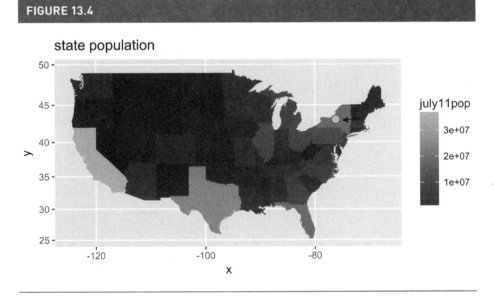

Note: Arrow has been added to indicate dot.

Adding a second point requires just a little more work:

```
> df.latlon <- data.frame(latlon)
> latlon <- geocode("colorado")
```

```
Source :
https://maps.googleapis.com/maps/api/geocode/json?
address=colorado
> df.latlon[2,] <- latlon
> df.latlon[3,] <- geocode("denver, colorado")
Source :
https://maps.googleapis.com/maps/api/geocode/json?
address=denver%2C%20colorado
> map.simple + geom _ point(data=df.latlon,aes(x = lon,
y =
+     lat))
Error in eval(expr, envir, enclos) : object 'state'
not found
```

As you can see, R gave an error, because it wanted our simple dataframe (df.latlon) to have a column state. So, although we are not using the state info, we can certainly supply a dummy column:

```
> df.latlon$state <- "?"
> map.popColor + geom _ point(data=
+     df.latlon, aes(x = lon, y = lat),
+     alpha = .5, color="darkred", size = 3)
```

Figure 13.5 has a map with three circles, one in New York and two in Colorado. You might be asking why the geocode function didn't give an error, since we just specified Colorado for one of the locations. Geocode (or, more specifically, Google) will do its best to figure out what you meant. In this case, it looks like Google gave us the location close to Denver (which is Colorado's state capital) but not exactly Denver.

A MAP VISUALIZATION EXAMPLE

Now, let's use our new knowledge to do a more advanced mashup. First, we need a source of data (points, locations) to add to our map. This could be anything that we're interested in: the locations of restaurants, crime scenes, colleges, and so on. In Google

FIGURE 13.5

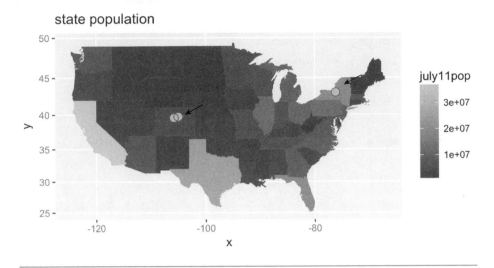

Note: Arrows have been added to indicate dots.

a search for filetype:xls or filetype:csv with appropriate additional search terms can provide interesting data sources. You might also have mailing lists of customers or clients. The most important thing is that we will need an address in order to geocode the addresses. For this example, we found a list of companies trying to leverage open data. You can look at the website (http://www.opendata500.com/) to get more info, but in brief, the website states, "The OD500 Global Network is an international network of organizations that seek to study the use and impact of open data." Since we are data scientists, this sounds like a good list to explore.

When we explore a new data set, it is often helpful to identify some interesting questions that one might try to answer when exploring the data set. In this situation, we can ask several questions, such as

Where are the companies located?

Are the companies bunched in one or two parts of the country (or spread out throughout the country)?

Are most of the companies large or small? Does the size of the company vary by geography?

While we could ask other questions, let's focus on these questions. First, we need to read in the file, which is located at http://www.opendata500.com/us/download/us_companies.csv:

```
> urlFile <- "http://www.opendata500.com/us/download/
+    us_companies.csv"
> od.companies <- read.csv(url(urlFile))
```

Let's look at the dataframe we just read into od.companies:

```
> str(od.companies)
'data.frame':    526 obs. of  22 variables:
 $ company_name_id       : Factor w/ 526 levels
 $ company_name          : Factor w/ 526 levels
 $ url                   : Factor w/ 526 levels "
 $ year_founded          : int
 $ city                  : Factor w/ 203
 $ state                 : Factor w/ 39 levels
 $ country               : Factor w/ 1 level
 $ zip_code              : int
 $ full_time_employees   : Factor w/ 8
 $ company_type          : Factor w/ 10 levels
 $ company_category      : Factor w/ 21 levels
 $ revenue_source        : Factor w/ 98 levels
 $ business_model        : Factor w/ 28 levels
 $ social_impact         : Factor w/ 12 levels
 $ description           : Factor w/ 526 levels
 $ description_short     : Factor w/ 526 levels
 $ source_count          : Factor w/ 5 levels
 $ data_types            : Factor w/ 38 levels
 $ example_uses          : Factor w/ 8 levels
 $ data_impacts          : Factor w/ 9 levels
 $ financial_info        : Factor w/ 142 levels
 $ last_updated          : Factor w/ 526 levels
```

Wow—that's a lot of columns of data. However, for now we can focus on city and state. We first make sure the city was not left blank:

```
> od.companies <-
+         od.companies[od.companies$city != "",]
```

Next we need to clean up the state abbreviations. In order to do this, we first remove Washington, D.C. Why do that? Because it's not a state, so ggplot2 will not know what to do with that info. Then we also need to change KA to KS (the postal service abbreviation for Kansas is KS, but sometimes it is known as KA.

```
> od.companies$state <-
+         as.character(od.companies$state)
> od.companies <- od.companies[od.companies$state !=
+         "DC",]
> od.companies$state <- ifelse(od.companies$state ==
+         "KA", "KS", od.companies$state)
```

Now we are ready to get our geocodes. We first create a new column that combines the city and state, and then pass that info to the geocode function. Since we have many geocodes, this might take several minutes—mainly due to the fact that Google throttles people using their web service.

```
> od.companies$cityState <- paste(od.companies$city,
+         od.companies$state)
> od.companies$geoCode <-
+         geocode(od.companies$cityState)
```

OK. Glad we only had to create the geocodes once, but now that we have them, we can show these locations on our maps!

```
> map.simple + geom _ point(data=od.companies,
+         aes(x = geoCode$lon, y = geoCode$lat), shape=1)
```

FIGURE 13.6

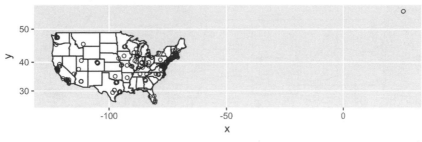

Basic map of continental USA

Oh no. What happened? If you look at Figure 13.6, you can see a point on the right—with a bad longitude location, that messes up the map (making the U.S. map much smaller). Which company is causing the issue? One way to find the company is to look at the company with a longitude greater than zero (0). We can see, with the following R code, that the company has a location of Vilnius, AL. However, there is no known city of Vilnius in Alabama. Instead, Google seems to have returned a city in Lithuania!

```
> bad <- od.companies[od.companies$geoCode$lon > 0, ]
> bad$cityState
[1] "Vilnius AL"
```

Since the city seems wrong, we can remove that company from our list, and then try to plot the points again.

```
> od.companies <-
+     od.companies[od.companies$geoCode$lon < 0, ]
> map.simple + geom _ point(data=od.companies,
+     aes(x = geoCode$lon, y = geoCode$lat), shape=1)
```

Now Figure 13.7 shows a better map, but it is still not that informative.

To make the map more useful, we can have the color of the mark (circle) represent the size of the company, in terms of the number of employees. Note that the size of the

FIGURE 13.7

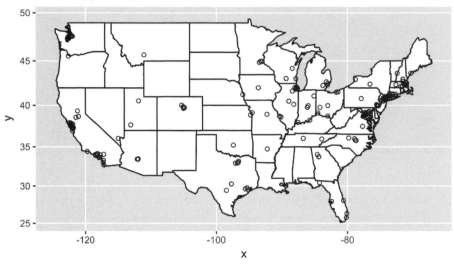

Basic map of continental USA

company is a factor (i.e., not an actual number), but we need to tell R the order of the full_time_employees so that the smaller number of employees are mapped to lighter circles. In order to show the colors, it will also be useful to use the RColorBrewer package (to get a good range of colors).

```
> library(RColorBrewer)
>  od.companies$sizes <-
+    factor(od.companies$full _ time _ employees,levels =
+      c("1-10", "11-50", "51-200", "201-500",
+        "501-1,000", "5,001-10,000", "10,001+"))
> myColors <- brewer.pal(numSizes,"Reds")
> names(myColors) <- levels(od.companies$sizes)
> myColors[1:3]
    1-10  11-50  51-200
"#FFF5F0" "#FEE0D2" "#FCBBA1"
```

You will see that the code created a variable called myColors that has a specific shade of color for each level of company size. The darkest circle in Figure 13.8 (most red if you run the code) represents the largest company. Note that as we start to use colors to represent data, we need to keep in mind that there are many people who are color-blind—going from light to dark will work for people that are color-blind. For our final map, we will go back to the map that had the populations for each state represented as the fill color of each state, and then overlay all our points on that map (note that the figure on your screen will look better than Figure 13.8, which is in black and white):

```
> map.popColor + geom_point(data=od.companies,
+     aes(x = geoCode$lon, y = geoCode$lat,
+     color=sizes)) + scale_colour_manual(name =
+     "sizeOfCompany", values = myColors) +
+     ggtitle("Open Data Company Analysis")
```

FIGURE 13.8

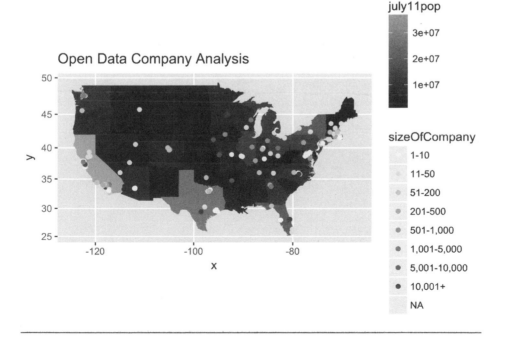

In the key, you can see that there is an NA as one of the sizes. This is because some of the data entries in the column full_time_employees were not known (and hence NA). R generated a warning when generating the image, because ggplot didn't know how to plot a size of NA. If we wanted to remove these rows, we could have used the na.omit() function.

This completes our focus on visualizations, until much later, when we explore interactive applications via the use of Shiny Apps. Next, we turn to text mining, which focuses on exploring unstructured data sets.

Chapter Challenge(s)

Find a census data set with additional information (https://www2.census.gov/programs-surveys/popest/datasets/2010-2016/national/totals/nst-est2016-alldata.csv). Parse the data set and then display the data in a useful manner, using the different visualization techniques we have covered in these last two chapters.

Sources

http://www.opendata500.com/

http://blog.programmableweb.com/2012/06/21/7-free-geocoding-apis-google-bing-yahoo-and-mapquest/

https://developers.google.com/maps/terms

http://en.wikipedia.org/wiki/Open_Mashup_Alliance

http://www.housingmaps.com/

R Functions Used in This Chapter

map_data()	Finds a map to be used by ggplot.
data.frame()	Creates a dataframe.
tolower()	Changes all uppercase letters to lowercase.
gsub()	Substitutes one string for another.
geocode()	Gets the latitude and longitude for an address.
read.csv()	Reads a CSV file.
as.character()	Treats a variable as a string.
paste()	Combines multiple strings into one string.
brewer.pal()	Creates a list of colors.
ggplot()	Creates a ggplot.
geom_map()	Creates a map visualization.
geom_point ()	Adds point(s) to a visualization.
expand_limits()	Defines the x and y for the map.
coord_map()	Makes sure the map does not show up stretched or distorted.
ggtitle()	Adds a title to a visualization.

WORD PERFECT

LEARNING OBJECTIVES

- Access and analyze unstructured data.
- Explain the purpose of word clouds.
- Apply the text mining and word cloud package to do basic text mining.
- Gain experience using the following R functions: readlines, scan, htmlTreeParse, xpathApply, VectorSource, corpus, tm_map, TermDocumentMatrix, sumRows.

Prior chapters focused on analysis of structured data and built on earlier knowledge of samples and distributions. Even our visualizations focused on understanding the analysis of structured data. This chapter switches gears to focus on manipulating so-called unstructured data, which in most cases means natural language texts. These unstructured data are everywhere and include speeches and web pages. Additional sources of text include Twitter (which companies can mine to understand positive and negative tweets about their products), product reviews (such as Yelp and TripAdvisor), and free-form answers to surveys.

So, let's start our exploration of words. The picture at the start of this chapter is an example of a text mining visualization. The visualization is a word cloud that was generated by R, using a famous speech as input. These colorful word clouds are fun to look at, but they also do contain some useful information. The geometric arrangement of words on the figure is partly random and partly designed and organized, and colored, to please the eye. The font size of each word, however, conveys some measure of its importance in the corpus of words that was presented to the word cloud graphics program. The word *corpus*, from the Latin word for "body," is a word that text analysts use to refer to a body of text material, often consisting of one or more documents. When thinking about a corpus of textual data, a set of documents could really be anything: web pages, word processing documents on your computer, a set of tweets, or government reports. In most cases, text analysts think of a collection of documents, each of which contains some natural language text, as a corpus if they plan to analyze all the documents together.

Similar to many other visualizations, word clouds are sometimes useful and sometimes not so useful. For example, when trying to get a quick understanding from free-form survey responses (such as "please let us know if you have any additional thoughts about using our product"), a word cloud can give a high-level view of how people are responding, or when someone is trying to get a quick view of a speech, a word cloud might be useful to show the frequently occurring words.

In this chapter, we will use some new R packages to enable us to investigate a speech and to create a word cloud like the one shown at the start of this chapter. Before beginning our work with the two new R packages, we need to read in a text source. In our case, let's explore a famous speech by Susan B. Anthony. Sadly, in the 1800s women in the United States had few legal rights and did not have the right to vote. Susan B. Anthony gave this speech after her arrest for casting a vote in the presidential election of 1872, an act that was unlawful at the time. She was tried and fined $100 but refused to pay. You can see the speech at http://www.historyplace.com/speeches/anthony.htm. You can save the actual speech into a text file by saving a simple text file, which can be done within a Microsoft Word document, using the save as command, and selecting txt. In addition, on a Mac, you could also do this using the Text Edit tool, or on a PC, by using the wordpad tool. Once we have the file, we need to read it into R.

READING IN TEXT FILES

To begin working on our word cloud, launch your copy of RStudio. The first order of business is to create a new RStudio project. A project in RStudio helps to keep all of the different pieces and parts of an activity together, including the data sets and variables that you establish as well as the functions that you write. For professional uses of R and RStudio, it is important to have one project for each major activity: This keeps different data sets and variable names from interfering with each other. So let's practice creating and using projects! Click on the Project menu in RStudio and then click on New Project. You will usually have a choice of three kinds of new projects: a brand-new, or clean, project; an existing directory of files that will get turned into a project folder; or a project that comes out of a version control system. Choose New Directory to start a brand-new project. You can call your project whatever you want, but because this project uses the word cloud package, you might want to just call the project wcloud. You also have a choice in the dialog box about where on your computer RStudio will create the new directory.

RStudio will respond by showing a clean console screen and, most important, an R workspace that does not contain any of the old variables and data that we created in previous chapters.

Now we can get started with our new project. The first task we need to do is to be able to read in a text file. As you are starting to see, there are several different ways to read data into R. Until now, we have used read.csv and read.xls (e.g., to read the census data set). These functions are useful for reading in structured data. Other functions, such as read.table and read.delim, are also useful for reading in structured data. But if we want to read in unstructured (text-based) data, scan and readLines are more appropriate. Since there are so many ways to read in data into R, let's review the different alternatives of reading data into R.

For reading in structured data, we can use read.table, read.delim, read.csv, or read.xls. These functions all allow us to read data into R and create dataframes. Note that these functions allow that the different columns can be different types, known in R as the mode of the column (such as a number, a factor or a string). Remember that all the rows in the column must be the same mode. How are these functions different? Well, read .table is the most basic of these functions, and the others are somewhat more specialized. For example, read.csv is basically a read.table command that defines that the separator is a comma, and assumes that the first line of the file is the header (i.e., that it contains the variable names for the dataframe). The function read.delim is similar to read.csv, but uses a tab as a separator (sep='\t'), as compared to read.csv's comma. The first, and only required, argument to these functions is a filename or URL. Some other potentially useful arguments include the following:

stringsAsFactors: Setting this argument to FALSE prevents R from converting character data into factors.

na.string: This argument is useful if missing values in your file are represented by something other than NA or NaN, or if you want to make sure that strings like NA or NaN are *not* treated as missing values

skip: This argument allows you to specify the number of lines in your file that should be ignored before reading the data.

Not surprisingly, read.xls is a specialized function that reads a file that is in the Microsoft Excel file format. The read.xls function has slightly different parameters, but the basics are the same in that the function will create a dataframe by reading the specified file.

Scan is a function for reading in vectors of data, where all the elements have the same mode, such as all numbers or all characters. Each element (word or number) needs to be separated from the others by one or more blanks or other defined character that acts as a separator (such as a comma). When using scan, the sep= argument can be used to specify a different separator. While we haven't used scan yet, we will use it in the next section on sentiment analysis. We can also try to use scan to read the speech, and as you can see below, the syntax is easy to understand. The character(0) parameter tells scan that, in this case, we are reading characters and not integers. The separator character is \n, since, in this situation, we want to read a line of characters at a time. Note that the sba.txt file was downloaded from the web and is a simple text file stored locally on the computer.

```
> sbaFile <- "sba.txt"
> sba <- scan(sbaFile, character(0),sep = "\n")
Read 8 items
> head(sba, 3)
> words[1]
[1] "Friends and fellow citizens: I stand before
you tonight under indictment for the alleged crime
of having voted at the last presidential election,
without having a lawful right to vote. It shall be
```

```
my work this evening to prove to you that in thus
voting, I not only committed no crime, but, instead,
simply exercised my citizen's rights, guaranteed to
me and all United States citizens by the National
Constitution, beyond the power of any state to deny."
> words[2]
[1] "The preamble of the Federal Constitution says:"
> words[3]
[1] "\"We, the people of the United States, in order
to form a more perfect union, establish justice,
insure domestic tranquillity, provide for the common
defense, promote the general welfare, and secure the
blessings of liberty to ourselves and our posterity,
do ordain and establish this Constitution for the
United States of America.\""
```

We also could have used the default separator (a space), which would have also worked. In this situation, our vector (sba) would have had many more elements (in fact 487 elements), and each element would have had just one word.

The third way to read a file is by using readLines. The readLines function provides a simple but flexible approach to obtaining text data from a source. One of the interesting aspects of readLine is the control parameter con (which means connection). The con parameter defaults to con=stdin()" where stdin() is the command line input to R. So readLines can be used to grab one or more lines of text typed by the R user. More commonly, we supply the readLines function with a filename as its first argument, and it returns a vector with as many elements as there are lines of text in that file. Unlike scan or read.table, readLines grabs each line and stores it as a character string in a vector of character strings. In the following code, the function readLines creates a character vector with as many elements as lines of text, with a line being defined as any string of text that ends with a newline character (\n). As you can see, the output is somewhat cleaner than the results from using the scan function, but both would work in this situation.

```
> sbaFile <- "sba.txt"
> sba <- readLines(sbaFile)
> head(sba, 3)
```

```
[1] "Friends and fellow citizens: I stand before you
tonight under indictment for the alleged crime of
having voted at the last presidential election,
without having a lawful right to vote. It shall be my
work this evening to prove to you that in thus
voting,
I not only committed no crime, but, instead, simply
exercised my citizen's rights, guaranteed to me and
all United States citizens by the National
Constitution, beyond the power of any state to deny."
[2] ""
[3] "The preamble of the Federal Constitution says:"
```

Finally, as shown next, we can read a web page directly. This means that we have to parse the HTML and convert that HTML into simple text. To do this, we can use the htmlTreeParse function to read a web page (page of HTML). We then parse the HTML document to look for paragraphs. HTML denotes paragraphs by using <p>, so we look for the p HTML tag, starting at the root of the document. Finally, we unlist the results to create a vector of character strings.

```
> sbaLocation <- URLencode(
+ "http://www.historyplace.com/speeches/anthony.htm")
> doc.html <- htmlTreeParse(sbaLocation,
+     useInternal = TRUE)
> sba <- unlist(xpathApply(doc.html, '//p', xmlValue))
> head(sba, 3)
[1] ""
[2] ""
[3] "Friends and fellow citizens: I stand before you
tonight under indictment\n     for the alleged crime
of having voted at the last presidential election,\n
without having a lawful\n     right to vote. It shall
be my work this evening to prove to you that in\n
thus voting, I not only committed no crime, but,
```

```
instead, simply exercised\n        my citizen's rights,
guaranteed to me and all United States citizens by\n
the National Constitution, beyond the power of any
state to deny."
```

Once we read in the speech (above, we stored the results into the variable sba, for Susan B. Anthony), we can see it is just a vector. However, each element in the vector can contain lots of words, since, as we can see in the output for sba, a given vector might contain several sentences.

USING THE TEXT MINING PACKAGE

Now that we have the text of the speech, we need to be able to process it to get it ready for the word cloud procedure. We can use the tm package to process our texts. The tm in this case refers to text mining and is a popular choice among the many text analysis packages available in R. By the way, text mining refers to the practice of extracting useful analytic information from corpora of text (the word *corpora* is the plural of *corpus*). Although some people use the terms "text mining" and "natural language processing" interchangeably, there are some couple subtle differences worth considering. First, the mining part of text mining refers to an area of practice that looks for patterns in large data sets, or what some people refer to as knowledge discovery in databases. In contrast, natural language processing reflects a more general interest in understanding how machines can be programmed (or can learn on their own) how to digest and make sense of human language. In a similar vein, text mining often focuses on statistical approaches to analyzing text data, using strategies such as counting word frequencies in a corpus. In natural language processing, one is more likely to hear consideration given to linguistics, and therefore to the processes of breaking text into its component grammatical components such as nouns and verbs. In the case of the tm add-on package for R, we are definitely in the statistical camp, where the main process is to break down a corpus into sequences of words and then to tally up the different words and sequences we have found.

To begin, make sure that the tm package is installed and libraried in your copy of R and RStudio. Once the tm package is ready to use, you should be able to run these commands:

```
> words.vec <- VectorSource(sba)
> words.corpus <- Corpus(words.vec)
```

```
> words.corpus
<<VCorpus>>
Metadata: corpus specific: 0, document level
(indexed): 0
Content:  documents: 15
> words.corpus <- tm _ map(words.corpus,
+     content _ transformer(tolower))
> words.corpus <- tm _ map(words.corpus,
+     removePunctuation)
> words.corpus <- tm _ map(words.corpus, removeNumbers)
> words.corpus <- tm _ map(words.corpus, removeWords,
+     stopwords("english"))
```

In the first step, we coerce our text file vector (sba) into a custom Class provided by the tm package and called a corpus, storing the result in a new data object called words.corpus. This is the first time we have directly encountered a class. The term *class* comes from an area of computer science called "object-oriented programming." Although R is different in many ways from object-oriented languages such as Java, it does contain many of the basic features that define an object-oriented language. For our purposes here, there are just a few things to know about a class. First, a class is nothing more or less than a definition for the structure of a data object. Second, classes use basic data types, such as numbers, to build up more-complex data structures. For example, if we made up a new Dashboard class, it could contain one number for Miles Per Hour, another number for RPM, and perhaps a third one indicating the remaining Fuel Level. That brings up another point about classes: Users of R can build their own. In this case, the author of the tm package, Ingo Feinerer, created a new class, called corpus, as the central data structure for text mining functions. (Feinerer is a computer science professor who works at the Vienna University of Technology in the Database and Artificial Intelligence Group.) Last, and most important for this discussion, a class not only contains definitions about the structure of data, but it also contains references to functions that can work on that class. In other words, a class is a data object that carries with it instructions on how to do operations on it, from simple things like add and subtract all the way up to complicated operations such as graphing.

In the case of the tm package, the corpus class defines the most fundamental object that text miners care about: a corpus containing a collection of documents. Once we have our texts stored in a corpus, the many functions that the tm package provides to us are available to use in processing and analyzing our textual data. The last four commands in the group above show the use of the tm_map() function, which is one of the powerful capabilities provided by tm. In each case where we call the tm_map() function, we are providing words.corpus as the input data, and then we are providing a command that undertakes a transformation on the corpus. We have done four transformations here, first making all of the letters lowercase, then removing the punctuation, then removing numbers, and finally taking out the so-called stop words.

The stop words deserve a little explanation. Researchers who developed the early search engines for electronic databases found that certain words interfered with how well their search algorithms worked. Words such as *the*, *a*, and *at* appeared so commonly in so many different parts of the text that they were useless for differentiating between documents. The unique and unusual nouns, verbs, and adjectives that appeared in a document did a much better job of setting a document apart from other documents in a corpus, such that researchers decided that they should filter out all of the short, commonly used words. The term *stop words* seems to have originated in the 1960s to signify words that a computer processing system would throw out or stop using because they had little meaning in a data processing task. To simplify the removal of stop words, the tm package contains lists of such words for different languages. In the last command on the previous page we requested the removal of all of the common stop words.

At this point we have processed our corpus into a nice uniform bag of words that contains no capital letters, punctuation, or stop words. We are now ready to conduct a kind of statistical analysis of the corpus by creating what is known as a term-document matrix. The following command from the tm package creates the matrix:

```
> tdm <- TermDocumentMatrix(words.corpus)
> tdm
<<TermDocumentMatrix (terms: 189, documents: 15)>>
Non-/sparse entries : 225/2610
Sparsity            : 92%
Maximal term length: 20
Weighting           : term frequency (tf)
```

A term-document matrix, also sometimes called a document-term matrix, is a rectangular data structure with terms as the rows and documents as the columns (in other uses you might also make the terms as columns and documents as rows). A term can be a single word, for example, "biology," or it could also be a compound word, such as "data analysis." The process of determining whether words go together in a compound word can be accomplished statistically by seeing which words commonly go together, or it can be done with a dictionary. The tm package supports the dictionary approach, but we have not used a dictionary in this example. So if a term like *data* appears once in the first document, twice in the second document, and not at all in the third document, then the column for the term *data* will contain 1, 2, 0.

The statistics reported when we ask for tdm on the command line give us an overview of the results. The TermDocumentMatrix() function extracted 189 terms. The resulting matrix mainly consists of zeros: Out of 2,610 cells in the matrix, only 225 contain non-zero entries, while the rest contain zeros. A zero in a cell means that that particular term did not appear in that particular document. Finally, the last line, starting with Weighting, indicates what kind of statistic was stored in the term-document matrix. In this case we used the default, and simplest, option that simply records the count of the number of times a term appears across all of the documents in the corpus. You can peek at what the term-document matrix contains by using the following inspect function:

inspect(tdm)

Be prepared for a large amount of output. Remember the term "sparse" in the summary of the matrix? Sparse refers to the overwhelming number of cells that contain zero—indicating that the particular term does not appear in a given document. Most term document matrices are quite sparse. This one is 92% sparse. In most cases, we will need to cull or filter the term-document matrix for purposes of presenting or visualizing it. The tm package provides several methods for filtering out sparsely used terms, but in this example we are going to leave the heavy lifting to the word cloud package.

CREATING WORD CLOUDS

As a first step we need to install and library() the wordcloud package. The wordcloud package was written by freelance statistician Ian Fellows, who also developed the Deducer user interface for R. Deducer provides a graphical interface that allows users who are more familiar with SPSS or SAS menu systems to be able to use R without resorting to the command line.

Once the wordcloud package is loaded, we need to do a little preparation to get our data ready to submit to the word cloud generator function. That function expects two vectors as input arguments: The first is a list of the terms, and the second is a list of the frequencies of occurrence of the terms. The list of terms and frequencies must be sorted with the most frequent terms appearing first. To accomplish this, we first have to coerce our text data back into a plain data matrix so that we can sort it by frequency. The first command below accomplishes this:

```
> m <- as.matrix(tdm)
> wordCounts <- rowSums(m)
> wordCounts <- sort(wordCounts, decreasing=TRUE)
> head(wordCounts)
women   citizens   oligarchy   people   states   blessings
   7          6           5        5        5           4

> cloudFrame<-data.frame(
+      word=names(wordCounts),freq=wordCounts)
> wordcloud(cloudFrame$word,cloudFrame$freq)
```

In the next two commands above, we first are calculating the sums across each row, which gives us the total frequency of a term across all of the different sentences/documents. We then are sorting the resulting values with the highest frequencies first. The result is a named list: Each item of the list has a frequency and the name of each item is the term to which that frequency applies. Finally, we can see the top words, in terms of frequency. For example, the word *women* was used seven times in Anthony's speech.

Now we are ready to create a word cloud. The wordcloud() function has lots of optional parameters for making the word cloud more colorful, controlling its shape, and controlling how frequent an item must be before it appears in the cloud, but we have used the default settings for all of these parameters for the sake of simplicity. We pass to the wordcloud() function the term list and frequency list that we just created and wordcloud() produces the nice graphic that you see in Figure 14.1.

Now, let's use some of the optional parameters to make a more visually appealing visualization. We can specify the minimum word frequency of 2, a maximum number of 50, the percentage of words rotates to be 35%. The brewer.pal() code below will make a nice range of colors, but in Figure 14.2 they show as shades of gray.

```
> wordcloud(names(wordCounts), wordCounts, min.freq=2,
+      max.words=50, rot.per=0.35, colors=brewer.pal(8,
+      "Dark2"))
```

To recap, in this chapter we explored the possible use of word clouds and learned how to create word clouds in R. In the next chapter we will move on to sentiment analysis, which is another text mining technique.

FIGURE 14.1

FIGURE 14.2

Chapter Challenge(s)

Create a word cloud for a recent document you created (a longer e-mail or a Word document). Save the file as a text file (a.txt file, if you are using Word) and then create a word cloud. Does the word cloud convey the key points of the document?

Sources

http://cran.r-project.org/web/packages/wordcloud/wordcloud.pdf

http://en.wikipedia.org/wiki/Document-term_matrix

http://en.wikipedia.org/wiki/Stop_words

http://en.wikipedia.org/wiki/Text_mining

http://stat.ethz.ch/R-manual/R-devel/library/base/html/colSums.html

http://www.jasondavies.com/wordcloud/

R Functions Used in This Chapter

readLines()	Reads all the lines of text in a file.
scan()	Reads a file.
htmlTreeParse()	Reads a web (HTML) web page.
xpathApply()	Parses an HTML file.
VectorSource()	Treats each element of the input vector as a document.
Corpus()	Creates a corpus of words (or bag of words).
tm_map()	Performs an operation on the bag of words (corpus).
TermDocumentMatrix()	Creates a tdm, given a corpus.
sumRows()	Sums the rows within a matrix.
wordcloud()	Creates a word cloud visualization.

© iStockphoto.com/tigermad

HAPPY WORDS?

Although word clouds are a good first step, another useful analysis technique for textual data is known as sentiment analysis. For example, how positive or negative are reviews (or tweets) about a product. Sentiment analysis sounds really complicated, and in fact, there are many ways to do sentiment analysis, but we will use a basic strategy. Our process will start with a "dictionary" of positive and negative words (that others have created) and then just count how many positive words there are in our text and how many negative words there are in our text. Given this, we can compute a positive score and a negative score for any text.

SENTIMENT ANALYSIS

Let's continue to use the same text as we used in the previous chapter (Susan B. Anthony's speech). Was it a positive speech? Let's find out. First, let's load the positive and negative files and clean them up to get ready to use. To find a positive and a negative word list, we can use a nice website on sentiment analysis: https://www.cs.uic.edu/~liub/FBS/sentiment-analysis.html

About halfway down the web page, you can see a section titled "Opinion Lexicon (or Sentiment Lexicon)." The first bullet in this section contains a link to a list of positive and negative opinion words or sentiment words for English. When you click on this link it downloads a compressed file that contains a folder that has both positive and negative words. Specifically, there will be one text file is for the positive words and one text file is for the negative words. Once you download those files, save them to a place where R can easily access them. Now let's get to the R coding:

```
> #define the name of the word files
> pos <- "positive-words.txt"
> neg <- "negative-words.txt"

> #read the files
> #separate each word
> p <- scan(pos, character(0),sep = "\n")
Read 2040 items
> n <- scan(neg, character(0),sep = "\n")
Read 4817 items
```

OK. Let's review what we just did. First, we read the text files. Note this code assumes the text files are in R's default directory. If you didn't know, you can get and set R's working directory with the getwd and setwd functions. The positive file had 2,040 words, and the negative file had 4,817 words, but some of this might have been headers. This seems to suggest that there are more ways to say something in a negative way than in a positive way. That's kind of interesting in itself, but let's press on and take a look at the start of the positive file:

```
> head(p, 10)
 [1] ";;;;;;;;;;;;;;;;;;;;;;;;;;;;;;;;;;;;;;;;;;;;;;;;;;;;;
;;;;;;;;;;;;;;;;;;;;;;;;;;;"
 [2] "; "
 [3] "; Opinion Lexicon: Positive"
 [4] ";"
 [5] "; This file contains a list of POSITIVE opinion
words (or sentiment words)."
 [6] ";"
 [7] "; This file and the papers can all be downloaded
from "
 [8] "; http://www.cs.uic.edu/~liub/FBS/sentiment-
analysis.html"
 [9] ";"
[10] "; If you use this list, please cite one of the
following two papers:"
```

Yup, as one might guess, we can see that there is useful (for humans, not our code) header information, so we need to remove those elements.

```
> p <- p[-1:-34]
> n <- n[-1:-34]

> head(p, 10)
[1] "a+" "abound" "abounds" "abundance" "abundant"
"accessable"
[7] "accessible" "acclaim" "acclaimed" "acclamation"

> head(n,10)
[1] "2-faced" "2-faces" "abnormal" "abolish"
```

```
"abominable" "abominably"
[7] "abominate" "abomination" "abort" "aborted"
```

That looks like the start of a good list of positive and negative words! Since we already have the word file we want to examine (from the previous chapter, the word-Counts variable), the next step is to count the total number of words in our text (stored in wordCounts).

```
#calculate the total number of words
> totalWords <- sum(wordCounts)

#have a vector that just has all the words
> words <- names(wordCounts)
```

Next, we somehow need to figure out how to count the number of positive and negative words in wordCounts. To do this, we need to use the match function, which returns a vector of the positions of (first) matches of its first argument in its second. When there is no match, we can specify to return a specific number (such as zero [0]).

```
> matched <- match(words, p, nomatch = 0)
> head(matched,10)
[1] 0      0      0      0      0      0      0      0      1083   0
```

We can see that the first eight words did not match, but the ninth word did match. This is confirmed with the code below, where we can see that the ninth word in "words" should be the same as the 1,083rd word in "p"—and indeed, they are both the word *liberty*.

```
> matched[9]
[1] 1083

> p[1083]
[1] "liberty"

> words[9]
[1] "liberty"
```

Now that we have the list of matched positive words, we just have to get the counts of all the words that did match.

```
> mCounts <- wordCounts[which(matched != 0)]
> length(mCounts)
[1] 12

> mWords <- names(mCounts)
> nPos <- sum(mCounts)
> nPos
[1] 17
```

So, we can see that there were 17 positive words (note that some of the words were repeated, and in fact, there were 12 unique positive words used in the speech—which is why there was only 12 items in mCounts). Now let's do the same for the negative words.

```
> matched <- match(words, n, nomatch = 0)
> nCounts <- wordCounts[which(matched != 0)]
> nNeg <- sum(nCounts)
> nWords <- names(nCounts)
> nNeg
[1] 13
> length(nCounts)
[1] 11
```

We can see that there were 13 negative words (and 11 unique negative words that were used). Great! After all this work, we have all the information we need to calculate the percentage of positive and negative words for this speech, which you can see in the following lines of R code:

```
#calculate the percentage of words that are positive
or negative
> totalWords <- length(words)
> ratioPos <- nPos/totalWords
> ratioPos
```

```
[1] 0.08994709
> ratioNeg <- nNeg/totalWords
> ratioNeg
[1] 0.06878307
```

Given this, we can see that Susan B. Anthony's speech was made up of about 9% positive and a little less than 7% negative words. What do you conclude about the nature of her speech?

OTHER USES OF TEXT MINING

While we have focused on using text mining for sentiment analysis, there are many other uses for text mining. While space does not allow use to discuss all the different possible uses of text mining, let's explore three different scenarios where text mining might be useful.

A very common example is to do text mining on tweets. When someone mines tweets, she can explore the frequency of a certain hashtag or how a specific tweet or hashtag can go viral (which is related to the phrase "trending on Twitter"). In addition, a company can use text mining to review tweets to get an understanding of how consumers view their product.

In a different example, text mining can also be used in call centers. For example, for an inbound call center (where people call into a call center with questions or to order a product), it is helpful to know what people are talking about on the phone. Using speech-to-text, an organization can generate text documents, which can then be analyzed using text mining to create a list of key words per call. The organization might show this list to the call center representative (so that person can select the most relevant keywords) or the organization might focus on the frequency of the key words used. Armed with these data for each call, the organization can then do analysis of what customers talk about during the call, and determine if these key words change over time. For example, a top 10 complaint list can be generated and the managers can see how this list changes over time. In a related use of text mining, notes about repairs (e.g., by a heating manufacturer) could be analyzed to determine if specific keywords (representing specific components in the system) are causing issues at a higher-than-expected rate.

In one last example, we can use text mining to do an analysis for a specific industry by text mining news feeds to extract the names of people, areas of focus, and companies that occur in the news—for example, those focusing on data science. The goal would be to try to infer who the key people are in that field or how different areas of focus change over time; for instance, maybe next year people will talk more about text mining, as compared to other data science techniques.

To recap, in this chapter we explored sentiment analysis, a text mining technique that attempts to determine how positive or negative an unstructured text document is. We also reviewed some other possible scenarios where text mining could be used, such as analyzing customer comments (via Twitter or other communication channels). In the next chapter, we will move on to more-advanced analytical models, focusing on more-structured data sets.

Chapter Challenge(s)

Generate positive and negative sentiment analysis across a range of speeches to see if there are patterns to when speeches (or parts of speeches) are positive or negative.

Sources

https://www.cs.uic.edu/~liub/FBS/sentiment-analysis.html

R Functions Used in This Chapter

scan()	Reads a data file.
sum()	Totals the numbers in the vector.
names()	Gets the names for each element in a vector (if there are names).
match()	Returns the positions of first matches of its first argument in its second.

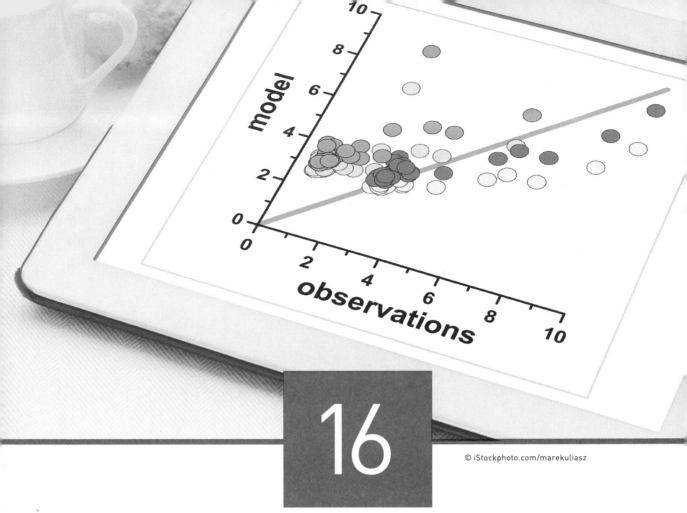

16

LINING UP
OUR MODELS

LEARNING OBJECTIVES

- Explain data science modeling techniques.
- Use models to interpret and understand the data.
- Utilize the lm package to create and interpret a linear regression model.

Finding relationships between sets of data is one of the key aims of data science. The question, "Does x influence y?" is of prime concern for data analysts: Are house prices influenced by incomes? Is the growth rate of crops improved by fertilizer? Do taller sprinters run faster? We can start the process of answering these kinds of questions by building models—in particular, linear prediction models, or what statisticians often call regression models.

WHAT IS A MODEL?

In order to build a model, we first need to understand what a model is. People use the word *model* in many ways. Some have nothing to do with data, such as using the term to connote a person who might appear in a magazine wearing a certain sweater, shirt, or watch. Another use of the word describes a small representation of an object (such as a model railroad). Even when we start talking about data, there are multiple uses of the word *model*. For example, in Chapter 4 we discussed data modeling. If you remember, data modeling (or data models) help data scientist follow and understand data that have been stored in a repository (such as a database). One example of a data model that was mentioned was an entity-relationship diagram, which describes the structure and movement of data in a system.

In this chapter, we do not want to discuss people that model clothes, miniature trains, or data models. We want to discuss prediction models that are created from a statistical analysis process (in our case, from procedures offered by R). These models analyze data that the user supplies (such as a dataframe of observations) and then calculate a set of numerical coefficients that help us with prediction.

LINEAR MODELING

A work-horse method used by statisticians to interpret data is linear modeling, also known as linear regression, which is a term covering a wide variety of methods, from the relatively simple to the very sophisticated. However, all these methods create a model that can be used for prediction. You can get an idea of how many different methods there are by looking at the regression analysis page in Wikipedia and checking out the number of models listed on the right-hand sidebar (and, by the way, the list is not exhaustive).

The original ideas behind linear regression were developed by some of the usual suspects behind many of the ideas we've seen already, such as Gauss, Galton, and Pearson. The biggest individual contribution was probably by Gauss, who used the procedure to predict movements of the other planets in the solar system when they were hidden from view and, hence, to correctly predict when and where they would appear again.

The basis of all these methods is the idea that for many kinds of data it is possible to fit a line to a set of data points that represents the connection between an independent variable and a dependent variable. It is easy to visualize how this works with one variable changing in step with another variable. Figure 16.1 shows a line fitted to a series of points, using the so-called least squares method (a relatively simple mathematical method of finding a best-fitting line). The chart shows how the relationship between an input (independent) variable—on the horizontal X-axis—relates to the output (dependent) values on the Y-axis. In other words, the output variable is dependent (is a function of) the independent variable.

FIGURE 16.1

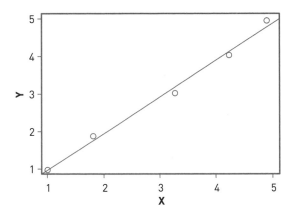

Note that although the line fits the points fairly well, with an even split (as even as it can be for five points!) of points on either side of the line, none of the points is precisely on the line—the data do not fit the line precisely. As we discuss the concepts in regression analysis further, we will see that understanding these discrepancies is just as important as understanding the line itself. The other important thing to note is that just because we have called the X-axis variable "independent" and the Y-axis variable "dependent" does not mean that X causes Y. Statisticians have an old saying that is very important to remember: "Correlation does not mean causation."

The mathematical idea that allows us to create lines of best fit for a set of data points like this is that we can find a line that will minimize the distance the line is from all the points. Once the model calculates the line that minimizes the distance for all the points, the model can represent the line with an equation you might remember from algebra:

$$Y = MX + B.$$

Do not worry if you have never taken an algebra course: All you need to understand is that the equation has two coefficients (numbers with specific values for each model) that describe the line (M and B). M describes the slope of the line and B describes the height of the line (more precisely, where the line crosses the Y-axis, also known as the Y-intercept). With M and B known, the equation can be used to predict Y values (for any given X value).

So, given a list of points, an algorithm (available in R) will generate what it thinks is the best-fitted line for the data points. In other words, the R can calculate the appropriate M and B. It is this computer code that generates our model (i.e., the values of M and B). If you know M and B, you can use any new X value, together with the equation for the line (Y = MX + B), to calculate a predicted Y value.

The details of how R calculates the values of M and B are not particularly difficult, but they are beyond the scope of this chapter. If you are curious to learn more, trying looking up the term "ordinary least squares." The ordinary least squares fitting method is one of the simplest and most commonly used strategies for figuring out the best-fitting line. When we use the lm() function in the material that follows, we are using the least squares method to discover the slope and intercept of the best-fitting line.

AN EXAMPLE—CAR MAINTENANCE

Is changing the oil of a car more frequently a good thing? Does it save money in the long run? Let's use linear regression to try and answer this question. In this example, we were just put in charge of maintaining a fleet of company cars. We know that the company replaces the cars every three years, and in fact the company just replaced the cars (i.e., bought a new fleet of cars). The person who was previously in charge of the car maintenance didn't have a schedule for when to change the oil but rather changed the oil whenever the car was available. Luckily, the maintenance records were available, and now we want to try and figure out, in a more data-driven approach, if changing the oil frequently is a good idea. The following R code defines our data set:

```
> oilChanges <- c(3,5,2,3,1,4,6,4,3,2,0,10,7,8)
> repairs <- c(300, 300, 500, 400, 700, 420, 100, 290,
+       475, 620, 600, 0, 200, 50)
> miles <- c(20100, 23200, 19200, 22100, 18400, 23400,
+       17900, 19900, 20100, 24100, 18200, 19600, 20800,
+       19700)
> oil <- data.frame(oilChanges, repairs, miles)
> View(oil)
```

TABLE 16.1			
	oilChanges	repairs	miles
1	3	300	20100
2	5	300	23200
3	2	500	19200
4	3	400	22100
5	1	700	18400
6	4	420	23400
7	6	100	17900
8	4	290	19900
9	3	475	20100
10	2	620	24100
11	0	600	18200
12	10	0	19600
13	7	200	20800
14	8	50	19700

First, let's look at Figure 16.1 at the data that were collected for the cars that were just replaced (i.e., our data set). The data have three columns of information. First, there is the number of oil changes that each car had during the past three years. The next column shows the total amount of repairs (in dollars). Finally, we have the miles driven by each car.

Given these data, let's figure out how the number of oil changes and miles driven are connected to repair costs. Our independent variables are oilChanges and miles. The dependent variable (the one we are trying to predict) is repairs. Before building a model, we can do some exploratory analysis, which data scientists often do prior to building a model. Figure 16.2 shows the plot of points created by the following R command:

```
> plot(oil$oilChanges, oil$repairs)
```

We can see a general trend: The repairs are high when the number of oil changes is low, and the repairs are low when the number of oil changes is high. There seems to be a pattern! Now let's explore miles and repairs:

```
> plot(oil$miles, oil$repairs)
```

FIGURE 16.2

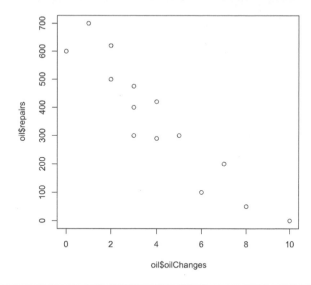

FIGURE 16.3

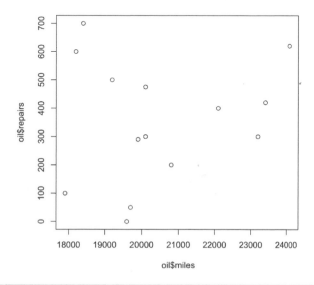

This doesn't look nearly as interesting: There does not appear to be a pattern. So let's build our first model in R with oilChanges as the independent variable. Below is the code for building a linear model:

```
> model1 <- lm(formula=repairs ~ oilChanges, data=oil)
```

The lm() command places its output in a data structure (the model that we just created), and we want to hang on to the model, so we store the results of lm() in the variable called model1. Note that the lm command takes two parameters: the first tells lm to use oilChanges to predict repairs. The squiggly line [~], which is called a tilde character, is part of the syntax that tells lm() which independent and dependent variables to include in the model. In this case you can read "repairs ~ oilChanges" as "use oilChanges to predict repairs." The other parameter tells lm the name of the dataframe we are using. In the next command, we request an overview of the contents of our model.

```
> summary(model1)

Call:
lm(formula = repairs ~ oilChanges, data = oil)

Residuals:
    Min       1Q    Median       3Q      Max
-136.208  -48.195   -0.211   54.782  119.803

Coefficients:
             Estimate Std.  Error t value Pr(>|t|)
(Intercept)   652.191        40.537  16.089 1.74e-09 ***
oilChanges    -71.994         8.202  -8.778 1.44e-06 ***
---
Signif. codes:  0 '***' 0.001 '**' 0.01 '*' 0.05 '.'
0.1 ' ' 1
```

```
Residual standard error: 82.72 on 12 degrees of
freedom
Multiple R-squared:  0.8653, Adjusted R-squared:
0.854
F-statistic: 77.05 on 1 and 12 DF,  p-value: 1.436e-06
```

Wow! That's a lot information that R has provided for us, and we need to use this information to decide whether we are happy with this model. Being happy with the model involves a variety of considerations, and there is no simple way of deciding what is a good model and what is not. To start, we will look at the R-squared value, also known as the coefficient of determination.

The R squared value—the coefficient of determination—represents the proportion of the variation that is accounted for in the dependent variable by the whole set of independent variables (in this case there is just one). An R-squared value of 1.0 would mean that the X variable(s) as a set perfectly predicted the Y (the dependent variable). An R-squared value of zero would indicate that the X variable(s) as a set did not predict the Y variable at all. R-squared cannot be negative. The R-squared of .8653 in this example means that the oilChanges variable accounts for about 87% of the variability in repair costs. Note that there is no absolute rule for what makes an R-squared value good. Much depends on the context and purpose of the analysis. In the analysis of human behavior, which is notoriously unpredictable, an R-squared of .20 or .30 could be considered extremely good. Then again, in predicting something more mechanical like engine repair costs, an R-squared of .60 or .70 might be considered very poor.

There is also a significance test on the value of R-squared. Significance testing is sufficiently complex that there are whole books written about it, but you will need a rule of thumb to make sense out of results like these. Whenever you see output from R that says something like p-value or Pr(>|t|) the corresponding numeric value refers to the probability of observing a result this extreme under the assumption that the "true" situation is that the result is really zero. Imagine if we had an omniscient understanding of all oil changes and repairs everywhere and we knew from having this super power that in fact there is absolutely no connection between oil changes and repairs. Given that reality, it would be extremely unlikely to observe a value of R-squared of .8653 because that value is so far from zero. The p-value quantifies that scenario. The rule of thumb is that when you observe a p-value that is less than 0.05, you can call that statistically significant, and you can take away a sense that your results were probably not due to randomness (specifically, a problem known as "sampling error").

While the R-squared is one of the first things you might examine in the model, let's also explore some of the other outputs. First, at the top of the output we can see the actual function call used to create the model. This is helpful if we are exploring a model, but didn't see the original R code used to create the model. Next, we can see the residuals, which are the difference between the actual observed values and the values that the model predicted (these are the "errors" that ordinary least squares tries to minimize). We see five summary points about residuals. One way to explore how well the model fits the data is to see if the residuals are symmetrically distributed across these five summary points and for the median to be close to zero.

The next section in the model output talks about the coefficients of the model. The coefficients are two unknown constants that represent the intercept and slope terms in the linear model (remember the equation Y=MX+B: the slope is M and the intercept is B). In this example, the coefficient estimate contains two rows; the first row is the intercept. The intercept, in our example, is essentially the expected value of the repairs when there were zero oil changes. The second row in the coefficients is the slope, or, in our example, the effect oil changes have on vehicle repairs. The slope term in our model is saying that for every additional oil change, the expected repairs decrease by about $72.

Both the slope and the Y-intercept have statistical significance tests associated with them. As described earlier, we are generally looking for values of p that are less than 0.05. In the output earlier, both the Y-intercept and the slope coefficient for oilChanges are statistically significant because the *p*-values for each are much smaller than 0.05. Note the signif. codes associated to each estimate. One, two, or three asterisks denote a significant p-value. Because both the R-squared value and the slope coefficient on oil-Changes are significant, we can "reject the null hypothesis" that oil changes and repairs are not connected. So this regression model provides evidence that as the number of oil changes rises, repair costs decline. Don't forget our caution about correlation and causation! These results certainly do not prove that doing more oil changes causes repair costs to go down, although that is one sensible possibility.

Next, Figure 16.4 shows the line of best fit (based on the model to the X-Y plot of repair costs against oil changes with this command:

```
> plot(oil$oilChanges, oil$repairs)
> abline(model1)
```

The model above suggests that we should do as many oil changes as possible. For example, it predicts very low (almost zero [0]) repairs if we do nine or more oil changes, but about $680 if we do no oil changes.

FIGURE 16.4

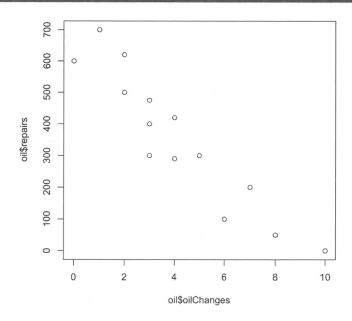

Next, let's try using both oilChanges and miles to calculate the linear model. This is sometimes known as multiple linear regression. Perhaps both variables could do a better job predicting repair costs (as opposed to just using oilChanges). We can test if using both oilChanges and miles improves the model with the following R code:

```
> m <- lm(formula=repairs ~ oilChanges + miles,
+          data=oil)
> summary(m)

Call:
lm(formula = repairs ~ oilChanges + miles, data = oil)

Residuals:
    Min       1Q    Median       3Q       Max
-130.488   -53.810   -1.712    46.301   151.182
```

```
Coefficients:
             Estimate Std. Error t value  Pr(>|t|)
(Intercept) 343.26567  231.42285   1.483     0.166
oilChanges  -71.98591    7.93052  -9.077  1.93e-06 ***
miles         0.01508    0.01114   1.354     0.203
---
Signif. codes:  0 `***' 0.001 `**' 0.01 `*' 0.05 `.'
0.1 ` ' 1

Residual standard error: 79.98 on 11 degrees of
freedom
Multiple R-squared:  0.8845, Adjusted R-squared:
0.8635
F-statistic: 42.12 on 2 and 11 DF,  p-value: 6.982e-06
```

Note that oilChanges is statistically significant but miles is not. You can see this because the p-value for miles, under the column labeled Pr(>|t|), is 0.203, considerably larger than our cutoff point of p less than 0.05. This result is not surprising, since our initial plot of data suggested that miles did not seem to connect with repair costs. So, in this case, we stick with our original model where we predict repair costs as a function of the number of oil changes.

Although we are done with the statistical piece of this analysis, there is one additional practical matter that we can explore. So far, we did not consider the cost of an oil change into our analysis. Let's pretend that oil changes are very expensive because when the car is not in service, the person that should be driving the car is not able to be productive. Let's say that after taking into account this lost productivity, the real cost of stopping to do an oil change is $350 per oil change. The following code creates additional columns in our data set to compute and show the total cost for each car (which is the cost of the repairs plus the cost of doing the oil changes). The code then creates a new linear model using the number of oilChanges to predict totalCost and plots the results (see Figure 16.5).

```
> oil$oilChangeCost <- oil$oilChanges * 350
> oil$totalCost <- oil$oilChangeCost + oil$repairs
> m <- lm(formula=totalCost ~ oilChanges, data=oil)
> plot(oil$oilChanges, oil$totalCost)
> abline(m)
```

FIGURE 16.5

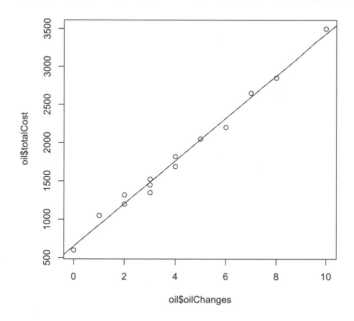

Wow—now the analysis shows that we shouldn't do any oil changes! To use this model for prediction, we can have R calculate the total repair costs for a given number of oil changes with the following R code:

```
> test = data.frame(oilChanges=0)
> predict(m,test, type="response")
652.191

> test = data.frame(oilChanges=5)
> predict(m,test, type="response")
2042.219

> test = data.frame(oilChanges=10)
> predict(m,test, type="response")
3432.247
```

We can see that as the number of oil changes increases, so does the predicted total cost of maintenance. Beware that because totalCost (the dependent variable) was calculated as a function of oilChanges (the independent variable), the R-squared value and its associated significance test is artificially inflated and should be ignored. Generally speaking, you should never include an independent variable in a regression analysis if it has a formulaic connection to the dependent variable. In this case, we just did that in order to get R to produce some calculated values for us that included the oil change cost.

Finally, we can see the same result using ggplot2 (see Figure 16.6):

```
> ggplot(oil, aes(x = oilChanges, y = totalCost)) +
+       geom _ point() +
+       stat _ smooth(method = "lm", col = "red")
```

FIGURE 16.6

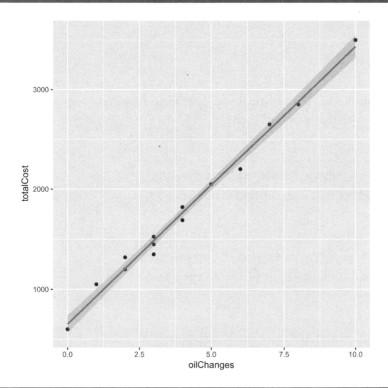

One additional note—in this scenario as well as other common research scenarios we might not have access to all the important information that needs to be modeled. For example, perhaps there was additional maintenance done on the car beyond oil changes? What if some drivers put more wear and tear on the cars than others? What if some cars operated in a dusty environment but others did not? These questions show the variety of possible influences that occur in real life versus the variables that we have actually measured to create the model. Very often we can develop a model, but we are not sure if the model covers all the data that could possibly impact the results of our analysis. That's another good reason to remember that correlation does not equal causation!

In this chapter, we explored how to model data using a linear model, also known as a regression model. Linear modeling works with two or more variables to ascertain the linear relationship that might exist between the independent variables (one or more X variables) and a dependent variable. This type of modeling can be applied when the data you have contain numeric measurements of some phenomenon. In the next chapter, we will explore a very different modeling technique known as association rules mining that works to discover patterns in lists of items.

Chapter Challenge

You might find it interesting to explore a write-up of some actual work done on predictive car maintenance. While, not surprisingly, the following blog post includes many techniques beyond linear modeling, it also demonstrates the challenge of collecting useful and actionable data. https://blog.pivotal.io/data-science-pivotal/products/the-data-science-behind-predictive-maintenance-for-connected-cars

As a chapter challenge in using lm, try to create a linear model of the supplied data set airquality. Which variable do you think is the dependent variable? What is the best model you can create? How good is that model?

Sources

http://stat.ethz.ch/R-manual/R-patched/library/stats/html/lm.html

http://www.ddiez.com/teac/r/linear_models.php

R Functions Used in This Chapter

abline()	Plots a best-fitting line on top of a scatter plot.
lm()	Stands for linear models and, for this chapter, multiple regression.
predict()	Uses a model to predict a variable (output).
plot()	Is a general purpose graphing function that has many uses in R.
ggplot()	Uses geom_point and stat_smooth.
View()	Shows a dataframe in an easy-to-read format.

© iStockphoto.com/Alashi

17

HI HO, HI HO—DATA MINING WE GO

LEARNING OBJECTIVES

- Understand and apply the four data mining processes (data preparation, exploratory data analysis, model development, interpretation of results).

- Understand and be able to use the association rules mining algorithm.

- Develop data mining R code using the arules package.

One famous example of data mining that gets mentioned quite frequently is the supermarket that analyzed patterns of purchasing behavior and found that diapers and beer were often purchased together. The supermarket manager decided to put a beer display close to the diaper aisle and supposedly sold more of both products as a result. Another familiar example comes from online merchant sites that say things like "People who bought that book were also interested in this book." By using an algorithm to look at purchasing patterns, vendors are able to create automatic systems that make these kinds of recommendations.

Over recent decades, statisticians and computer scientists have developed many different algorithms that can search for patterns in different kinds of data. As computers get faster and the researchers do additional work on making these algorithms more efficient, it becomes possible to look through larger and larger data sets looking for promising patterns. Today we have software that can search through massive data haystacks looking for lots of interesting and usable needles.

Some people refer to this area of research as machine learning. Machine learning focuses on creating computer algorithms that can use preexisting inputs to refine and improve their own capabilities for dealing with future inputs. Machine learning is very different from human learning. When we think of human learning, like learning the alphabet or learning a foreign language, we see that humans can develop flexible and adaptable skills and knowledge that are applicable to a range of different contexts and problems. Machine learning is more about figuring out patterns of incoming information that correspond to a specific result. For example, given lots of examples like this—input: 3, 5, 10; output: 150—a machine-learning algorithm could figure out on its own that multiplying the input values together produces the output value.

Machine learning is not exactly the same thing as data mining. Not all data mining techniques rely on what researchers would consider machine learning. Likewise, machine learning is used in areas like robotics that we don't commonly think of when we are thinking of data analysis or data mining.

DATA MINING OVERVIEW

Data mining typically includes four processes: (1) data preparation, (2) exploratory data analysis, (3) model development, and (4) interpretation of results. Although this sounds like a neat, linear set of steps, there is often a lot of back and forth through these processes, and especially among the first three. The other point that is interesting about these four steps is that Steps 3 and 4 seem like the most fun, but Step 1 usually takes the most time. Step 1 involves making sure that the data are organized in the right way, that missing data fields are filled in, that inaccurate data are located and repaired or deleted, and that data are recoded as necessary to make them amenable to the kind of analysis we have in mind.

Step 2 is very similar to activities we have done in earlier chapters of this book: getting to know the data using histograms and other visualization tools and looking for preliminary hints that will guide our model choice. The exploration process also involves figuring out the right values for key parameters. We will see some of that activity in this chapter.

Step 3—choosing and developing a model—is by far the most complex and most interesting of the activities of a data miner. It is here where you test out a selection of the most appropriate data mining techniques. Depending on the structure of a data set, there could be dozens of options, and choosing the most promising one has as much art in it as science. We had some practice performing model development in Chapter 16.

For the current chapter we are going to focus on just one data mining technique, albeit one that is quite powerful and applicable to a range of very practical problems. So we will not really have to do Step 3 because we will not have two or more different mining techniques to compare. The technique we will use in this chapter is called "association rules mining," and it is the strategy that was used to find the diapers and beer association described earlier.

Step 4—the interpretation of results—focuses on making sense out of what the data mining algorithm has produced. This is the most important step from the perspective of the data user, because this is where an actionable conclusion is formed. When we discussed the example of beer and diapers, the interpretation of the association rules that were derived from the grocery purchasing data is what led to the discover of the beer–diapers rule and the use of that rule in reconfiguring the displays in the store.

ASSOCIATION RULES DATA

Let's begin by talking a little about association rules. Have a look at all of the boxes and arrows in Figure 17.1.

From the figure you can see that each supermarket customer has a grocery cart that contains several items from the larger set of items that the grocery store stocks. The association rules algorithm (also sometimes called affinity analysis or market-basket analysis) tries out many different propositions, such as "If diapers are purchased, then beer is also purchased." The algorithm uses a data set of transactions (in the example above, these are the individual carts) to evaluate a long list of these rules for a value called support. Support is the proportion of times that a particular pairing occurs across all shopping carts. The algorithm also evaluates another quantity called confidence, which is how frequently a particular pair occurs among all the times when the first item is present. If you look back at the figure again, we had support of 0.67 (the diapers–beer association

FIGURE 17.1

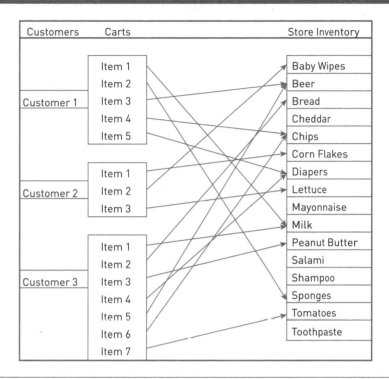

occurred in two out of the three carts) and confidence of 1.0 ("beer" occurred 100% of the time with "diapers"). In practice, both support and confidence are generally much lower than in this example, but even a rule with low support and smallish confidence might reveal purchasing patterns that grocery store managers could use to guide pricing, coupon offers, or advertising strategies.

ASSOCIATION RULES MINING

We can get started with association rules mining very easily using the R package known as arules. In RStudio, you can get the arules package ready using the following commands:

```
> install.packages("arules")
> library(arules)
```

We will begin our exploration of association rules mining using a data set that is built in to the arules package. For the sake of familiarity, we will use the Groceries data set. Note that by using the Groceries data set we have relieved ourselves of the burden of data preparation, because the authors of the arules package have generously made sure that Groceries is ready to be analyzed. So we are skipping right to Step 2 in our four-step process—exploratory data analysis. You can make the Groceries data set ready with this command:

```
> data(Groceries)
```

Next, let's run the summary() function on Groceries so that we can see what is in there:

```
> summary(Groceries)
transactions as itemMatrix in sparse format with
 9835 rows (elements/itemsets/transactions) and
 169 columns (items) and a density of 0.02609146

most frequent items:
      whole milk   other vegetables   rolls/buns
                2513               1903         1809
          soda             yogurt       (Other)
          1715               1372         34055

element (itemset/transaction) length distribution:
sizes
   1     2     3     4     5     6     7     8     9    10    11
      2159  1643  1299  1005   855   645   545   438   350   246   182
  12    13    14    15    16    17    18    19    20    21    22
 117    78    77    55    46    29    14    14     9    11     4
  23    24    26    27    28    29    32
   6     1     1     1     1     3     1

   Min. 1st Qu.  Median    Mean 3rd Qu.    Max.
  1.000   2.000   3.000   4.409   6.000  32.000
```

```
      includes extended item information - examples:
         labels  level2            level1
1   frankfurter sausage meat and sausage
2        sausage sausage meat and sausage
3     liver loaf sausage meat and sausage
```

Right after the summary command line we see that Groceries is an itemMatrix object in sparse format. So what we have is a nice, rectangular data structure with 9,835 rows and 169 columns, where each row is a list of items that might appear in a grocery cart. The word *matrix*, in this case, is just referring to this rectangular data structure. The columns are the individual items. A little later in the output we see that there are 169 columns, which means that there are 169 items. The reason the matrix is called sparse is that very few of these items exist in any given grocery basket. By the way, when an item appears in a basket, its cell contains a one (1), while if an item is not in a basket, its cell contains a zero (0). So in any given row, most of the cells are zero and very few are one, and this is what is meant by sparse. We can see from the Min, Median, Mean, and Max outputs that every cart has at least one item, half the carts have more than three items, the average number of items in a cart is 4.4, and the maximum number of items in a cart is 32.

The output also shows us which items occur in grocery baskets most frequently. If you like working with spreadsheets, you could imagine going to the very bottom of the column that is marked "whole milk" and putting in a formula to sum up all of the ones in that column. You would come up with 2,513, indicating that there are 2,513 grocery baskets that contain whole milk. Remember that every row/basket that has a one in the whole milk column contains whole milk, whereas every row/basket with a zero does not contain whole milk. You might wonder what the data field would look like if a grocery cart contained two gallons of whole milk. For the present data mining exercise, we can ignore that problem by assuming that any non-zero amount of whole milk is represented by a one. Other data mining techniques could take advantage of knowing the exact amount of a product, but association rules does not need to know that amount—just whether the product is present or absent.

Another way of inspecting our sparse matrix is with the itemFrequencyPlot() function. This produces a bar graph that is similar in concept to a histogram: It shows the relative frequency of occurrence of different items in the matrix. When using the itemFrequencyPlot() function, you must specify the minimum level of support needed to include an item in the plot. Remember the mention of support earlier in the chapter—in this case it simply refers to the relative frequency of occurrence of something. We can make a guess as to what level of support to choose based on the results of the summary() function we ran earlier in the chapter. For example, the item "yogurt" appeared in 1,372 out of 9,835 rows, or in about 14% of cases. So we can set the support parameter to somewhere around 10% and 15% in order to get a manageable number of items:

```
> itemFrequencyPlot(Groceries,support=0.1)
```

This command produces the plot in Figure 17.2:

FIGURE 17.2

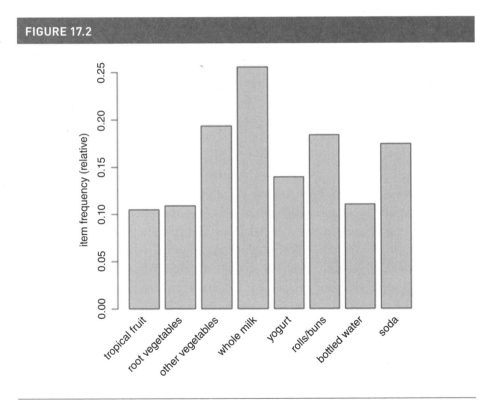

We can see that yogurt is right around 14% as expected, and we also see a few other items not mentioned in the summary such as bottled water and tropical fruit.

You should experiment with using different levels of support, just so that you can get a sense of the other common items in the data set. If you show more than about 10 items, you will find that the labels on the X-axis start to overlap and obscure one another. Use the cex.

names parameter to reduce the font size on the labels. This will keep the labels from overlapping at the expense of making the font size much smaller (see Figure 17.3). Here's an example:

```
> itemFrequencyPlot(Groceries,
+         support=0.05,cex.names=0.5)
```

FIGURE 17.3

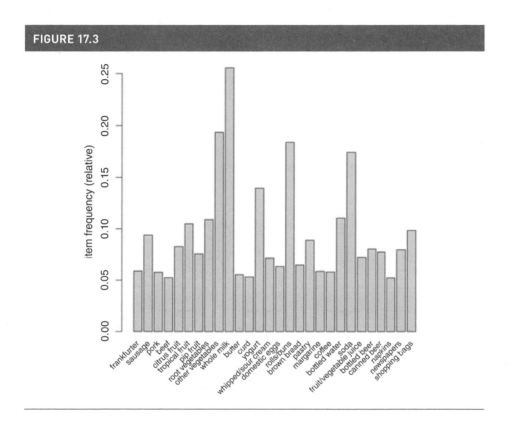

This command yields about 25 items on the X-axis. Without worrying too much about the labels, you can also experiment with lower values of support, just to get a feel for how many items appear at the lower frequencies. We need to guess at a minimum level of support that will give us quite a substantial number of items that can potentially be part of a rule. Nonetheless, it should also be obvious that an item that occurs only very rarely in the grocery baskets is unlikely to be of much use to us in terms of creating meaningful rules. Let's pretend, for example, that the item "Venezuelan Anteater Cheese" occurred only once in the whole set of 9,835 carts. Even if we did end up with a rule about this item, it won't apply very often, and is therefore unlikely to be useful to store managers or others. So we want to focus our attention on items that occur with some meaningful frequency in the data set. Whether this is 1% or 0.005, or something somewhat larger or smaller will depend on the size of the data set and the intended application of the rules.

Before we generate some rules, let's take a step back and explore the type of data object that itemFrequencyPlot (and the other associated functions with arules) needs. You might have noticed that it is *not* a dataframe (you can see this by doing the str command on the Groceries data set). In fact, you can see it is a transactions data set. But what if we have a dataframe: Can we convert it to a transactions data set? Yes, sometimes this is possible, but it depends on the dataframe. Let's look at a different dataframe and convert it to a transactions data set. This time, we will use the AdultUCI data set. If you want to explore what the columns in the data set mean, you can do the help(AdultUCI) command at the R console to get some additional information. In any event, you can see that we first need to convert any numbers or strings into factors. Also note that since some of the column names have a hyphen (-), we need to quote that column name, so R does not get confused and think, for example, that we want to subtract num from AdultUCI$education. After doing all this work, we can finally convert the dataframe into a transactions data set, which we can then use to generate an itemFrequencyPlot (see Figure 17.4).

```
> data(AdultUCI)
> AdultUCI.t <- AdultUCI
> AdultUCI.t$age <- as.factor(AdultUCI.t$age)
> AdultUCI.t$fnlwgt <- as.factor(AdultUCI.t$fnlwgt)
> AdultUCI.t$'education-num' <-
+    as.factor(AdultUCI.t$'education-num')
> AdultUCI.t$'capital-gain' <-
+    as.factor(AdultUCI.t$'capital-gain')
> AdultUCI.t$'capital-loss' <-
+    as.factor(AdultUCI.t$'capital-loss')
> AdultUCI.t$'hours-per-week' <-
+    as.factor(AdultUCI.t$'hours-per-week')
> AdultUCI.trans <- as(AdultUCI.t, "transactions")
> itemFrequencyPlot(AdultUCI.trans,support=0.2,
+    cex.names=1.1)
```

FIGURE 17.4

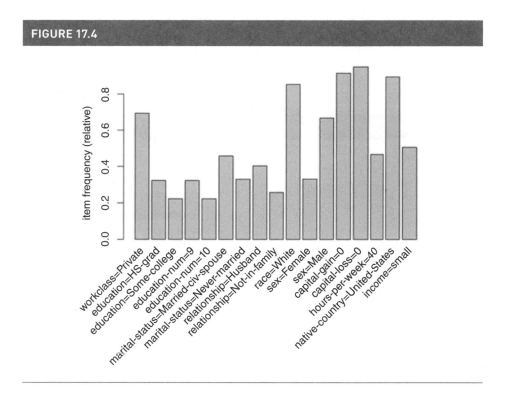

OK, now that we understand a little more about the transactions data set, we are ready to generate some rules with the apriori() command. The term "apriori" refers to the specific algorithm that R will use to scan the data set for appropriate rules. Apriori is a very commonly used algorithm, and it is quite efficient at finding rules in transaction data.

EXPLORING HOW THE ASSOCIATION RULES ALGORITHM WORKS

Apriori uses an iterative approach known as level-wise search. Basically, at the first level, we have one-item sets (i.e., individual items such as bread or milk), which are frequently found (i.e., have sufficient support, as defined in the apriori command). At the next level, the two-item sets we need to consider must have the property that each of their subsets must be frequent enough to include (i.e., they have sufficient support). The algorithm keeps going up levels until there is no more analysis to do. So, for example, as shown in Table 17.5, if we know at Level 2 that the sets {Milk Tea}, {Bread Tea}, {Bread Fish} and {Tea Fish} are the only sets with sufficient support, then at Level 3 we join these with each other to produce {Milk Tea Bread}, {Milk Tea Fish}, {Milk Bread Fish} and {Bread Tea Fish}. But we only need to consider {Bread Tea Fish}, since the others each have subsets with insufficient support—such as {Milk Fish} or {Milk Bread}.

FIGURE 17.5

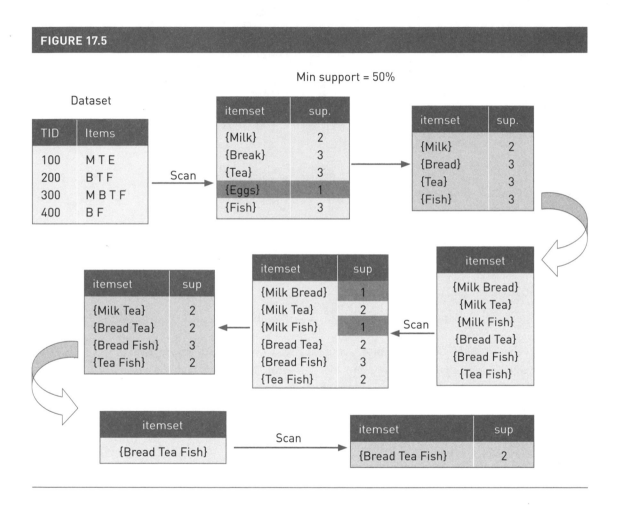

Apriori rules are in the form of "if LHS, then RHS." The abbreviation LHS means "left-hand side," and naturally, RHS means "right-hand side." So each rule states that when the thing or things on the left-hand side of the equation occur(s), the thing on the right-hand side occurs a certain percentage of the time. To reiterate a definition provided earlier in the chapter, support for a rule refers to the frequency of cooccurrence of both members of the pair, that is, LHS and RHS together. The confidence of a rule refers to the proportion of the time that LHS and RHS occur together versus the total number of appearances of LHS. For example, if Milk and Bread occur together in 10% of the grocery carts (i.e., support), and Milk (by itself, ignoring Bread) occurs in 25% of the carts, then the confidence of the Milk/Bread rule is 0.10/0.25 = 0.40.

There are a couple of other measures that can help us zero in on good association rules—such as lift and conviction—but we will put off discussing these until a little later.

One last note before we start using apriori(). For most of the work the data miners do with association rules, the RHS part of the equation contains just one item, like Bread. On the other hand, the LHS part can and will contain multiple items. A simple rule might just have Milk in LHS and Bread in RHS, but a more complex rule might have Milk and Bread together in LHS with Tea in RHS. OK, let's give it a try:

```
> apriori(Groceries,parameter=list(support=0.005,
+         confidence=0.5))
Apriori

parameter specification:
 confidence minval smax   arem  aval originalSupport
        0.5    0.1    1   none FALSE            TRUE
    support minlen maxlen  target     ext
      0.005      1     10   rules   FALSE


Algorithmic control:
 filter tree heap memopt load sort verbose
    0.1 TRUE TRUE  FALSE TRUE    2    TRUE


Absolute minimum support count: 49

set item appearances ...[0 item(s)] done [0.00s].
set transactions ...[169 item(s), 9835 transaction(s)]
done [0.00s].
sorting and recoding items ... [120 item(s)] done
[0.00s].
creating transaction tree ... done [0.01s].
checking subsets of size 1 2 3 4 done [0.01s].
writing ... [120 rule(s)] done [0.00s].
creating S4 object  ... done [0.00s].
set of 120 rules
```

We set up the apriori() command to use a support of 0.005 (half a percent) and confidence of 0.5 (50 percent) as the minimums. These values are confirmed in the first few lines of output. Some other confirmations, such as the value of minval and smax are not relevant to us right now—they have sensible defaults provided by the apriori() implementation. The minlen and maxlen parameters also have sensible defaults: These refer to the minimum and maximum length of item set that will be considered in generating rules. Obviously you can't generate a rule unless you have at least one item in an item set, and setting maxlen to 10 ensures that we will not have any rules that contain more than 10 items. If you recall from earlier in the chapter, the average cart only has 4.4 items, so we are not likely to produce many rules involving more than 10 items.

In fact, a little later in the apriori() output above, we see that the apriori() algorithm only had to examine subsets of size one, two three, and four. Apparently, no rule in this output contains more than four items. At the very end of the output we see that 120 rules were generated. Later on we will examine ways of making sense out of a large number of rules, but for now let's agree that 120 is too many rules to examine. Let's move our support to 0.01 (1 percent) and rerun apriori(). This time we will store the resulting rules in a data structure called ruleset:

```
> ruleset <- apriori(Groceries, parameter =
+         list(support = 0.01,confidence = 0.5))
```

If you examine the output from this command, you should find that we have slimmed down to 15 rules, quite a manageable number to examine one by one. We can get a preliminary look at the rules using the summary function, like this:

```
> summary(ruleset)
set of 15 rules

rule length distribution (lhs + rhs):sizes
 3
15


    Min. 1st Qu.  Median   Mean 3rd Qu.   Max.
       3       3       3      3       3      3
```

```
summary of quality measures:
    support             confidence            lift
 Min.    :0.01007   Min.    :0.5000   Min.    :1.984
 1st Qu. :0.01174   1st Qu. :0.5151   1st Qu. :2.036
 Median  :0.01230   Median  :0.5245   Median  :2.203
 Mean    :0.01316   Mean    :0.5411   Mean    :2.299
 3rd Qu. :0.01403   3rd Qu. :0.5718   3rd Qu. :2.432
 Max.    :0.02227   Max.    :0.5862   Max.    :3.030


mining info:
      data ntransactions support confidence
 Groceries          9835     0.01        0.5
```

Looking through this output, we can see that there are 15 rules in total. The line starting with "rule length distribution" shows that all 15 of the rules have exactly three elements (counting both the LHS and the RHS). Then, under summary of quality measures, we have an overview of the distributions of support, confidence, and a new parameter called lift.

Researchers have done a lot of work trying to come up with ways of measuring how interesting a rule is. A more interesting rule could be a more useful rule because it is more novel or unexpected. Lift is one such measure. Without getting into the math, lift takes into account the support for a rule, but also gives more weight to rules where the LHS and/or the RHS occurs less frequently. In other words, lift favors situations where LHS and RHS are not abundant but where the relatively few occurrences always happen together. The larger the value of lift, the more interesting the rule may be.

Now we are ready to take a closer look at the rules we generated. The inspect() command gives us the detailed contents of the dta object generated by apriori():

```
> inspect(ruleset)
   lhs
   rhs                         support confidence     lift
1  {curd,yogurt}
=> {whole milk}            0.01006609  0.5823529 2.279125
2  {other vegetables,butter}
```

```
=> {whole milk}        0.01148958  0.5736041 2.244885
3  {other vegetables,domestic eggs}
=> {whole milk}        0.01230300  0.5525114 2.162336
4  {yogurt, whipped/sour cream}
=> {whole milk}        0.01087951  0.5245098 2.052747
5  {other vegetables,whipped/sour cream}
=> {whole milk}        0.01464159  0.5070423 1.984385
6  {pip fruit,other vegetables}
=> {whole milk}        0.01352313  0.5175097 2.025351
7  {citrus fruit,root vegetables}
=> {other vegetables} 0.01037112  0.5862069 3.029608
8  {tropical fruit,root vegetables}
=> {other vegetables} 0.01230300  0.5845411 3.020999
9  {tropical fruit, root vegetables}
=> {whole milk}        0.01199797  0.5700483 2.230969
10 {tropical fruit, yogurt}
=> {whole milk}        0.01514997  0.5173611 2.024770
11 {root vegetables, yogurt}
=> {other vegetables} 0.01291307  0.5000000 2.584078
12 {root vegetables, yogurt}
=> {whole milk}        0.01453991  0.5629921 2.203354
13 {root vegetables,rolls/buns}
=> {other vegetables} 0.01220132  0.5020921 2.594890
14 {root vegetables, rolls/buns}
=> {whole milk}        0.01270971  0.5230126 2.046888
15 {other vegetables, yogurt}
=> {whole milk}        0.02226741  0.5128806 2.007235
```

You can see that each of the 15 rules shows the LHS, the RHS, the support, the confidence, and the lift. Rules 7 and 8 have the highest level of lift: the fruits and vegetables involved in these two rules have a relatively low frequency of occurrence, but their support and confidence are both relatively high. Contrast these two rules with Rule 1, which also has high confidence but low support. The reason for this contrast is that milk is a frequently occurring item, so there is not much novelty to that rule. On the other hand, the combination of fruits, root vegetables, and other vegetables suggests a need to find out more about customers whose carts contain only vegetarian or vegan items.

Now it is possible that we have set our parameters for confidence and support too stringently, and as a result we have missed some truly novel combinations that might lead us to better insights. We can use a data visualization package to help explore this possibility. The R package called arulesViz has methods of visualizing the rule sets generated by apriori() that can help us examine a larger set of rules. First, install and library the arulesViz package:

```
> install.packages("arulesViz")
> library(arulesViz)
```

These commands will give the usual raft of status and progress messages. When you run the second command you might find that three or four data objects are masked. As before, these warnings generally will not compromise the operation of the package.

Now let's return to our apriori() command, but we will be much more lenient this time in our minimum support and confidence parameters:

```
> ruleset <- apriori(Groceries,
+     parameter=list(support=0.005, confidence=0.35))
```

We brought support back to 0.005, and confidence down to 35%. When you run this command, you should find that you now generate 357 rules. That is way too many rules to examine manually, so let's use the arulesViz package to see what we have. We will use the plot() command that we have also used earlier in the book. You might ask yourself why we needed to library the arulesViz package if we are simply going to use an old command. The answer to this conundrum is that arulesViz has put some extra plumbing into place so that when the plot() command runs on a data object of type rules (as generated by apriori) it will use some of the code that is built into arulesViz to do the work. So by installing arulesViz we have put some custom visualization code in place that can be used by the generic plot() command. The command is very simple:

```
> plot(ruleset)
```

Figure 17.6 contains the result:

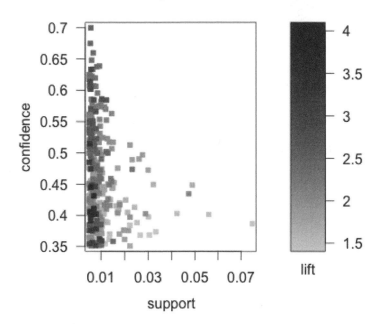

FIGURE 17.6

Even though we see a two-dimensional plot, we actually have three variables represented here. Support is on the X-axis and confidence is on the Y-axis. All else being equal, we would like to have rules that have high support and high confidence. We know, however, that lift serves as a measure of interestingness, and we are also interested in the rules with the highest lift. On this plot, the lift is shown by the darkness of a dot that appears on the plot. The darker the dot, the closer the lift of that rule is to 4.0, which appears to be the highest lift value among these 357 rules.

The other thing we can see from this plot is that although the support of rules ranges from somewhere below 1% all the way up above 7%, all of the rules with high lift seem to have support below 1%. On the other hand, there are rules with high lift and high confidence, which sounds quite positive.

Based on this evidence, let's focus on a smaller set of rules that have only the very highest levels of lift. The following command makes a subset of the larger set of rules by choosing only those rules that have lift higher than 3.5:

```
> goodrules <- ruleset[quality(ruleset)$lift > 3.5]
```

Note that the use of the square brackets with our data structure ruleset allows us to index only those elements of the data object that meet our criteria. In this case, we use the expression quality(ruleset)$lift to tap into the lift parameter for each rule. The inequality test > 3.5 gives us just those rules with the highest lift. When you run this line of code you should find that goodrules contains just nine rules. Let's inspect those nine rules:

```
> inspect(goodrules)
  lhs
  rhs                       support   confidence    lift
1 {herbs}
=> {root vegetables} 0.007015760  0.4312500 3.956477
2 {onions, other vegetables}
=> {root vegetables} 0.005693950  0.4000000 3.669776
3 {beef, other vegetables}
=> {root vegetables} 0.007930859  0.4020619 3.688692
4 {tropical fruit, curd}
=> {yogurt}          0.005287239  0.5148515 3.690645
5 {citrus fruit, pip fruit}
=> {tropical fruit}  0.005592272  0.4044118 3.854060
6 {pip fruit, other vegetables, whole milk}
=> {root vegetables} 0.005490595  0.4060150 3.724961
7 {citrus fruit, other vegetables, whole milk}
=> {root vegetables} 0.005795628  0.4453125 4.085493
8 {root vegetables, whole milk, yogurt}
=> {tropical fruit}  0.005693950  0.3916084 3.732043
9 {tropical fruit, other vegetables, whole milk}
=> {root vegetables} 0.007015760  0.4107143 3.768074
```

When you look over these rules, it seems evident that shoppers are purchasing particular combinations of items that go together in recipes. The first three rules really seem like soup! Rules 4 and 5 seem like a fruit platter with dip. The other four rules might also connect to a recipe, although it is not quite as obvious what.

The key takeaway point here is that using a good visualization tool to examine the results of a data mining activity can enhance the process of sorting through the evidence and making sense of it. If we were to present these results to a store manager (and we would certainly do a little more digging before formulating our final conclusions) we might recommend that recipes could be published along with coupons and popular recipes, such as for homemade soup, might want to have all of the ingredients group together in the store along with signs saying, "Mmmm, homemade soup!"

Chapter Challenge

The arules package contains other data sets, such as the Epub data set with 3,975 transactions from the electronic publication platform of the Vienna University of Economics. Load up that data set, generate some rules, visualize the rules, and choose some interesting ones for further discussion.

Sources

http://en.wikipedia.org/wiki/Association_rule_learning

http://jmlr.csail.mit.edu/papers/volume12/hahsler11a/hahsler11a.pdf

http://journal.r-project.org/archive/2009-2/RJournal_2009-2_Williams.pdf

http://www.r-bloggers.com/examples-and-resources-on-association-rule-mining-with-r/

http://rattle.togaware.com

http://www.statsoft.com/textbook/association-rules/

Reference

Michael Hahsler, Kurt Hornik, and Thomas Reutterer. (2006). "Implications of probabilistic data modeling for mining association rules." In M. Spiliopoulou, R. Kruse, C. Borgelt, A. Nuernberger, and W. Gaul (Eds.), *From data and information analysis to knowledge engineering, studies in classification, data analysis, and knowledge organization* (pp. 598–605). Berlin: Springer-Verlag.

R Functions Used in This Chapter

apriori()	Uses the algorithm of the same name to analyze a transaction data set and generate rules.
itemFrequencyPlot()	Shows the relative frequency of commonly occurring items in the spare occurrence matrix.
inspect()	Shows the contents of the data object generated by apriori() that generates the association rules.
install.packages()	Loads package from the CRAN repository.
summary()	Provides an overview of the contents of a data structure.

© iStockphoto.com/DNY59

18

WHAT'S YOUR
VECTOR, VICTOR?

SUPERVISED AND UNSUPERVISED LEARNING

Data mining techniques fall into two large categories: supervised learning techniques and unsupervised learning techniques. The association rules mining example we examined in the previous chapter was an unsupervised learning technique. This means that there was no particular criterion that we were trying to predict, but rather, we were just looking for patterns that would emerge from the data naturally. In this chapter, we will examine a supervised learning technique called a support vector machine (SVM). The reason SVMs are considered a supervised learning technique is that we train the algorithm on an initial set of data (the supervised phase) and then we test it out on a brand-new set of data. If the training we accomplished worked well, then the algorithm should be able to predict the right outcome most of the time in the test data.

Take the weather as a simple example. Some days are cloudy, some are sunny. The barometer rises some days and falls others. The wind might be strong or weak, and it might come from various directions. If we collect data across several days and use those data to train a machine learning algorithm, the algorithm might find that cloudy days with a falling barometer and the wind from the east signal that it is likely to rain. Next, we can collect more data on some other days and see how well our algorithm does at predicting rain on those days. The algorithm will make mistakes. The percentage of mistakes is the error rate, and we would like the error rate to be as low as possible.

This is the basic strategy of supervised machine learning: Have a substantial number of training cases that the algorithm can use to discover and mimic the underlying pattern, and then use the results of that process on a test data set in order to find out how well the algorithm and parameters perform in a cross-validation. Cross-validation, in this instance, refers to the process of verifying that the trained algorithm can carry out is prediction or classification task accurately on novel data.

SUPERVISED LEARNING VIA SUPPORT VECTOR MACHINES

In this chapter, we will develop an SVM to classify e-mails into spam or nonspam. Hence, the SVM needs to segregate the data into two classes (spam and nonspam). But how does SVM best segregate the two classes within the data?

SVM tries to create a hyperplane to divide the data. If we keep the discussion to a two-dimensional piece of paper, we can think of the hyperplane as a line dividing the two categories of data. The goal is to choose a hyperplane (the line in two dimensions) with

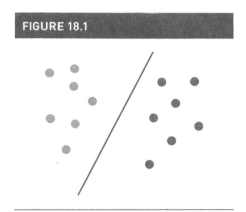

FIGURE 18.1

the greatest possible margin between the hyperplane and any point within the training set, giving a greater chance of new data being classified correctly. In Figure 18.1, you can think of the light blue dots as being spam and the dark blue dots as being nonspam.

However, this can get tricky if the data are not this cleanly divided; most data sets are not this clean. Figure 18.2 shows an even more complicated challenges, but you should be aware that real data sets are often even messier than this.

So, how does an SVM solve this challenge? An SVM maps a low-dimensional problem into a higher-dimensional space with the goal of being able to describe geometric boundaries between different regions. The input data (the independent variables) from a given case are processed through a mapping algorithm called a kernel (the kernel is simply a formula that is run on each case's vector of input data), and the resulting kernel output determines the position of that case in multidimensional space.

A simple mapping example can illustrate how this works. We can take a messy two-dimensional set of dots and try to map them to a third dimension, making it much easier to separate the two cases. You can see how this might be done in Figure 18.3.

Another way to think about it is to imagine looking at a photograph of a snowcapped mountain photographed from high above the earth, such that the mountain looks like a small, white circle completely surrounded by a region of green trees. Using a pair of

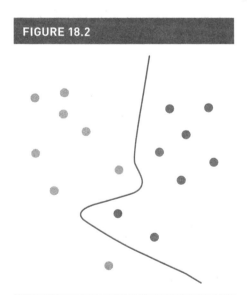

FIGURE 18.2

scissors, there is no way of cutting the photo on a straight line so that all of the white snow is on one side of the cut and all the green trees are on the other. In other words, there is no simple linear separation function that could correctly separate or classify the white and green points given their two-dimensional positions on the photograph.

Next, instead of a piece of paper, think about a realistic three-dimensional clay model of the mountain. Now all the white points occupy a cone at the peak of the mountain and all of the green points lie at the base of the mountain. Imagine inserting a sheet of cardboard through the clay model in a way that divides the snowcapped peak from the green-tree-covered base. It is much easier to do now because the white points are sticking up into the high altitude and the green points are all at a lower altitude on the base of the mountain.

FIGURE 18.3

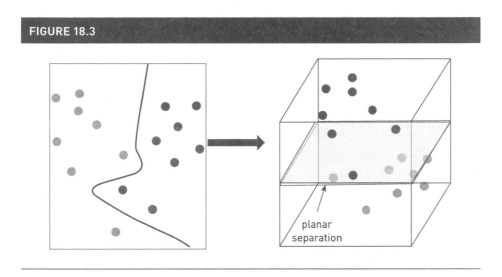

planar
separation

The position of that piece of cardboard is the planar separation function that divides white points from green points. An SVM analysis of this scenario would take the original two-dimensional point data and search for a projection into three dimensions that would maximize the spacing between green points and white points. The result of the analysis would be a mathematical description of the position and orientation of the cardboard plane. Given inputs describing a novel data point, the SVM could then map the data into the higher dimensional space and then report whether the point was above the cardboard (a white point) or below the cardboard (a green point). The so-called support vectors contain the coefficients that map the input data for each case into the high-dimensional space.

SUPPORT VECTOR MACHINES IN R

To get started with SVMs, we can load one of the R packages that supports this technique. We will use the kernlab package. Use the commands below:

```
> install.packages("kernlab")
> library(kernlab)
```

Remember to use the double quotes in the first command, but not in the second command. The data set that we want to use is built into this package. The data come from a study of spam e-mails received by employees at the Hewlett-Packard company. Load the data with the following command:

```
> data(spam)
```

This command does not produce any output. We can now inspect the spam data set with the str() command:

```
> str(spam)
'data.frame':     4601 obs. of   58 variables:
 $ make    : num  0 0.21 0.06 0 0 0 0 0.15 0.06 ...
 $ address: num  0.64 0.28 0 0 0 0 0 0 0.12 ...
 $ all     : num  0.64 0.5 0.71 0 0 0 0 0.46 0.77 ...
 $ num3d   : num  0 0 0 0 0 0 0 0 0 ...
 .

 .

 .
 $ charDollar  : num  0 0.18 0.184 0 0 0 0.054 0 0.203
0.081 ...
 $ charHash    : num  0 0.048 0.01 0 0 0 0 0 0.022 0
...
 $ capitalAve  : num  3.76 5.11 9.82 3.54 3.54 ...
 $ capitalLong : num  61 101 485 40 40 15 4 11 445 43
...
 $ capitalTotal: num  278 1028 2259 191 191 ...
 $ type        : Factor w/ 2 levels "nonspam","spam":
2 2 2 2 2 2 2 2 2 ...
```

Some of the lines of output have been dropped from the material above. You can also use the dim() function to get a quick overview of the data structure:

```
> dim(spam)
[1] 4601    58
```

The dim() function shows the dimensions of the data structure. The output of this dim() function shows that the spam data structure has 4,601 rows and 58 columns. If you inspect a few of the column names that emerged from the str() command, you will see that each e-mail is coded with respect to its contents. There is lots of information available about this data set here: http://archive.ics.uci.edu/ml/datasets/Spambase

For example, just before the word "type" at the end of the output of the str() command on the previous page, we see a variable called capitalTotal. This is the total number of capital letters in the whole e-mail. Right after that is the criterion variable, type, that indicates whether an e-mail was classified as spam by human experts. Let's explore this variable some more:

```
> table(spam$type)
nonspam    spam
   2788    1813
```

We use the table function because type is a factor rather than a numeric variable. The output shows us that there are 2,788 messages that were classified by human experts as nonspam, and 1,813 messages that were classified as spam. What a great data set!

To make the analysis work we need to divide the data set into a training set and a test set. There is no universal way to do this, but as a rule of thumb you can use two thirds of the data set to train and the remainder to test. Let's first generate a randomized index that will let us choose cases for our training and test sets. In the following command, we create a new list/vector variable that samples at random from a list of numbers ranging from 1 to the final element index of the spam data (4,601).

```
> randIndex <- sample(1:dim(spam)[1])
> summary(randIndex)
   Min. 1st Qu.  Median    Mean 3rd Qu.    Max.
      1    1151    2301    2301    3451    4601
> length(randIndex)
[1] 4601
```

The output of the summary() and length() commands above show that we have successfully created a list of indices ranging from 1 to 4,601 and that the total length of our index list is the same as the number of rows in the spam data set: 4,601. We can confirm that the indices are randomized by looking at the first few cases:

```
> head(randIndex)
[1]  2073   769  4565   955  3541  3357
```

Since this is a random set of numbers, based on the sample function, it is possible that you might get different numbers in your randIndex. Of course, your numbers will still be random; they just might be in a different order than what we have shown in our code. It is important to randomize your selection of cases for the training and test sets in order to ensure that there is no systematic bias in the selection of cases. We have no way of knowing how the original data set was sorted (if at all)—in case it was sorted on some variable of interest, we do not just want to take the first two thirds of the cases as the training set.

Next, let's calculate the cut point that would divide the spam data set into a two-thirds training set and a one-third test set:

```
> cutPoint2 _ 3 <- floor(2 * dim(spam)[1]/3)
> cutPoint2 _ 3
[1] 3067
```

The first command in this group calculates the two-thirds cut point based on the number of rows in spam (the expression dim(spam)[1] gives the number of rows in the spam data set). The second command reveals that that cut point is 3,067 rows into the data set, which seems very sensible given that there are 4,601 rows in total. Note that the floor() function chops off any decimal part of the calculation. We want to get rid of any decimal because an index variable needs to be an integer.

Now we are ready to generate our test and training sets from the original spam data set. First we will build our training set from the first 3,067 rows:

```
> trainData <- spam[randIndex[1:cutPoint2 _ 3],]
```

We make the new data set, called trainData, using the randomized set of indices that we created in the randIndex list, but only using the first 3,067 elements of randIndex (The inner expression in square brackets, 1:cutPoint2_3, does the job of selecting the first 3,067 elements. From here you should be able to imagine the command for creating the test set:

```
> testData <-
+    spam[randIndex[(cutPoint2 _ 3+1):dim(spam)[1]],]
```

The inner expression now selects the rows from 3,068 all the way up to 4,601 for a total of 1,534 rows. So now we have two separate data sets, representing a two-thirds training and one-third test breakdown of the original data. We are now in good shape to train our support vector model. The following command generates a model based on the training data set:

```
> svmOutput <- ksvm(type ~., data=trainData,  kernel =
+      "rbfdot",kpar="automatic",C=5,cross=3,
+       prob.model=TRUE)

Using automatic sigma estimation (sigest) for RBF or
laplace kernel
```

Let's examine this command in some detail. The first argument, type ~., specifies the model we want to test. Using the word "type" in this expression means that we want to have the type variable (i.e., whether the message is spam or nonspam) as the outcome variable that our model predicts. The tilde character (~) in an R expression simply separates the left-hand side of the expression from the right-hand side. Finally, the dot character (.) is a shorthand that tells R to use all of the other variables in the dataframe to try to predict type.

The data parameter lets us specify which dataframe to use in the analysis. In this case, we have specified that the procedure should use the trainData training set that we developed.

The next parameter is an interesting one: kernel="rbfdot". You will remember from the earlier discussion that the kernel is the customizable part of the SVM algorithm that lets us project the low-dimensional problem into higher-dimensional space. In this case, the rbfdot designation refers to the radial basis function. One simple way of thinking about the radial basis function is this: Think of a point on a regular X,Y coordinate system: The distance from the origin to the point is like a radius of a circle. The dot in the name refers to the mathematical idea of a dot product, which is a way of multiplying vectors together to come up with a single number such as a distance value. In simplified terms, the radial basis function kernel takes the set of inputs from each row in a data set and calculates a distance value based on the combination of the many variables in the row. The weighting of the different variables in the row is adjusted by the algorithm in order to get the maximum separation of distance between the spam cases and the nonspam cases.

The kpar argument refers to a variety of parameters that can be used to control the operation of the radial basis function kernel. In this case, we are depending on the goodwill of the designers of this algorithm by specifying automatic. The designers came up with some heuristics (guesses) to establish the appropriate parameters without user intervention.

The C argument refers to the so-called cost of constraints. Remember back to our example of the white top on the green mountain? When we put the piece of cardboard (the planar separation function) through the mountain, what if we happen to get one green point on the white side or one white point on the green side? This is a kind of mistake that influences how the algorithm places the piece of cardboard. We can force these mistakes to be more or less costly and thus to have more influence on the position of our piece of cardboard and the margin of separation that it defines. We can get a large margin of separation—but possibly with a few mistakes—by specifying a small value of C. If we specify a large value of C we might get fewer mistakes but only at the cost of having the cardboard cut a very close margin between the green and white points: the cardboard might get stuck into the mountain at a very weird angle just to make sure that all of the green points and white points are separated. On the other hand, if we have a low value of C we will get a generalizable model, but one that makes more classification mistakes.

In the next argument, we have specified cross=3. Cross refers to the cross-validation model that the algorithm uses. In this case, our choice of the final parameter, prob. model=TRUE, dictates that we use a so-called threefold cross-validation in order to generate the probabilities associated with whether a message is or isn't a spam message. Cross-validation is important for avoiding the problem of overfitting. In theory, many of the algorithms used in data mining can be pushed to the point where they essentially memorize the input data and can perfectly replicate the outcome data in the training set. The only problem with this is that the model based on the memorization of the training data will almost never generalize to other data sets. In effect, if we push the algorithm too hard, it will become too specialized to the training data and we won't be able to use it anywhere else. By using k-fold (in this case threefold) cross-validation, we can rein in the fitting function so that it does not work so hard and so that it does create a model that is more likely to generalize to other data.

Let's have a look at what our output structure contains:

```
> svmOutput
Support Vector Machine object of class "ksvm"


SV type: C-svc   (classification)
 parameter : cost C = 5
```

```
Gaussian Radial Basis kernel function.
 Hyperparameter : sigma =  0.0287825580201687


Number of Support Vectors : 953


Objective Function Value : -1750.51
Training error : 0.027388
Cross validation error : 0.076296
Probability model included.
```

Most of this is technical detail that will not necessarily affect how we use the SVM output, but a few things are worth pointing out. First, the sigma parameter mentioned was estimated for us by the algorithm because we used the automatic option. Thank goodness for that, because it would have taken a lot of experimentation to choose a reasonable value without the help of the algorithm. Next, note the large number of support vectors. These are the lists of weights that help to project the variables in each row into a higher-dimensional space. The training error at about 2.7% is quite low. Naturally, the cross-validation error is higher, because a set of parameters never performs as well on subsequent data sets as it does with the original training set. Even so, a 7.6% cross-validation error rate is pretty good for a variety of prediction purposes.

We can take a closer look at these support vectors with the following command:

```
> hist(alpha(svmOutput)[[1]])
```

The alpha() accessor reveals the values of the support vectors. Note that these are stored in a nested list, hence the need for the [[1]] expression to access the first list in the list of lists. Because the particular data set we are using only has two classes (spam or nonspam), we need only one set of support vectors. If the type criterion variable had more than two levels (e.g., spam, not sure, and nonspam), we would need additional support vectors to be able to classify the cases into more than two groups. The histogram in Figure 18.4 shows the range of the support vectors from 0 to 5.

The maximum value of the support vector is equal to the cost parameter that we discussed earlier. We can see that about half of the support vectors are at this maximum value while the rest cluster around zero. Those support vectors at the maximum represent the most difficult cases to classify. With respect to our mountain metaphor, these are the white points that are below the piece of cardboard and the green points that are above it.

FIGURE 18.4

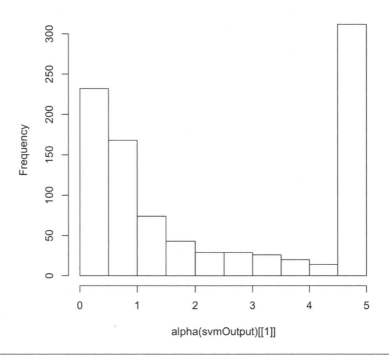

Histogram of alpha(svmOutput)[[1]]

If we increase the cost parameter we can get fewer of these problem points but only at the cost of increasing our cross-validation error:

```
> svmOutput <- ksvm(type ~., data=trainData,
+       kernel = "rbfdot",kpar="automatic",C=50,cross=3,
+       prob.model=TRUE)
> svmOutput
Support Vector Machine object of class "ksvm"

SV type: C-svc  (classification)
 parameter : cost C = 50

Gaussian Radial Basis kernel function.
 Hyperparameter : sigma =  0.0299992970259353

Number of Support Vectors : 850
```

```
Objective Function Value : -6894.635
Training error : 0.008803
Cross validation error : 0.085424
Probability model included.
```

In the first command, the C=50 is what we changed from the earlier command. The output here shows that our training error went way down, to 0.88% but that our cross-validation error went up from 7.6% in our earlier model to 8.5% in this model. We can again get a histogram (see Figure 18.5) of the support vectors to show what has happened, and this time, we improve the title and axis labels.

```
> hist(alpha(svmOutput)[[1]],
+     main="Support Vector Histogram with C=50",
+     xlab="Support Vector Values")
```

FIGURE 18.5

Support Vector Histogram with C=50

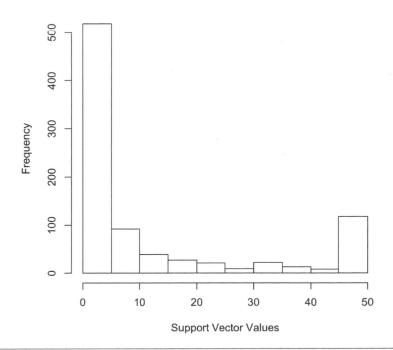

Now there are only about 100 cases where the support vector is at the maxed-out value (in this case 50, because we set C = 50 in the ksvm() command). Again, these are the hard cases that the model could not get to be on the right side of the cardboard (or that were precisely on the cardboard). Meanwhile, the many cases with the support vector value near zero represent the combinations of parameters that make a case lie very far from the piece of cardboard. These cases were so easy to classify that they really made no contribution to positioning the hyperplane that separates the spam cases from the nonspam cases.

We can poke our way into this a little more deeply by looking at a couple of instructive cases. First, let's find the index numbers of a few of the support vectors that were near zero:

```
> alphaindex(svmOutput)[[1]][alpha(svmOutput)[[1]] <
+      0.05]
 [1]   90   98  289   497   634   745 1055 1479 1530 1544
  1646 1830 1948 2520 2754
```

This monster of a command is not as bad as it looks. We are tapping into a new part of the svmOutput object, this time using the alphaindex() accessor function. Remember that we have 850 support vectors in this output. Now imagine two lists of 850 right next to each other: The first is the list of support vectors themselves; we get at that list with the alpha() accessor function. The second list, lined right up next to the first list, is a set of indices into the original training data set, trainData. The left-hand part of the expression in the command above lets us access these indices. The right-hand part of the expression, where it says alpha(svmOutput)[[1]]<0.05, is a conditional expression that lets us pick from the index list just those cases with a very small support vector value. You can see the output above, just underneath the command: about 15 indices were returned. Just pick off the first one, 90, and take a look at the individual case it refers to:

```
> trainData[90,]
make address all num3d our over remove
   0         0   0     0   0    0      0
internet order mail receive will
      0     0    0       0    0

 .

 .

 .

charExclamation charDollar charHash capitalAve
          1.123          0        0        2.6
```

```
capitalLong capitalTotal              type
         16           26           nonspam
```

The command requested row 90 from the trainData training set. A few of the lines of the output were left off for ease of reading and almost all of the variables thus left out were zero. Note the very last two lines of the output, where this record is identified as a nonspam e-mail. So this was a very easy case to classify because it has virtually none of the markers that a spam e-mail usually has (e.g., as shown earlier, no mention of Internet, order, or mail). You can contrast this case with one of the hard cases by running this command:

```
> alphaindex(svmOutput)[[1]][alpha(svmOutput)[[1]] ==
+   50]
```

You will get a list of the 92 indices of cases where the support vector was maxed out to the level of the cost function (remember C = 50 from the latest run of the ksvm() command). Pick any of those cases and display it, like this:

```
> trainData[11,]
```

This particular record did not have many suspicious keywords, but it did have long strings of capital letters that made it hard to classify (it was a nonspam case, by the way). You can check out a few of them to see if you can spot why each case might have been difficult for the classifier to place.

The real acid test for our support vector model, however, will be to use the support vectors we generated through this training process to predict the outcomes in a novel data set. Fortunately, because we prepared carefully, we have the testData training set ready to go. The following commands will give us some output known as a confusion matrix:

```
> svmPred <- predict(svmOutput, testData, type =
+   "votes")
> compTable <- data.frame(testData[,58],svmPred[1,])
> table(compTable)
              svmPred.1...
testData...58.   0    1
      nonspam   38  854
      spam      574  68
```

The first command in the confusion matrix uses our model output from before, namely, svmOutput, as the parameters for prediction. It uses the testData, which the support vectors have never seen before, to generate predictions, and it requests votes from the prediction process. We could also look at probabilities and other types of model output, but for a simple analysis of whether the ksvm() function is generating good predictions, votes will make our lives easier.

The output from the predict() command is a two-dimensional list. You should use the str() command to examine its structure. Basically there are two lists of vote values side by side. Each list is 1,534 elements long, corresponding to the 1,534 cases in our testData object. The left-hand list has one (1) for a nonspam vote and zero (0) for a spam vote. Because this is a two-class problem, the other list has just the opposite. We can use either one because they are mirror images of each other.

In the second command above, we make a little dataframe, called compTable, with two variables in it: The first variable is the 58th column in the test data, which is the last column containing the type variable (a factor indicating spam or nonspam). Remember that this type variable is the human judgments from the original data set, so it is our ground truth. The second variable is the first column in our votes data structure (svm-Pred), so it contains ones for nonspam predictions and zeros for spam predictions.

Finally, applying the table() command to our new dataframe (compTable) gives us the confusion matrix as output. Along the main diagonal, we see the erroneous classifications: 38 cases that were nonspam but were classified as spam by the support vector matrix, and 68 cases that were spam but were classified as nonspam by the support vector matrix. On the counter-diagonal, we see 854 cases that were correctly classified as nonspam and 574 cases that were correctly classified as spam.

Overall, it looks like we did a pretty good job. There are a bunch of different ways of calculating the accuracy of the prediction, depending on what you are most interested in. The simplest way is to sum the 68 + 38 = 106 error cases and divide by the 1,534 total cases for a total error rate of about 6.9%. Interestingly, that is a tad better than the 8.5% error rate we got from the k-fold cross-validation in the run of ksvm() that created the model we are testing. Keep in mind, though, that we might be more interested in certain kinds of error than others. For example, consider which is worse: an e-mail that gets mistakenly quarantined because it is not really spam or a spam e-mail that gets through to someone's inbox? It really depends on the situation, but you can see that you might want to give more consideration to either the 68 misclassification errors or the other set of 38 misclassification errors.

This completes our focus on modeling. Hopefully, at this point, you understand the difference between the models that we have been able to create in R (using lm, apriori, and ksvm). There are many other models that might be useful, such as clustering observations in a data set into groups based on the data within the dataframe. These other models are also available within R. Alas, the exploration of these other models is beyond our scope—but feel free to explore!

Chapter Challenge

Look up the term *confusion matrix* and then follow up on some other terms such as *Type I error, Type II error, sensitivity,* and *specificity.* Think about how the SVM model could be modified to do better at either sensitivity or specificity.

For an additional challenge, try using another data set with the kernlab svm technology. Specifically, there is a data set called promotergene that is built into the kernlab package. Promotergene is a data set of E. coli promoter gene sequences (DNA) with 106 observations and 58 variables that was originally made available at the UCI Machine Learning repository. Your goal is to explore the promotergene data set and to try to be able to predict promoters (which is a column in the data set). In case you were wondering, promoters have a region where a protein makes contact with the helical DNA sequence and that contact region spatially aligns.

Sources

http://cbio.ensmp.fr/~jvert/svn/tutorials/practical/svmbasic/svmbasic_notes.pdf

http://cran.r-project.org/web/packages/kernlab/kernlab.pdf

http://en.wikipedia.org/wiki/Confusion_matrix

http://stackoverflow.com/questions/9480605/what-is-the-relation-between-the-number-of-support-vectors-and-training-data-and

http://www.louisaslett.com/Courses/Data_Mining/ST4003-Lab7-Introduction_to_Support_Vector_Machines.pdf

http://www.jstatsoft.org/v11/i09/paper

R Functions Used in This Chapter

predict()	Uses a model to predict an outcome.
table()	Creates tabular results for a given list of categorical (factor) variables.
ksvm()	Runs support vector machine analysis in the kernlab package.
hist()	Creates a histogram for a given vector.
dim()	Provides the dimension (size) of a vector or dataframe.
sample()	Chooses elements at random from a vector.

19

SHINY® WEB APPS

LEARNING OBJECTIVES

- Build an interactive R application.
- Deploy an interactive R application on the web.
- Create a Shiny web app within RStudio.

Shiny is a trademark of RStudio, Inc.

Sometimes, when we use R to develop code, it is helpful to actually create an application and have that application be interactive. Happily, there is a very easy way to create interactive web applications in R. Let's get started!

CREATING WEB APPLICATIONS IN R

The first step, within RStudio, is to create a new file, but rather than an R source file, we want to click the File menu, then New File, then Shiny Web App . . . ." When you see this dialog window, press the Create button.

FIGURE 19.1

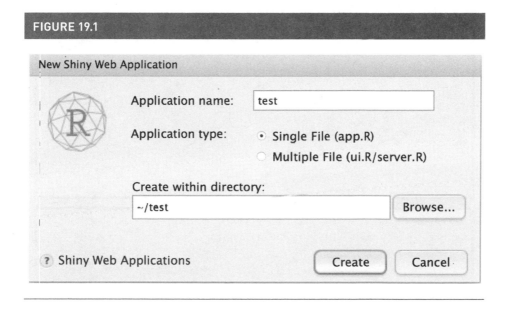

After creating a new app (select single file as the application type), an R file (app.r) will be created. This code will be visible as a tab in your R source RStudio window (i.e., in the upper-left-hand part of RStudio). Wow, a lot of code was created! But let's explore the code; it's easy to understand. There are three main components of the code. First is the user interface (ui), then the code that does the R calculations (the server), and, finally, the code that tells R/Shiny our ui and server variables.

```r
library(shiny)

# Define UI for application that draws a histogram
ui <- fluidPage(

    # Application title
    titlePanel("Old Faithful Geyser Data"),

    # Sidebar with a slider input for number of bins
    sidebarLayout(
        sidebarPanel(
            sliderInput("bins",
                        "Number of bins:",
                        min = 1,
                        max = 50,
                        value = 30)
        ),

        # Show a plot of the generated distribution
        mainPanel(
            plotOutput("distPlot")
        )
    )
)

# Define server logic required to draw a histogram
server <- function(input, output) {
    output$distPlot <- renderPlot({
        # generate bins based on input$bins from ui.R
        x    <- faithful[, 2]
        bins <- seq(min(x), max(x), length.out =
              input$bins + 1)

        # draw the histogram with the specified number
        # of bins
        hist(x, breaks = bins, col = 'darkgray', border
            = 'white')
    })
}

# Run the application
shinyApp(ui = ui, server = server)
```

As we can see, first there is the code that creates the user interface (this is the code that lets a user adjust the application, such as selecting an attribute). That code defines the object ui. Then there is the code that generates the server code (think of this as the code that performs the functions needed to display the appropriate information on a web page). This is defined in the server object. Finally, there is one line that actually runs the code, the shinyApp, which is the last line in the file. It is important (not now, but when we go to create a web-based application) for this shinyApp function to be the last line in the file.

We can name ui any variable name we want. We can also name server any name we want. The shinyApp lets R know the names of our two key components. So if we changed ui to myUI, the shinyApp would be changed to

```
shinyApp(ui = myUI, server = server)
```

Note that in RStudio, there no longer is the Run button (to run the code). Instead, there is the Run App button. Since the code has been pre-generated, you can press the Run App button and the code will run.

FIGURE 19.2

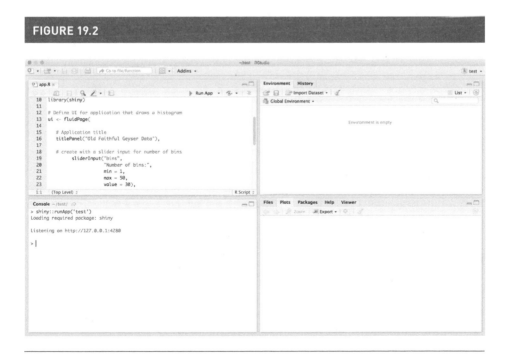

Since we are now running applications, RStudio can launch the app in a new window, a window in your browser or in the viewer window (the lower-right window in RStudio). You can choose to have the app launch in one of these by clicking on the icon to the right of the Run App button. RStudio will give you a pulldown menu to select how you want to display the app.

With our application running (e.g., in your browser or in your viewer window), we can change the number of bins used to create the histogram, and then the picture adjusts. One important note is that while this can be run in your web browser, it is not yet a web application (we will get to that later). For now, it is an interactive application, running locally on your machine.

FIGURE 19.3

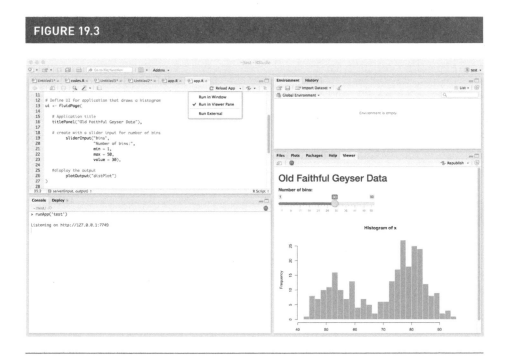

A minor issue occurs sometimes: After closing the application window (e.g., the window tab in a web browser where the R code was running), RStudio might not terminate the application. So if you hit enter in the console of RStudio, you might not see the >. If this is the case, then it is likely the case that R is still running. If this happens, all you need to do his press the Stop button, in the middle of the RStudio screen (in the upper-right part of the console window). This button is visible only when R is running. So if you see the Stop button and are not actively running your R code, then it makes sense to hit the Stop button (which will cause the Stop button to go away).

FIGURE 19.4

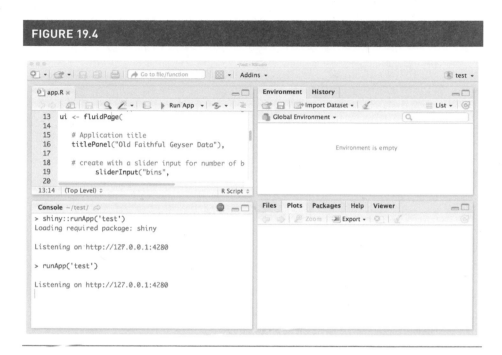

OK. Now that we got the code to run, and then stop, let's explore the code in more detail. First, for the ui, we can see there are two areas defined. First there is the slider area that defines the number of bins to be used, and next is the main panel area where we will plot (draw) the histogram.

The server function takes the variable input$bins, which supplies the information from the slider, and uses that value to define the number of bins in the histogram. The input$bins is defined by the fact that the number is from input (so that explains "input" in the variable), but the "bins" part of the variable is defined in the ui. Take a look at the slider input, where bins are defined as the output of the slider.

We can also see that the plotOutput in the ui uses distPlot, and that variable is defined in the server code. So distPlot is a variable that is used as the output of the renderPlot function, and shows the actual histogram.

Note that we can simplify the code to make it easier to follow:

```r
library(shiny)

# Define UI for application that draws a histogram
ui <- fluidPage(
```

```r
    # Application title
    titlePanel("Old Faithful Geyser Data"),

    # Sidebar with a slider input for number of bins
        sliderInput("bins",
                    "Number of bins:",
                    min = 1,
                    max = 50,
                    value = 30),


      # Show a plot of the generated distribution
            plotOutput("distPlot")
)


# Define server logic required to draw a histogram
server <- function(input, output) {

   output$distPlot <- renderPlot({
      # generate bins based on input$bins from ui.R
      x    <- faithful[, 2]

      # draw the histogram with the specified number
      # of bins
      hist(x, breaks = input$bins, col = 'darkgray',
          border = 'white')
   })
}


# Run the application
shinyApp(ui = ui, server = server)
```

To show these variables, we can change the code somewhat to show our important variables. We can change bins to myBins and distPlot to myPlot. You can see where myPlot and myBins are used. This provides a template on how to create Shiny apps.

```
library(shiny)

# Define UI for application that draws a histogram
ui <- fluidPage(

    # Application title
    titlePanel("Old Faithful Geyser Data"),

    # Define a slider input for number of bins
            sliderInput("myBins",
                        "Number of bins:",
                        min = 1,
                        max = 50,
                        value = 30),

        # Show a plot of the generated distribution
            plotOutput("myPlot")
)

# Define server logic required to draw a histogram
server <- function(input, output) {

    output$myPlot <- renderPlot({
        # generate bins based on input$bins from ui.R
        x       <- faithful[, 2]

        # draw the histogram with the specified number
        # of bins
        hist(x, breaks = input$myBins, col = 'darkgray',
            border = 'white')
    })
}

# Run the application
shinyApp(ui = ui, server = server)
```

DEPLOYING THE APPLICATION

Although this code works within RStudio, and can be run in a web browser, it is still not a web application. We still have to deploy our application so it can be run on the web. There are many ways to deploy the app, and one of the easiest is to use the hosting service available at http://www.shinyapps.io/, which is free for testing small apps. What makes shinyapps.io so nice is that it is integrated with RStudio. In fact, we have already done almost all the work required to deploy a Shiny app.

To get our interactive web page to work, we first need to create an account at shiny apps.io, and then follow the instructions. We first need to install rsconnect (via the normal install.packages command in the RStudio console).

```
> install.packages("rsconnect")
> library(rsconnect)
```

Then, we need to use the command setAccountInfo, as explained (on the shinyapps. io website), after getting a shinyapps account. Note that the parameters to this command are specific to your account. So make sure to appropriately copy the code to R and then run the line of code in the R console. You might have to Show secret so that the code is copied correctly.

```
> setAccountInfo(name='xxx',
+    token='yyyyyyyyyyyyyyyyyyyyyyyyyyyyyyyyyyyyyyyyyyyy',
+    secret=zzzzzzzzzzzzzzzzzzzzzzzzzzzzzzzzzzzzzzzz')
```

Remember, the xxx, yyy . . . yyy, and zzz . . . zzz are placeholders for values you get on the shinyapps.io website after we have logged into the system. This process is explained in a small shinyapps tutorial available at http://shiny.rstudio.com/articles/shinyapps.html

Once these two steps are completed, we can publish the application (instead of Run App) from within RStudio. Publish Application is the icon next to Run App and is circled in Figure 19.5.

When we use Publish Application, RStudio will create a new tab in the lower-left window. Now, in addition to the console, there will be a Deploy tab. After publishing, you should see something similar to the following (in the deploy window):

Preparing to deploy application . . . DONE

Uploading bundle for application: 146349 . . . DONE

FIGURE 19.5

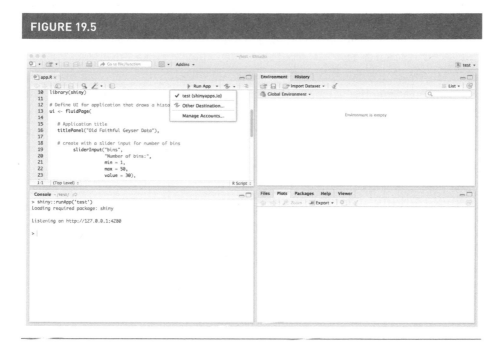

Deploying bundle: 655321 for application: 146349 . . .

Waiting for task: 317406782

building: Parsing manifest

building: Installing packages

building: Installing files

building: Pushing image: 645493

deploying: Starting instances

rollforward: Activating new instances

success: Stopping old instances

Application successfully deployed to https://xxx.shinyapps.io/test/

Deployment completed: https://xxx.shinyapps.io/test/

As you can see, we just deployed a public test of a simple R application. Note that when you deploy, the xxx will be replaced with your account. That's it! We now have a real web-based application.

Of course, there are many ways to configure/define input within Shiny—a slider is just one possibility. Our small application was just a way to test how to deploy an application.

Let's build a slightly more-advanced application, using the map visualizations that we previously created. Within this new application, we will use a different input method to build an application that will allow the user to define how to color-code our map. For this input, we will have a predefined list of possible choices, so a choice menu makes the most sense. To do this, we need to create a new Shiny app (from the File, New File, menu in RStudio).

Once we have this new application, the ui code is similar to our initial example, but rather than a sliderInput input, we have a selectInput (which will create a choice menu). When we create a choice menu, for each menu choice we define two items. The first item is what is shown to the user and can be any text string. The second item is the variable name we want to use in our R code. In this example, the choice menu is letting the user select a column in our dataframe, so the different choices have the appropriate column name as the second item for each choice selection.

The code to define the server function is somewhat more complicated but is very similar to the code that we have previously created to display the map. In fact, the only real difference is the use of input$variable to define the column we want to color the map: Where previously we had coded that to a specific column, now the code is more general, based on what the user selects. You may notice that we also use the exact same readCensus function. So, while this is a lot of code, almost all of it should look familiar.

```r
library(shiny)
library(ggmap)
library(ggplot2)

ui <- fluidPage(
  selectInput("variable", "Variable:",
              c("july population" = "july11pop",
                "region of country" = "region",
                "change in population" = "popChange",
                "Percent change in population" =
                "percentChange")),
  plotOutput("plot")
)
```

```r
server <- function(input, output) {
  dfStates <- readCensus()
  dfStates <- dfStates[dfStates$stateName !=
                "District of Columbia", ]

  dfStates$region <- state.region
  dfStates$stateName <-
          tolower(dfStates$stateName)

  dfStates$popChange <- dfStates$july11pop -
                            dfStates$july10pop
  dfStates$percentChange <-
      dfStates$popChange/dfStates$july10pop * 100

  us <- map_data("state")

  output$plot <- renderPlot(
    ggplot(dfStates, aes(map_id = state)) +
      geom_map(map = us,
          aes(fill=dfStates[,input$variable])) +
      expand_limits(x = us$long, y = us$lat) +
      coord_map() + ggtitle("state population") +
      guides(fill=guide_legend(title=input$variable))
  )
}

#read in the census data set. This function
#is the same as the one previously defined
readCensus <- function() {
  urlToRead <-
  "http://www2.census.gov/programs-surveys/
    popest/tables/2010-2011/state/totals/
    nst-est2011-01.csv"
```

```
#do the basic cleanup
testFrame <- read.csv(url(urlToRead))
testFrame<-testFrame[-1:-8,]
testFrame<-testFrame[,1:5]
testFrame$stateName <- testFrame[,1]
testFrame<-testFrame[,-1]
testFrame<-testFrame[-52:-58,]

#remove the 'dot' from the state name
testFrame$stateName <- gsub("\\.","",
        testFrame$stateName)

#convert columns to numbers and rename columns
testFrame$april10census <-Numberize(testFrame$X)
testFrame$april10base <-Numberize(testFrame$X.1)
testFrame$july10pop <-Numberize(testFrame$X.2)
testFrame$july11pop <-Numberize(testFrame$X.3)
testFrame <- testFrame[,-1:-4]

#remove the old rownames, which are now confusing
rownames(testFrame) <- NULL

return(testFrame)
}




# Run the application
shinyApp(ui = ui, server = server)
```

If you encounter an error when trying to run the application, Shiny app might generate a Disconnected from Server error (and then not show the web page). When this happens, or if you are just curious about how the app is doing, one trick is to look at the output log by typing the showLogs command within the R console:

```
> rsconnect::showLogs()
```

You can see the double colons (::) between the rsconnect and the showLogs. This full line makes sure we are using the rsconnect's showLogs function. Since there might be other packages that use a showLogs function, explicitly telling R we want to use the rsconnect function makes sure we get the function we wanted.

To recap, in this chapter we explored how to create web-based applications, written in R, that anyone can see with a web browser. These applications allow interactive R visualizations.

Chapter Challenge(s)

Try to create a scatter plot interactive application. In this application, use the census data from earlier in the book, and let the user determine the X-axis, the Y-axis, the color, and the size based on what the user would like to see. To do this, you will need multiple-choice menus, one for each selection the user needs to make.

Sources

http://shiny.rstudio.com/articles/shinyapps.html

http://www.shinyapps.io/

R Functions Used in This Chapter

setAccountInfo()	Enables the creation of web-based hosted applications.
shinyApp()	Runs the shiny application, defining the ui and the server.
Run App	Is a new way to run an application, not just R code.

20

BIG DATA? BIG DEAL!

LEARNING OBJECTIVES

- Explain the characteristics of big data.

- Explain the importance of big data in business and other sectors.

- Demonstrate a distributed computing R application across a cluster of computers (perhaps virtual machines running on one computer).

On May 14, 2012, Informatica (a data integration software provider) published an article with the title "Big Data Equals Big Business Opportunity Say Global IT and Business Professionals," and the subtitle, "70 Percent of Organizations Now Considering, Planning or Running Big Data Projects According to New Global Survey." The technology news has been full of similar articles for several years. Given the number of such articles it is hard to resist the idea that big data represents some kind of revolution that has turned the whole world of information and technology topsy-turvy. But is this really true? Does big data change everything?

WHAT IS BIG DATA?

In 2001, business analyst Doug Laney suggested that three characteristics make big data different from what came before: volume, velocity, and variety. Volume refers to the sheer amount of data. Velocity focuses on how quickly data arrive as well as how quickly those data become stale. Finally, Variety reflects the fact that there can be many different kinds of data. Together, these three characteristics are often referred to as the three Vs model of big data. Note, however, that even before the dawn of the computer age we've had a variety of data, some of which arrives quite quickly, and that can add up to quite a lot of total storage over time. Think, for example, of the large variety and volume of data that have arrived annually at the Library of Congress since the 1800s! So it is difficult to tell, just based on someone saying that she has a high-volume, high-velocity, and high-variety data problem, that big data is fundamentally a brand-new thing.

With that said, there are certainly many changes afoot that make data problems qualitatively different today from what they were a few years ago. Let's list a few things that are pretty accurate:

The decline in the price of sensors (like barcode readers) and other technology over recent decades has made it cheaper and easier to collect a lot more data. Similarly, the declining cost of storage has made it practical to keep lots of data hanging around, regardless of its quality or usefulness.

Many people's attitudes about privacy seem to have accommodated the use of Facebook and other platforms where we reveal lots of information about ourselves.

Researchers have made significant advances in the machine learning algorithms that form the basis of many data mining techniques.

When a data set gets to a certain size (into the range of thousands of rows), conventional tests of statistical significance are meaningless, because even the most tiny and trivial results (or effect sizes, as statisticians call them) are statistically significant.

Keeping these points in mind, there are also a number of things that have not changed throughout the years:

Garbage in, garbage out: The usefulness of data depends heavily on how carefully and well they were collected. After data were collected, the quality depends on how much attention was paid to suitable preprocessing: data cleaning and data screening.

Bigger equals weirder: If you are looking for anomalies—rare events that break the rules—then larger is better. Low-frequency events often do not appear until data collection goes on for a long time and/or encompasses a large enough group of instances to contain one of the bizarre cases.

Linking adds potential: Stand-alone data sets are inherently limited by whatever variables are available. But if those data can be linked to some other data, new vistas can suddenly open up. No guarantees, but the more you can connect records here to other records over there, the more potential findings you have.

Items on both of the lists above are considered pretty commonplace and uncontroversial. Taken together, however, they do shed some light on the question of how important big data might be. We have had lots of historical success using conventional statistics to examine modestly sized (i.e., 1,000 rows or fewer) data sets for statistical regularities. Everyone's favorite basic statistic, the Student's t-test, is essential a test for differences in the central tendency of two groups. If the data contain regularities such that one group is notably different from another group, a t-test shows it to be so.

Big data does not help us with these kinds of tests. We don't even need 1,000 records for many conventional statistical comparisons, and having 1 million or 100 million records won't make our job any easier (it will just take more computer memory and storage). Think about what you read earlier in the book: We were able to start using a basic form of statistical inference with a data set that contained a population with only 51 elements. In fact, many of the most commonly used statistical techniques, like the Student's t-test, were designed specifically to work with very small samples.

On the other hand, if we are looking for needles in haystacks, it makes sense to look (as efficiently as possible) through the biggest possible haystack we can find, because it is much more likely that a big haystack will contain at least one needle and maybe more.

Keeping in mind the advances in machine learning that have occurred over recent years, we begin to have an idea that good tools together with big data and interesting questions about unusual patterns could indeed provide some powerful new insights.

Let's couple this optimism with three very important cautions. The first caution is that the more complex our data are, the more difficult it will be to ensure that the data are clean and suitable for the purpose we plan for them. A dirty data set is worse in some ways than no data at all because we might put a lot of time and effort into finding an insight and find nothing. Even more problematic, we might put a lot of time and effort and find a result that is simply wrong! Many analysts believe that cleaning data—getting it ready for analysis, weeding out the anomalies, organizing the data into a suitable configuration—actually takes up most of the time and effort of the analysis process.

The second caution is that rare and unusual events or patterns are almost always, by their nature, highly unpredictable. Even with the best data we can imagine and plenty of variables, we will almost always have a lot of trouble accurately enumerating all of the causes of an event. The data mining tools might show us a pattern, and we might even be able to replicate the pattern in some new data, but we might never be confident that we have understood the pattern to the point where we believe we can isolate, control, or understand the causes. Predicting the path of hurricanes provides a great example here: Despite decades of advances in weather instrumentation, forecasting, and number crunching, meteorologists still have great difficulty predicting where a hurricane will make landfall or how hard the winds will blow. The complexity and unpredictability of the forces at work make the task exceedingly difficult.

The third caution is about linking data sets. The third point above suggests that linkages could provide additional value. With every linkage to a new data set, however, we also increase the complexity of the data and the likelihood of dirty data and resulting spurious patterns. In addition, although many companies seem less and less concerned about the idea, the more we link data about living people (e.g., consumers, patients, voters, etc.), the more likely we are to cause a catastrophic loss of privacy. Even if you are not a big fan of the importance of privacy on principle, it is clear that security and privacy failures have cost companies dearly in both money and reputation. Today's data innovations for valuable and acceptable purposes might be tomorrow's crimes and scams. The greater the amount of linkage between data sets, the easier it is for those people with malevolent intentions to violate privacy.

Putting this altogether, we can take a sensible position that *high-quality* data, in abundance, together with tools used by intelligent analysts in a secure environment, could provide worthwhile benefits in the commercial sector, in education, in government, and in other areas. The focus of our efforts as data scientists, however, should not be on achieving the largest possible data sets, but rather on getting the right data and the right amount of data for the purpose we intend. There is no special virtue in having a lot of data if those data are unsuitable to the conclusions that we want to draw. Likewise, simply getting data more quickly does not guarantee that what we get will be highly relevant to our problems. Finally, although it is said that variety is the spice of life, complexity is often a danger to reliability and trustworthiness: the more complex the linkages among our data, the more likely it is that problems could crop up in making use of those data or in keeping them safe.

THE TOOLS FOR BIG DATA

We can think of big data as the next step beyond remote databases—it leverages distributed computing across a cluster of computers. This combines the remote access to data that we previously demonstrated via SQL with additional computational capabilities. As of this writing, one of the most popular systems for large-scale distributed storage and computing is Hadoop (named after the toy elephant of the young son of the developer).

Hadoop is not a single thing but is rather a combination of pieces of software combined into a library. Hadoop is developed and maintained by the same people who maintain the Apache open source web server. There are about a dozen different parts of the Hadoop framework, but the Hadoop distributed files system (HDFS) and Hadoop MapReduce framework are two of the most important frameworks.

HDFS is easy to explain. Imagine your computer and several other computers at your home or workplace. If we could get them all to work together, we could call them a cluster and we could theoretically get more use out of them by taking advantage of all of the storage and computing power they have as a group. Running HDFS, we can treat this cluster of computers as one big hard drive. If we have a really large file—too big to fit on any one of the computers—HDFS can divide up the file and store its different parts in different storage areas without us having to worry about the details. With a proper configuration of computer hardware, such as an IT department could supply, HDFS can provide an enormous amount of throughput (i.e., a very fast capability for reading and writing data) as well as redundancy and failure tolerance.

MapReduce is somewhat more complicated, but it follows the same logic of trying to divide up work across multiple computers. The term "MapReduce" is used because there are two big processes involved: map and reduce. For the map operation, a big job is broken up into lots of separate parts. For example, if we wanted to create a search index for all of the files on a company's intranet servers, we could break up the whole indexing task into a bunch of separate jobs. Each job might take care of indexing the files on one server.

In the end, though, we don't want dozens or hundreds of different search indices. We want one big one that covers all the files our company owns. This is where the reduce operation comes in. As all of the individual indexing jobs finish up, a reduce operation combines them into one big job. This combining process works on the basis of a so-called key. In the search indexing example, some of the small jobs might have found files that contained the word *fish*. As each small job finishes, it mentioned whether or not *fish* appeared in a document and perhaps how many times *fish* appeared. The reduce operation uses *fish* as a key to match up the results from all of the different jobs, thus creating an aggregated summary listing all of the documents that contained *fish*. Later, if anyone searched on the word *fish*, this list could be used to direct them to documents that contained the word.

In short, map takes a process that the user specifies and an indication of which data it applies to, and divides the processing into as many separate chunks as possible. As the results of each chunk become available, reduce combines them and eventually creates and returns one aggregated result.

Founded in 2007, an organization called RevolutionAnalytics has developed an R interface, or wrapper, for Hadoop that is called RHadoop. This package is still a work in progress in the sense that it does not appear in the standard CRAN package archive, not because there is anything wrong with it, but rather because RevolutionAnalytics wants to continue to develop it without having to provide stable versions for the R community. There is good information available here:

https://github.com/RevolutionAnalytics/RHadoop/wiki

We will break open the first example presented in a tutorial authored by Hugh Devlin just to provide further illustration of the use of MapReduce. As with our MySQL example in Chapter 11, this is a rather trivial activity that would not normally require the use of a large cluster of computers, but it does show how MapReduce can be put to use.

The tutorial example first demonstrates how a repetitive operation is accomplished in R without the use of MapReduce. In prior chapters we have used tapply() function. The lapply() or list-apply is one of the simplest. You provide an input vector of values and a function to apply to each element, and the lapply() function does the heavy lifting. The example in the RHadoop tutorial squares each integer from 1 to 10. This first command fills a vector with the input data:

```
> small.ints <- 1:10
> small.ints
 [1]  1  2  3  4  5  6  7  8  9  10
```

Next we can apply the squaring function (just using the ^ operator) to each element of the list:

```
> out <- lapply(small.ints, function(x) x^2)
> out
[[1]]
[1]  1

[[2]]
[1]  4
... (shows all of the values up to [[10]] [1]  100)
```

In the first command above, we have used lapply() to perform a function on the input vector small.ints. We have defined the function as taking the value x and returning the value x^2. The result is a list of 10 vectors (each with just one element) containing the squares of the input values. Because this is such a small problem, R was able to accomplish it in a tiny fraction of a second.

Explaining how to install and use Hadoop and RHadoop would take an entire book, so our goal in this chapter is to give you a feel for Hadoop and how you might use Hadoop within an R environment. Installing Hadoop, and then RHadoop, is no simple task. In fact, that is our challenge at the end of this chapter. Note that installing Hadoop must be done outside of R, in a manner similar to how you would install a database that R might then use. In addition, since RHadoop is not an official package, that software must also be downloaded outside of R. Note that RHadoop actually consists of several packages, with the three most important being rmr, rhdfs, and rhbase. Rmr, actually the rmr2 package, provides the Hadoop MapReduce functionality in R, rhdfs provides HDFS file management in R, and rhbase provides HBase database management from within R. You can download these packages from the RevolutionAnalytics repository. The RevolutionAnalytics web page noted previously has details on the packages and provides help on downloading and installing RHadoop.

After installing both Hadoop and RHadoop—which, again, is not an official package, and therefore has to be installed manually—we can perform this same operation with two commands:

```
> small.ints <- to.dfs(1:10)
> out <- mapreduce(input = small.ints, map =
+    function(k,v) keyval(v, v^2))
```

In the first command, we again create a list of integers from 1 to 10. But rather than simply storing them in a vector, we are using the distributed file system, or dfs, class that is provided by RHadoop. Note that in most cases we would not need to create this ourselves because our large data set would already exist on the HDFS. We would have connected to HDFS and selected the necessary data much as we did earlier in this chapter with dbConnect().

In the second command, we are doing essentially the same thing as we did with lapply(). We provide the input data structure (which, again, is a dfs class data object, a kind of pointer to the data stored by Hadoop in the cluster). We also provide a map function, which is the process that we want to apply to each element in our data set. Notice that the function takes two arguments, k and v. The k refers to the key that we mentioned earlier in the chapter. We actually don't need the key in this example because we are not supplying a reduce function. There is, in fact, no aggregation or combining activity that needs to occur because our input list (the integers) and the output list (the squares of those integers) are lists of the same size. If we had needed to aggregate the results of the map function, say by creating a mean or a sum, we would have had to provide a reduce function that would do the job.

The keyval() function is characterized as a helper function in the tutorial. In this case, it is clear that the first argument to keyval, v, is the integer to which the process must be applied, and the second argument, v^2, is the squaring function that is applied to each argument. The data returned by mapreduce() is functionally equivalent to that returned by lapply(): In other words, it is a list of the squares of the integers from 1 to 10.

The following is another, slightly more elaborate, example of using RHadoop that generates the mean for a particular column in the iris data set, which is another data set built into R. As you can see, the basic structure is similar to the earlier example—the use of a map and then reduce function.

```
# Run MapReduce job and get result
val <- mapreduce(input = "iris/car2.csv", input.format
    = make.input.format("csv", sep = ","), map =
    cyl.map, reduce = cyl.reduce)
from.dfs(val)

# csv file includes header in first row - remove it
# before processing
cyl.map = function (k, v) {
    # Check first row, if having header name as
    # "model", delete it
```

```
        if (v[1,1] == "model") {
            v <- v[-1,]
        }
        k <- v[[3]]     # Take variable V3 as key
        V5 <- v[[5]]    # alternative: k <- v$V3
                        #(Take variable V3 as value)
        V5 <- as.integer(V5)# Convert value variable
                            # into integer
        keyval(k, V5)
    }
cyl.reduce = function (k, v) {
    keyval(k, mean(v))
}
```

Obviously, there is no point in harnessing the power of a cluster of computers to calculate something that could be done with a pencil and a paper in a few seconds. If, however, the operation was more complex and the list of input data had millions of elements, the use of lapply() would be impractical because it would take your computer quite a long time to finish the job. On the other hand, the second strategy of using mapreduce() could run the job in a fraction of a second, given a sufficient supply of computers and storage.

On a related note, Amazon, the giant online retailer, provides virtual computer clusters that can be used for exactly this kind of work. Amazon's product is called the Elastic Compute Cloud, or EC2, and at this writing it is possible to create a small cluster of Linux computers for as little as five cents per hour.

To summarize this chapter, although there are many analytical problems that require only a small amount of data, the wide availability of larger data sets has added new challenges to data science. As a single user program running on a local computer, R is well suited for work by a single analyst on a data set that is small enough to fit into the computer's memory. We can retrieve these small data sets from individual files stored in human-readable (e.g., CSV) or binary (e.g., XLS) formats.

To be able to tackle the larger data challenges, however, we need to be able to connect R with remote computational resources. Hadoop, which provides the potential for both massive storage and parallel computational power, promises to make very large data sets available for processing and analysis in R.

This chapter gave an overview of Hadoop, but we should consider some other strategies for working with very large data sets. One simple technique is to down-sample the data. For example, one might reduce the size of a data set by a factor of 100 through randomly sampling 10,000 records from a data set containing 1 million records. The smaller data set would be more likely to fit into your computer's memory, and in many scenarios there would not be a meaningful impact on the quality of your analytical results. (One key exception is the needle-in-the-haystack analysis described at the top of the chapter; down-sampling can interfere with the analysis of unusual events.)

Another strategy for working with very large data sets lies in getting a bigger computer: R keeps its data in the computer's main memory—the so-called RAM (random access memory)—so getting a computer with a larger memory means that more data can be stored. Although in theory a modern 64-bit computer can address 16 exabytes of memory (about 1 million terabytes), the operating systems used in today's computers generally create much smaller limits. In fact, on a 64-bit Windows machine, R can address no more than eight terabytes of data. Still, this is quite a large amount of data, so more memory is a workable strategy for dealing with large data sets in some cases.

A third option is to use one of the packages that R authors have developed for addressing data on mass storage devices (e.g., a large hard drive) instead of in memory. Hard disk drives are ridiculously cheap—a recent look showed an eight-terabyte hard drive available for about $250—making it easy to store a very large data set. Many functions in R, however, such as mean() and sd(), assume that a data object is stored in memory. Packages such as ffbase get around this problem. Two statisticians from Europe, Edmin de Jonge and Jan Wijffels, created the ffbase package to simplify the analysis of large data frames stored on a computer's mass storage device. Other options that are similar to ffbase include the bigmemory package and the RevoScaleR product from Revolution Analytics.

Deciding which of these techniques to use can be tricky. Generally, for any data set larger than 10 gigabytes, a parallel processing solution such as Hadoop will work best. Data sets between 2 gigabytes and 10 gigabytes can work with one of the hard drive solutions such as ffbase. Finally, for data sets smaller than two gigabytes, upgrading a computer's memory to sufficient size to handle the data may provide the simplest approach.

Chapter Challenge

Hadoop is a software framework designed for use with Apache, which is first and foremost a Linux server application. Yet there are development versions of Hadoop available for Windows and Mac as well. These are what are called single node instances—that is, they use a single computer to simulate the existence of a large cluster of computers. See if you can install the appropriate version of Hadoop for your computer's operating system.

As a bonus activity, if you are successful in installing Hadoop, then get a copy of the RHadoop package from Revolution Analytics and install that. If you are successful with both, you should be able to run the MapReduce code presented in this chapter.

Sources

http://aqua.nasa.gov/doc/pubs/Wx_Forecasting.pdf

http://en.wikipedia.org/wiki/Big_data

http://en.wikipedia.org/wiki/Data.gov

https://www.informatica.com/about-us/news/news-releases/2012/05/20120514-big-data-equals-big-business-opportunity-say-global-it-and-business-professionals.html#fbid=0md1UhhoUXd

http://en.wikipedia.org/wiki/Mapreduce

https://github.com/RevolutionAnalytics/rmr2/blob/master/docs/tutorial.md

R Functions Used in This Chapter

lapply()	Applies a function to all elements within a given list.
to.dfs()	Stores data in a distributed file system (dfs).
mapreduce()	Maps and reduces via a key value function.

INDEX

Acquisition, data, 2
Aggregates in visualizations, 140
Allaire, Joseph J., 61
Amazon, 268
American Standard Code for Information
    Interchange (ASCII), 11
Analysis, data, 3
    and analysis, 4
    exploratory, 211–212
Annotation in visualizations, 139
Apriori, 219–228
Archiving, data, 3
Argument, 69
Association rules
    algorithm process, 219–228
    data, 212–213
    mining, 213–219
Attention to quality, 4

Bar charts, 89–91, 141–142, 241 (figure)
Bare-Bones R: A Brief Introductory Guide, 24
Berners-Lee, Tim, 9
Big data
    defined, 261–264
    tools for, 264–269
"Bigger equals weirder," 262
Binary Hand Dance, 11
Bytes, 11–13

Call centers, 193
Car maintenance linear regression model,
    199–209
Causation, 198
Central limit theorem, 101–105
Central tendency, measures of, 83
Cleaning up data elements, 54–57
Color in visualizations, 139
Columns
    accessed in dataframes, 43–46
    in CSV text files, 49
    removing rows and, 51–53

renaming rows and, 53–54
    rows and, 35–36
Comparison
    of samples, 105–108
    in visualizations, 140
Complexity, data, 263
Connections in visualizations, 140
Correlation, 198
Cost of constraints, 238
Crockford, Douglas, 128
Cross-validation model, 238
CSV files, 49–51, 111
    accessing Excel data and, 114–120
    importing data from, 112–114

Darwin, Charles, 81
Data
    accessing Excel, 114–120
    combining bytes into larger structures in,
        11–13
    high-quality, 263–264
    imported using RStudio, 112–114
    linking of, 262, 263
    models, 32–33
    preparation, 211
    sets created in R, 13–14
    storage, 10–11, 111–112
    understanding existing sources of, 31–32
Databases, accessing of, 120–124
Dataframes
    accessing columns in, 43–46
    cleaning up elements of, 54–57
    creating, 36–39
    exploring, 39–43
    sorting, 57–58
Data mining, 211
    association rules data and, 212–213
    association rules mining, 213–219
    exploring how association rules algorithm
        works and, 219–228
    four processes in, 211–212

overview, 211–212
replicating patterns found in, 263
supervised and unsupervised
learning, 231
Data munging
cleaning up the elements in, 54–57
defined, 49
reading a CSV text file and, 49–51
removing rows and columns in, 51–53
renaming rows and columns in, 53–54
sorting dataframes in, 57–58
using descriptive statistics in, 85–88
Data problems
exploring risk and uncertainty
in identifying, 19–20
looking for the exception
in identifying, 18–19
talking to subject matter
experts about, 17–18
Data science
defined, 1–2
skills needed to do, 3–5
steps in doing, 2–3
Data storage, 10–11, 111–112
accessing a database and, 120–124
accessing Excel data and, 114–120
accessing JSON data and, 128–136
comparing SQL and R for accessing
data set and, 124–128
computer RAM and, 269
devices, 269
importing data using RStudio and, 112–114
Degrees of freedom, 84
De Jonge, Edmin, 269
Density in visualizations, 140
Deployment, web application, 254–259
Descriptive statistics
understanding, 83–85
using, 85–88
Devlin, Hugh, 265
Dispersion, measures of, 84
Distributions
normal, 91–94, 102
using histograms to understand, 88–91
Down-sample data, 268–269

EC2, 268
Elastic Compute Cloud, 268

Encoding, 140
Ethical reasoning, 4
Eugenics, 81
Excel data, accessing of, 114–120
Exceptions, looking for, 18–19
Experts, subject matter, 17–18
Exploratory data analysis, 211–212

Facebook, 5, 261
ffbase, 269
Fisher, Ronald, 81, 82, 83
Frequencies, 89
Functions
created in R, 69–73
installing a package to access, 77–78
testing, 73–76
why create and use, 69

Galton, Francis, 81, 197
"Garbage in, garbage out," 262
Gauss, Carl Friedrich, 91, 197
Getting Started with R-studio, 62
ggplot2, 142–149
advanced visualizations, 150–155
creating map visualizations with, 159–161,
162 (figure)
Google, 5
geocoding API, 128–130, 163–164,
163–165
Gossett, William Sealy, 81, 82
Grinstein, Georges, 139

Hadoop distributed files systems (HDFS),
264, 266–269
Hard disk drives, 269
Hart, Vi, 11
Hashtags, 193
High-quality data, 263–264
Histograms, 88–91, 141–142, 241 (figure)
Hogan, Thomas P., 24
HousingMaps, 159

Importing of data using RStudio, 112–114
Industry news, text mining of, 193–194
Integrated development
environment (IDE), 61–62
Interactive Data Visualization, 139
Interpretation of results of data mining, 211, 212

JSON data, 128–136, 163

Keim, Daniel, 139
Khan Academy, 5, 11

Laney, Doug, 261
Law of large numbers, 101–105
Linear modeling, 197–209
    car maintenance example, 199–209
"Linking adds potential," 262
Linking of data sets, 263

Macy's, 4–5, 19
MapReduce, 264–265
Map(s)
    mashup, 159, 165–172
    showing points on, 162–165
    visualization example, 165–172
    visualizations with ggplot2, 159–161,
        162 (figure)
Mashup, map, 159, 165–172
Mass storage devices, 269
Mean, 83
Median, 83
Microsoft products, 111, 121
    accessing Excel data and, 114–120
Mining, data, 211
    association rules data and, 212–213
    association rules mining, 213–219
    exploring how association rules algorithm
        works and, 219–228
    four processes in, 211–212
    overview, 211–212
    replicating patterns found in, 263
    supervised and unsupervised
        learning, 231
Mode, 83
Model(s), 32–33
    cross-validation, 238
    defined, 197
    development in data mining, 211, 212
    linear, 197–209
MongoDB, 121
Moore's Law, 111
Munging, data
    cleaning up the elements in, 54–57
    defined, 49
    reading a CSV text file and, 49–51

removing rows and columns in, 51–53
renaming rows and columns in, 53–54
sorting dataframes in, 57–58
using descriptive statistics in, 85–88
MySQL, 120–124
    for big data, 265

Normal distributions, 91–94
    law of large numbers and, 102

OpenDocument format, 111–112
Open Mashup Alliance, 159
Oracle, 120–124

Pareto, Vilfredo, 91
Patterns versus details, 140
Pearson, Karl, 81, 197
Points, map, 162–165
Population sampling, 82–83
PostgreSQL, 120–124
Preparation, data, 211
Problems, data
    exploring risk and uncertainty in
        identifying, 19–20
    looking for the exception
        in identifying, 18–19
    talking to subject matter
        experts about, 17–18
Proximity in visualizations, 139

R, 5, 20, 23
    apriori algorithm, 219–228
    association rules mining in, 213–219
    basic plots in, 141–142
    big data tools, 265–269
    compared to SQL for accessing a data,
        124–128
    creating a data set in, 13–14
    creating and using vectors in, 25–29
    creating functions in, 69–73
    creating web applications in, 247–253
    histogram generated by, 91–92
    installing, 24
    linear regression example, 199–209
    sampling in, 97–98
    support vector machines (SVM) in,
        233–245
    text mining package, 180–183

using, 24, 25 (figure)
See also RStudio
RAM (random access memory), 269
Range, 83
Ranges in visualizations, 140
Reading in RStudio text files, 176–180
Regression, linear. *See* Linear modeling
Renaming of rows and columns, 53–54
Repetition, sampling, 99–101
RevolutionAnalytics, 265
RHadoop, 265–269
Risk and uncertainty, exploring, 19–20
Rows and columns, 35–36
    in CVS text files, 49
    removing, 51–53
    renaming, 53–54
R scripts, 62–66
RStudio, 4–5, 24
    creating R scripts, 62–66
    creating web applications in, 247–253
    importing data using, 112–114
    installing, 62
    installing packages for accessing functions
        in, 77–78
    reading in text files with, 176–180
    text mining package, 180–183
    using integrated development
        environment and, 61–62
    See also R

Sampling, 97–98
    comparing two samples after, 105–108
    down, 268–269
    law of large numbers and the central limit
        theorem, 101–105
    population, 82–83
    in R, 98–99
    repeating, 99–101
Sentiment analysis, 189–193
Shannon, Claude, 9
Size of visualizations, 139
Skills needed to do data science, 3–5
Social media
    Facebook, 5, 261
    Twitter, 193
Sorting dataframes, 57–58
Sources, existing data, 31–32
SQL, 124–128
    for big data, 264

SQlite, 121
Standard deviation, 84–85
Statistics
    historical perspective of, 81–82
    normal distributions, 91–94
    sampling a population and, 82–83
    understanding descriptive, 83–85
    using descriptive, 85–88
    using histograms to understand a
        distribution in, 88–91
Steps in doing data science, 2–3
Stoll, Clifford, 9
Stop words, 182
Storage, data, 10–11, 111–112
    accessing a database and, 120–124
    accessing Excel data and, 114–120
    accessing JSON data and, 128–136
    comparing SQL and R for accessing data
        set and, 124–128
    computer RAM and, 269
    devices, 269
    importing data using RStudio and, 112–114
Subject matter experts, 17–18
Supervised learning
    unsupervised and, 231
    via support vector machines (SVM), 231–233
Support vector machines (SVM), 231
    in R, 233–245
    supervised learning via, 231–233
System architects, 2

Testing functions, 73–76
Text
    file reading, 176–180
    mining, other uses of, 193–194
    mining package, 180–183
Texture in visualizations, 139
Transformation, data, 4, 140
Tufte, Edward, 140
Twitter, 193

Uncertainty and risk, exploring, 19–20
Unsupervised learning, 231
U.S. Census Bureau, 49

Variance, 84
Variety, data, 261
Vectors, creating and using, 25–29
Velocity, data, 261

Verzani, John, 62
Visualizations, 4
  advanced ggplot2, 150–155
  ggplot2, 142–149
  map, 159–161, 162 (figure), 165–172
  overview, 139–141
Volume, data, 261

Ward, Matthew, 139
Web applications
  created in R, 247–253
  deploying, 254–259
Wijffels, Jan, 269
Wikipedia, 5, 197

Word clouds, 175–176
  creation, 183–184, 185 (figure)
  reading in text files and, 176–180
  using the text mining package for,
    180–183
Words and sentiment analysis, 189–193

XML, 111–112

Yourdon, Ed, 32